First Course in C++
D0755923
KINGSTON COLLEGE
00115148

# First Course in C++
## A Gentle Introduction

Mark Harman
*University of North London*

Ray Jones
*University of North London*

The McGraw-Hill Companies

**London** · New York · St Louis · San Francisco · Auckland
Bogotá · Caracas · Lisbon · Madrid · Mexico · Milan
Montreal · New Delhi · Panama · Paris · San Juan · São Paulo
Singapore · Sydney · Tokyo · Toronto

Published by
McGraw-Hill Publishing Company
Shoppenhangers Road, Maidenhead, Berkshire, SL6 2QL, England
Telephone 01628 23432
Fax 01628 770224

---

**British Library Cataloguing in Publication Data**
Harman, Mark
First course in C++: a gentle introduction
1. C++ (Computer program language) 2. Programming (Electronic computers)
I. Title II. Jones, Ray
005.1'33

ISBN 0–07–709–1949

**Library of Congress Cataloging-in-Publication Data**
The CIP data of this title is available from the Library of Congress, Washington DC, USA.



*McGraw-Hill*

*A Division of The* ***McGraw-Hill*** *Companies*



Typeset by Mark Harman and Ray Jones.
Printed and bound in Great Britain at the University Press, Cambridge.
Printed on permanent paper in compliance with ISO Standard 9706.

*To Amy, Celina, Daniel, Kathy, Matthew and Naomi*

# Contents

# Preface

This is a book about programming in the C++ language, which has been designed to be used by those completely new to programming.

C++ is a language which has evolved from its predecessors to include the major strengths (and perhaps, a few of the weaknesses) of the programming languages which have preceded it. That it is a popular language of growing importance is beyond question, and its increasingly widespread use means that many aspiring programmers will learn about programming for the first time, using C++.

As C++ has absorbed the features and linguistic constructions and concepts of the past forty years of language design it is an extremely powerful language. Sadly, the other, unavoidable, consequence of this process of absorption has been the creation of a language with many complex, intricate and potentially dangerous features, which presents the novice with an almost insurmountable barrier of understanding. It has often been observed that the learning curve for a programmer starting out with C++ is far steeper and longer than that pertaining to any of the foregoing programming languages.

Given the size and complexity of C++ full treatment of the language would, of necessity, be either voluminous or terse in its treatment of the generic fundamentals of programming. By focusing our attention on a carefully selected subset of the language we are able to ensure that the reader is provided with a thorough grounding in these fundamentals — the control structure 'building blocks' and parameter passing mechanisms common to almost all currently used programming languages.

On completing the book, the reader should feel comfortable with and fluent in the language, secure in the knowledge that they can write effective C++ programs to tackle any programming problem which they may face. On completing the course set out in the main text of the book, the reader should also feel that a solid foundation has been laid for the further study of the advanced features of C++ covered in the book's appendices and in other longer texts on the subject.

We would like to thank Ross Paterson, Ronnie Burton, Sandra Hartley, Bala and Yoga Sivagurunathan and our students on the C++ course at the University of North London for reading and commenting on earlier drafts of this book. All errors, naturally, remain the sole responsibility of the authors. We would also like to thank Celina and Kathy for their patience during the preparation of the book and Ros, Elizabeth and Rupert at McGraw-Hill for their help with the book's production.

# Guidelines for Readers

## Introduction

This book is intended for beginners, but can also be read by those programmers who are already familiar with the C programming language, and by those familiar with other languages. The book might also be of interest to project managers, who, though perhaps unconcerned with the precise details of the language, would like to familiarise themselves with some of the more important aspects of the language.

Readers with some prior knowledge of programming will not need to read every chapter in detail. Here we try to provide a feeling for the way in which we have organised the content of the book, in an effort to save the reader unnecessary effort.

## Guidelines for novice programmers

If you are a novice programmer, with little or no prior experience of programming in any language, you should follow the book sequentially from Chapter 1. We have designed the book specifically with you in mind and have organised the material in a way that makes it easy for the beginner to gradually build up, from a starting point with no prior knowledge of programming, to a point at which you will be capable of writing sophisticated C++ programs.

Each chapter builds upon the ideas presented in the preceding chapters, so you should use the exercises at the end of each chapter to ensure that you are ready to move on to the next. The exercises tend to become progressively harder; you should find the first exercise of each chapter relatively trivial, while the last might require some thought and effort. If you have managed over half the exercises in any chapter, then you will probably have mastered enough of the material to allow you to go on to the following chapter. Of course, in a practical subject such as programming, there is no substitute for practice, so we recommend that you attempt all exercises before moving on. It is important to try out the programs and exercises in the book.

One approach which seems to work particularly well for beginners is to modify working programs a little. Add a few new lines to a program from the book, or alter a couple of lines and see what happens when you compile and run the new program.

## Guidelines for C programmers

The first three chapters cover aspects of the language which deviate only mildly from the C language. You should briefly read Chapter 1, concerning input and output, but may comfortably omit Chapters 2 and 3, which cover selection and repetition. Both these subjects are identical in C and C++.

You should read the section on the class data structure in Chapter 4, but may omit the rest of this chapter and all of Chapter 5, apart from the sections on `new` and `delete`, which, in C++, corresponds to the use of `malloc` in C to dynamically allocate storage.

Chapters 6 and 7 cover parameterless functions and value parameter passing, with which you will be familiar, so you may safely omit these chapters. You should skim through Chapter 8, as it covers reference parameter passing, which is handled differently in C++ and C. Chapter 9 covers functions which return values and may be omitted.

You will need to read thoroughly Chapters 10, 11 and 12, which cover the object-oriented heart of the C++ language and its file access mechanism. You might also like to read Appendix B, which introduces the polymorphic features of C++, but may omit Appendix A, which covers recursion.

## Guidelines for non-C programmers

You should skim through the first three chapters which cover the basic procedural control structures of the language. These offer the same semantics as those found in languages such as Pascal, COBOL, Ada and FORTRAN, though the syntax varies a little from these languages. You should also skim through Chapters 4 and 5, which cover the basic data structures of C++. These structures correspond to record and array types in other languages, but once again, the precise details vary.

Chapters 6, 7, 8 and 9 describe the procedural abstraction mechanism of C++. In the language you are familiar with, that which is termed a 'function' in C++, may be called a 'procedure', 'function', 'subroutine' or 'perform'. In particular there is little distinction between a value-returning routine (a function proper) and a 'procedure' (i.e. a routine which does not return a value). You should read through these four chapters, focusing upon the examples, to see how procedural abstraction is achieved in C++.

Chapters 10, 11 and 12 cover the object-oriented features of C++, and you will need to read these in some detail. You might also like to read Appendix B, which covers polymorphism, but may omit Appendix A, if the language you are familiar with allows recursion.

## Guidelines for managers

It is the object-oriented nature of C++ which makes it different from other languages used in industry. You can see what this involves by reading Chapters 10, 11 and 12 and also Appendix B. Of slightly less significance are the features C++ has inherited from its predecessor, the C language. If this language is not familiar to you, you might also like to skim through the rest of the book, in particular Chapters 1 and 8.

## Guidelines for instructors

We have designed the content and structure of the book to fit a single semester programming course using C++. The text is ideally suited to a course in which C++ is taught as the *first* programming language, but the text could also be used on C++ programming courses where C++ is *not* the first language.

### C++ as a first language

The material has been organised into twelve chapters so that it can be easily followed sequentially on a 'C++ as a first language' course with a simple mapping from week number to chapter number(s).

We recommend a 'chapter-per-week' approach. Although more advanced students will find the pace of the first few chapters a little slow, we have found that beginners are likely to lose confidence if the treatment of this essential material is too rapid. This problem is exacerbated when one finds oneself teaching classes of mixed ability and experience, which is why we have included the two appendices. These will give the more advanced students something to get their teeth into, while their less experienced colleagues are progressing more steadily throughout the book.

### C++ as a second or subsequent language

For a 'second language' course, in which students have already met a procedural programming language, we recommend that the first three chapters are taken together in one go, and that the fourth and fifth chapters likewise are treated together. We find that two weeks is sufficient to cover all the material up to Chapter 6, on a 'second language' course, as the material is essentially merely new syntax for old semantics.

We find that students always have trouble appreciating and fully exploiting procedural abstraction, so even for a 'second language' course, we would recommend that Chapters 6, 7, 8 and 9 (which describe functions) be treated in some detail.

Where a week is the 'unit of study', we find that Chapters 6 and 7 can be taken together in a single week, whilst Chapters 8 and 9 should be covered individually — one week each.

Chapters 10, 11 and 12, which describe class abstraction, inheritance and files, should each be given a week of the course. Following the book will therefore occupy eight weeks of a 'second language' course. We have found it useful to devote the remaining weeks to object-oriented design, backed up by a group project, in which the students follow the entire process from OO design through to C++ coding.

# 1

# Programming Fundamentals and Object-oriented Programming

## Aims

The aim of this chapter is to acquaint the reader with the concepts of computers, programs, and program design, and to introduce the C++ programming language.

After reading this chapter you should be able to:

- understand the relationship between computers and programs
- understand the methods of program design
- understand the basic structure of computer programs
- understand the concepts of *data* and *operations*
- understand the form of a simple C++ program
- construct a working C++ program that performs simple arithmetic

## Introduction

Computers are a part of everyone's life, these days. But in order for them to be useful, someone has to write the programs to make them work. The aim of this book is to introduce you to the art of computer programming in C++. We shall assume that you have little or no knowledge of either computers or programming, so to start with we will give a brief introduction to both.

## Computers

A computer often consists of three main parts, a display screen and keyboard for communication with the user, and a processor (or, often, a microprocessor) that is the heart (or rather, brain) of the computer.

Normally, there will also be disks for storing programs and data; these generally come in two varieties, fixed disks that are found inside the computer and are an integral part of the computer hardware, and diskettes (or *floppy disks*), which are small portable devices that are designed to fit into a diskette drive that is accessible from the outside of the computer. Both types of disk are used for storing data and programs, and the differences between the two are that the fixed disk normally has a much higher capacity than the diskette and the diskette, being portable, can be used in more than one computer.

There are also normally peripheral devices attached to the computer: these are used to either give data to the computer or to enable the computer to provide data to the user. Often there is a printer, for producing a paper copy of the results of a program or printing the programs themselves. Some computers are designed for specialist applications, and these might well have more, or different, peripheral devices attached to them. For example, modern supermarket checkouts are computerised and have bar code readers incorporated into the computer that can read the code on items being purchased. This is an example of a peripheral device providing data to the computer.

## Programs

Computer programs are normally designed for problems that would be difficult or impossible to solve by other means, or to automate processes that already are achieved by other means but can be done more efficiently with a computer. Here are some examples:

- Stock control programs can help keep an optimum level of stock of items in a shop or warehouse; they can also keep up to date pricing information and be integrated with a Point of Sale retailing system.

- Satellite control would probably be impossible without on-board computers to correctly orient the satellite into the right orbit and handle the transmission of data.

- Language translation is a job traditionally done by manual means but this can be a slow and laborious process. There are now programs that can make a reasonable attempt at translation from one language to another. Although very far from perfect, they can reduce, significantly, the amount of work that a human translator needs to do.

- Computer games could not exist without computers to design and run them. They range from relatively simple 'platform' games to highly sophisticated simulations.

## Programming languages

Fundamentally, a computer program is a set of instructions, written in a special language, that tells the computer what to do. Computers, as you might expect, do not directly understand the natural language of humans; they are designed to respond to specific instructions coded in a language that consists, not of words, but of numbers. These, so called, *machine languages* are very difficult for humans to read and understand, so, in order to ease the process of writing a computer program, a number of *high level* languages have been designed.

A high level programming language is one that is designed to be much easier for humans to use and to read than machine language. However, to be useful to the computer, the high level language must be translated into the machine language that the computer understands. This translation can be achieved in two ways. One way is to read the program, instruction by instruction, and translate each of them into machine language instructions, which the processor can execute. This method is called interpreting a program.

A second way is to translate the whole of the program into machine code thus producing a new program that can control the computer directly. This is called compilation.

The `C++` language is normally compiled; thus to run a program you must first write it in `C++`, then compile it into machine code, and finally the compiled program can be run by the computer. The exact manner in which the programmer controls this process is dependant on the manufacturer of the language compiler, so it is important that you become familiar with the particular `C++` compiler on the computer that you are going to use. Many compilers are highly sophisticated, offering the programmer facilities to organise the development of their programs. These will help you later, but initially, you should establish a simple method of modifying and running your programs.

# Program design

Most, if not all, programs of any significance are too complex to construct without some form of design work being performed first. Some first-time programmers find this strange. They think that in order to produce a program all you need do is to sit at the keyboard and start typing. This is definitely not the case.

If you wanted to build a boat, and started by cutting some timber and nailing it together, you would end up with a pretty crude vessel. On the other hand, if you first drew up plans and cut your timber according to these, the result would be much better. The same principle applies to the construction of computer programs.

The evolution of computer program design has gone through a number of different stages. Originally, programs were written as single monolithic entities, but these, by today's standards, were simple programs that could be easily managed by a single programmer. As the complexity of the problem increases, it became clear that what programmers needed was some way of breaking up a program into smaller, more manageable, chunks. There are two reasons for this: first, human beings can cope only with a certain level of complexity; beyond what might be called a *headful* of information, programmers begin to lose track of the way they have constructed a program and are more prone to making mistakes. By concentrating upon smaller chunks, or *modules*, a complete program can be designed so that each of its modules can be made small enough to be easily understood.

A second reason for modularisation is the potential for reusability. Modules written as part of one program, if properly designed, can be used as part of other programs thus, potentially, saving a great deal of time and effort in the development of new programs. For some time, programmers have used so-called top-down methods of program development. Using these methods a single program is written that comprises the whole of a software system (as large complex programs tend to be called), but is constructed in a modular way.

The modules form a hierarchy that looks a little like a family tree, where the modules at the top of the tree use the modules further down to perform particular tasks. (A simple program hierarchy is shown in Figure 1.1.) Top-down methods are supported by a generation of programming languages, such as Pascal and C, that provide facilities to allow a program to be broken down into such a hierarchy of smaller units called procedures or functions. The ideas that contributed to top-down design have not been abandoned in the new object-oriented paradigm, rather they have been augmented and incorporated within new frameworks.

While top-down methods are a distinct improvement over previous *ad-hoc* methods of designing programs, they are themselves being augmented (at least in some areas of application) by newer object-oriented methods of program design. In order to support these newer methods another generation of programming languages has been developed. One of these languages is C++.

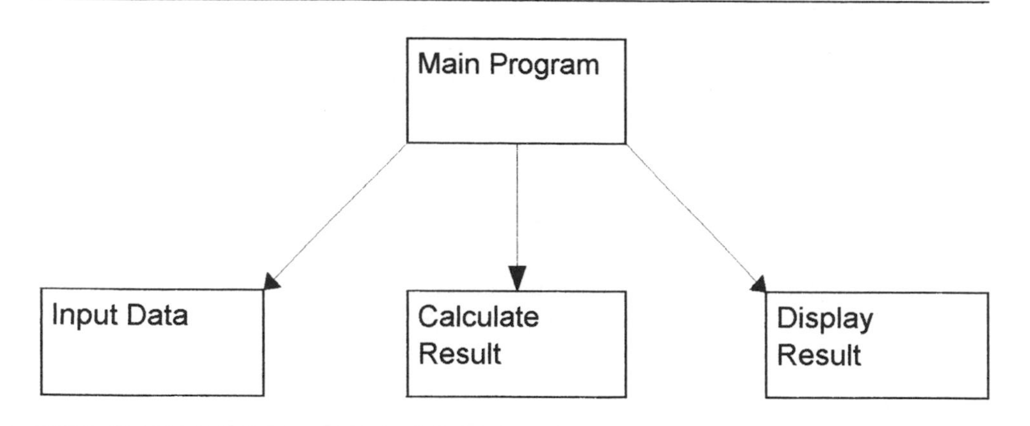


**Figure 1.1** A simple program hierarchy

## Object-oriented program design

Using the object-oriented way of thinking, programs are still split up into chunks. But rather than dividing them up into separate procedures and functions, they are divided into *classes*.

An object is a component of a computer program that is completely self-contained and, often, represents an object in the real world. For example, a program to keep track of the business of a car hire company might contain objects that represent cars and others that represent customers. In effect, an object-oriented program is like a set of smaller programs, each of which represents a component of a system, and these smaller programs communicate with each other to perform the overall function of the complete program.

Using object-oriented techniques the construction of a large program can be developed like any other engineered product. If you think of the construction of a bicycle, you would be thinking in terms of wheels, handlebars, the saddle, pedals and a number of other components: these are the objects from which the bicycle is made; they fit together to make a bicycle but they are each individually designed and manufactured parts. Object-oriented programs are built in the same way; each part is designed to fit with the others but they are specified and created individually.

`C++` is a programming language that supports the ideas of object-oriented programming and we will be dealing with the facilities that it provides later in the book. However, before we get too deep into the construction of object-oriented programs, we must first cover the basic concepts that are common to all programming languages. These features of `C++` are found in all programming languages, although often the notation is slightly different. You should therefore find that learning your second programming language takes far less time than learning your first.

All programming starts with a few fundamental concepts and programming constructs; the remainder of this chapter and much of the rest of this book is devoted to these. We shall, however, be returning to the subject of object-orientation in Chapter 10.

## Program = data + operations

Now we shall take a closer look at the way in which programs are constructed. Programs do their job by manipulating data. For example, a payroll program manipulates time and salary data to produce a monthly wage; a word processor manipulates characters and layout data to produce a document in a required format.

Most programs follow the same basic pattern:

1. get some data

2. perform some operation(s) on that data

3. provide a result

A simple program to add two numbers together would first get the two numbers (the data), then add them together (the operation) and finally display the result on the display screen (the result).

As you might be able to deduce from the above, all programs consist of two fundamental elements: *data objects*, which contain values (e.g. numbers) and *instructions*, which perform the operations on the data.

### Data

There are two fundamental forms of data that we use, textual and numeric, e.g. a person's name is textual data, while a number that represents a person's age is an example of numeric data.

Most computer programming languages include facilities for dealing with both types of data. In C++ we can represent textual data in two ways: as characters or strings. A character is a single letter, digit or other special character (e.g. punctuation and layout), while a string is a single entity that comprises a number of characters 'strung' together (e.g. a name, or a sentence).

C++ also caters for numbers. These, too, may be in more than one form. One form of number is an integer: an integer is a number that has no decimal part (i.e. a whole number). A number that does have a decimal part (e.g. 3.14159) is known as a real number, and is called a `float` in C++.

In addition to these simple forms of data, we can also invent our own more complex types. For example, in a program that acts as a name and address database, we might want to use a data object that represents a combination of numeric and textual data, e.g. an address that consists of a house number and a street name. Yet again, C++ gives us the facilities to deal with these new varieties of data by constructing new types of data object.

For the time being, however, we shall be concerned with simple data; in Chapter 4, we shall see how we can create and manipulate more complex data types.

### Operations

In order to produce a result from our original data, we need to perform operations on it. An operation might be to add two numbers together, e.g.

```
13 + 24
```

To add two numbers together you simply write the two numbers with a plus symbol between them. The plus symbol is known as the *addition operator* as it performs the addition operation. The combination of data and operations, in this way, is called an expression. *An expression always yields a value*, e.g. the expression `13 + 24` yields the value 37.

We will be looking in more detail at data types and operators later in this chapter, but first, we shall put into practice the concepts that we have covered so far.

## A first C++ program

We can use an expression to display its value on the computer screen, e.g.

```
cout << 2 + 2;
```

The line above is a C++ statement that displays the value of the expression `2 + 2`. The word `cout` (pronounced see-out) represents what is known as the *output stream* (you should imagine this being the computer display) and the chevrons are the operator that sends the value to the output stream.

Note that the direction of the chevrons shows the direction of movement of the data: the value to be displayed is on the right of the chevrons, and the chevrons point towards the output stream.

In order to make a complete program from this instruction, we will need to add a few extra lines.

```
// A program to display 2 + 2
#include <iostream.h>
void main()
{
        cout << 2 + 2;
}
```

This is a complete C++ program. If you type this program exactly as you see it here (making sure that the *case* of the letters is correct, e.g. you must type `main` not `Main`) you should find that, when compiled and run, it will display the value 4 on the computer screen.

There are a few things in this program that we have not encountered before, so we shall now go through it line by line.

The first line of the program begins with a symbol consisting of two oblique characters (`//`): this means that everything on that line after the symbol is a comment. A comment in a program has no effect on the program itself, rather we include it to document the program for the human reader. All programs should have comments in them to show what they do and to document parts of the program whose purpose is not immediately obvious. For example, it is good practice to insert comments into a program, detailing who wrote the program and when.

The next line is

```
#include <iostream.h>
```

This is an instruction to include references to the input/output library (this is one of a number of libraries that are provided with all C++ compilers). Effectively, this allows the use of instructions that will get data from the keyboard and display it on the screen. We cannot use any input or output functions (e.g. sending data to `cout`) without this directive in a program. The main part of the program appears between the lines:

```
void main()
      {
```

and the last line of the program

```
      }
```

Between these lines you can see the instruction to display `2 + 2`. The lines that are around the main part of the program are required to tell the C++ compiler where the program is to start.

```
void main()
{
      // the rest of the program would go here
}
```

At the moment, the need for this may not be apparent, but it will become clearer in Chapter 6. For the moment, you should simply accept that all the programs that you write, for now, will be in this form.

The combination of instructions, operators and data makes up what is known as a statement, and in C++ statements end with a semicolon. This makes sure that there is no ambiguity about where one statement ends and another begins. You will notice that the output statement in our program ends with a semicolon.

The layout of a C++ program is very flexible; although it is normally good practice to write only one statement on each line, C++ does not insist on this. The output statement in the program above could have just as well have been written:

```
cout
<<
2 + 2;
```

or even

```
cout
<<
2
+
2
;
```

or in any other format that did not split words over more than one line.

It must be stressed that the symbol << is a single entity in C++ and as such may not be separated by a new line or any other character. There are a number of other symbols like << that consist of two characters (e.g. ++, ==, !=); they must be treated in the same way as words like `cout` (they just happen to be made up of characters that are not in the alphabet).

In this book we have tried to adopt a style that takes advantage of the flexibility of layout that C++ allows us and, thereby, enhances the readability of a program. We suggest that you adopt a similar style.

## String constants

We have mentioned previously, that *strings* are a number of characters strung together. In C++, we construct strings by enclosing the characters in double quotation marks, e.g. "Hello Mother". We can print out strings to give the user information about what our programs are doing. Using output in this simple way is a first step towards making our programs 'user-friendly'.

Here is a slightly friendlier version of our first program:

```
// A more friendly program to display 2 + 2
#include <iostream.h>

void main()
{
        cout << "Two plus two equals: "
        cout << 2 + 2;
}
```

## Variables

Our first program was not particularly useful, except as an illustration of how a program is constructed. Useful programs, as we have mentioned before, consist of three stages: getting some data, manipulating that data in some way, and then providing a result.

We have already seen how we can output data from a program but in order to input data and manipulate it, we need to be able to store its values in the computer's memory. We do this by creating simple data objects called variables (known as such because they may take a variety of values).

To create a variable, we use a C++ *definition* statement. This simply gives the variable a name by which we can refer to it, and specifies the *type* of the variable.

In C++ we can define variables of a number of different types (e.g. a whole number, called an `int` in C++ and a decimal number, called a `float` in C++); we do this by preceding the name of the variable with the C++ word that represents its type. So the line:

```
int firstNum;
```

defines a variable called `firstNum` of type `int`.

As in the next program, variables are often given names that reflect their rôle in a program. This is a very good practice as, although the computer does not care what the variables are called, it makes the program much more easy to understand for the human reader.

You can normally give a variable any name you want, as long as it consists only of letters, numbers and the underscore character (_). However, the name of a variable must not start with a number and it must not be a word from the C++ language. (Also, it is normally unwise to start them with the underscore character, as the names may then clash with variables used elsewhere.)

The C++ language is *case sensitive*. This means that if we change the case of a letter (from upper case to lower case, or vice versa) then we change the meaning of the word that it appears in. In other words, if we define a variable `firstNum`, we cannot afterwards refer to it as `firstnum` or `FirstNum`. Both the spelling of the name and the case of its constituent letters are significant. We shall see how variables are used in the next program.

## An addition program

The program in Figure 1.2 takes two numbers typed in at the keyboard, adds them together and displays the sum on the display screen. The program consists of four parts and it is laid out and commented to reflect this.

The first part the program tells us that we will be using three variables called `firstNum`, `secondNum` and `result`, and that these will be used to store integer numbers.

The second part of the program gets the values that need to be added from the keyboard. The line

```
cin >> firstNum;
```

accepts an integer number from the keyboard and puts the value of that number in the variable `firstNum`; `secondNum` is given a value in the same way.

You will have noticed that the instruction to input data is similar in format to the one that outputs data. Here, the word `cin` represents the *input stream* (you can imagine this to be the data typed in at the computer keyboard) and the chevrons are the operator that moves data from `cin` to the variable on its right. Note that, like `cout`, the chevrons point in the direction that the data moves in, but that this time it is from the input stream to the variable, *the opposite direction to those used with* `cout`.

The third section does the manipulation of the data: it calculates the sum of the numbers and puts this value in the variable `result`. Here, we use the value of an expression to give a new value to a variable.

```
result = firstNum + secondNum;
```

The variable `result` has been given the value of the expression `firstNum + secondNum`, using the assignment operator, =. The fourth and final part of the program displays the value of the variable result on the computer screen:

```
cout << result;
```

```
//
// This is a program that will accept two integers and
// print out their sum
//
#include <iostream.h>

void main()
{
	// This is where the data will be stored
	int firstNum;
	int secondNum;
	int result;


	// Get the two numbers from the keyboard
	cin >> firstNum;
	cin >> secondNum;

	// Do the addition and store the sum
	result = firstNum + secondNum;

	// Display the result on the screen
	cout << result;
	cout << endl;
}
```

**Figure 1.2** A C++ program that performs addition

This is similar to the output statement in our first program, except that it is the value of the variable that is being output rather than the number four. The last line of this part of the program moves the screen cursor down one line:

```
	cout << endl;
```

This is the normal `cout` statement but using a special word, `endl`. It has a similar effect to pressing the *carriage return* key on a typewriter. The next line of text to be printed will appear one line further down in the output.

## More operators

You will probably not be surprised to learn that there are other operators that we can use in C++ programs to perform arithmetic operations. These are listed in Table 1.1. Of these arithmetic operators, the ++ and -- operators might seem a little odd. They are included in the C++ language as a convenience: it is often the case that we wish to increase, or decrease, the value of a variable by one.

The statements:

```
a++;
b--;
```

can be regarded as shorthand for:

```
a = a + 1;
b = b - 1;
```

You might have noticed that these increment and decrement operators appear twice in the table. This is because they can be used in two ways.

**Table 1.1** C++ Arithmetic operators

| Operator | Name | Example C++ statement | Meaning of statement |
|---|---|---|---|
| + | addition | `a = b + c;` | a is given the value yielded by b+c |
| ++ | pre-increment | `++a;` | increase the value of a by 1 |
| ++ | post-increment | `a++;` | increase the value of a by 1 |
| - | subtraction | `a = b - c;` | a is given the value yielded by b-c |
| -- | pre-decrement | `--a;` | decrease the value of a by 1 |
| -- | post-decrement | `a--;` | decrease the value of a by 1 |
| * | multiplication | `a = b * c;` | a is given the value yielded by b*c |
| / | division | `a = b / c;` | a is given the value yielded by b/c |
| % | modulus | `a = b % c;` | a is given the value yielded by b%c |

You will have noticed that the statements a++; and ++a; have the same effect — they increase the value of a by one. Similarly, the statements a--; and --a; have the same effect — they decrease the value of the variable a by one. Writing ++a is called pre-increment, while a++ is called post-increment. Writing --a is called pre-decrement, while writing a-- is called post-decrement. As statements, the pre- and post-forms of the two operators are identical. It is only when the operators are used in *expressions* that we notice a difference in the value yielded. A couple of examples should make things clear:

```
a = b++;            // a takes the value of b
                    // and then b is incremented

x = ++y;            // y is incremented and then
                    // x takes the new value of y
```

```
a = c * b++;          // a takes the value of
                      // c multiplied by b and
                      // then b is incremented
```

Similarly, when the -- operator appears on the left of the variable that it decrements, the operation is performed first, before the evaluation of the remainder of any expression in which it appears. On the other hand, if the operator appears after the variable, the decrement is performed last, after any expression in which it appears. Again, a couple of examples should make things clear:

```
a = b--;              // a takes the value of b
                      // and then b is decremented

x = --y;              // y is decremented and then
                      // x takes the new value of y

x = --y + z;          // y is decremented and then
                      // x takes the value of
                      // y plus z
```

The C++ language was derived from the C language, but with extra facilities added to it (such as the object-oriented extensions). Now, perhaps, you can see how C++ got its name!

## Precedence and bracketed expressions

In C++ certain operators take precedence over others, for instance, multiplication is performed before addition (such precedence is a convention used in most programming languages, as well as in mathematics). Here is an example:

```
a = b * c + d;
```

In C++, where there are no round brackets[1], the multiplication operator is always evaluated before an addition operator, so the calculation above means that a takes the value of the product of b and c plus the value of d.

However, we can change the order of the evaluation by putting brackets around parts of an expression. The sub-expression in the brackets is evaluated before the evaluation of the expression in which it appears. For example, look at the following statement, which contains a sub-expression in brackets:

```
a = b * (c + d);
```

This means, a takes the value of b multiplied by the sum of the values of c and d.

[1]The technical term for a round bracket is a parenthesis.

It is sometimes a good idea to put unnecessary brackets into expressions. So, though the brackets have no effect, you could write:

```
a = (b * c) + d;
```

This is the equivalent of the first example; the use of brackets has no effect on the program but make it obvious that you intend the multiplication to be performed first.

If an arithmetic expression contains only operators of the same precedence and no bracketing, then the expression is evaluated from left to right, e.g.

```
b - c - d
```

means subtract `c` from `b` and then subtract `d` from the result.

## A little more about variables

We have seen that a variable is used to hold a value but we must always be aware of the limitations of the type of variable that we are using.

A variable is simply a name that refers to a location in the computer's memory. This location has a limited capacity and so there is a limit to the size of the number that it can hold. We may find, on a small computer, that a variable of type `int` must be within the range −32768 to +32767.

Similarly, a real number will be represented in a memory location with a finite capacity, so it is only possible to store a real number with a fixed amount of precision. Thus a real number, or variable of type `float`, is often an approximation to any calculated value (although it may be exact).

As you may know, a computer stores all its data as numbers, in fact, as binary numbers. This normally has no effect on the way we write our programs because the programming language that we use hides all the necessary conversions that enable us to deal with integers, real numbers, text strings, characters, etc.

Computer memory is normally organised in chunks of 8 binary digits, or bits, and these chunks are called bytes (most modern personal computers have millions of bytes, or megabytes, of memory). Each variable that we define in our `C++` program is allocated a position in the computer's memory; when we use that variable's name, we are actually referring to its memory location.

The amount of memory allocated to a variable depends on its type: a variable of type `char` is normally accommodated in one byte of memory, whereas one of type `int` might be allocated two bytes.

Two variables are defined below, the first is an integer, or `int` type variable and the second is a variable that can hold the value of a single character, or `char` type variable (for example, the letter `'a'` or the space character `' '`). Each variable definition is terminated by a semicolon.

```
int firstNum;
char lineType;
```

They might be allocated memory locations as in Figure 1.3.

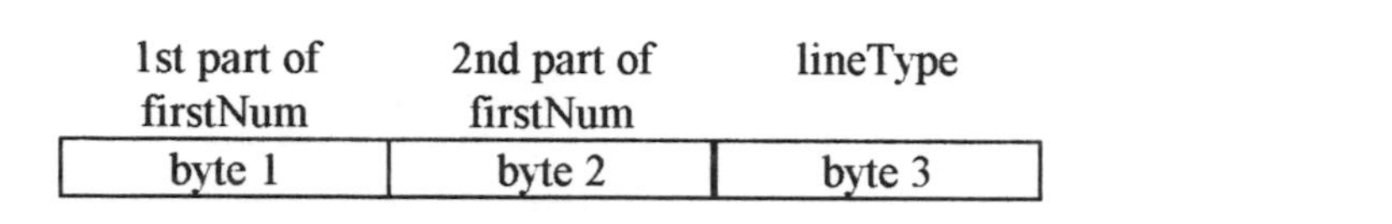


**Figure 1.3** Variables in computer memory

Figure 1.4 lists some of the types of variable that you can use in a C++ program, the amount of memory that they use and the range of values that they can take (these are based on a typical compiler that runs on a personal computer; other compilers may differ).

| Type | Size in bytes | Range of possible values | Comment |
|---|---|---|---|
| `char` | 1 | −128 to 127 | usually used for characters, although a `char` is in fact a type of integer |
| `int` | 2 | −32768 to 32767 | an integer double the size of a `char` |
| `long` | 4 | −2,147,483,648 to 2,147,483,647 | an integer double the size of an `int` |
| `float` | 4 | $-3.4\times10^{-38}$ to $3.4\times10^{38}$ | a type for holding real values |
| `double` | 8 | $-1.7\times10^{-308}$ to $1.7\times10^{308}$ | a `float` but double the size |

**Figure 1.4** Some C++ variable types

## The char variable

You may find it odd to see that the type char is described as being a type of integer. The reason for this is that, in a computer, characters are usually represented by integer numbers. For example, the number for the space character is usually 32 and, for the character 'C', it is usually 67. So when the compiler encounters a statement such as

```
char ch = 'C';
```

it actually assigns the decimal value 67 to the variable ch. If we were to write the line

```
char ch = 67;
```

the effect would be exactly the same. Consequently, it is quite possible to use char variables as integers with a restricted range of values. Unless there is an overriding reason for doing so, however, it is best to stick to using char variables for characters.

Not all computers use the same set of numbers (or codes) for characters. The most common, however, are the *ASCII*, or *Extended ASCII*, set of codes. So you may come across the phrase 'the ASCII value', meaning the integer code that represents a character. ASCII, by the way, stands for the American Standard Code for Information Interchange.

## Variable definitions

We have already seen that we need to define the variables that we are going to use in a program and, although these definitions may appear almost anywhere in a program, they are normally placed at the beginning of the section where they are going to be used: this is often at the beginning of the program. We will now look more closely at variable definitions.

Variables can be defined by giving a type followed by a *list* of variable names with optional initialisers. So if we want to define more than one variable of the same type, we can do this in the same statement, e.g.

```
// Three variables of type int
int   a, b, c;
```

and we can initialise those that we need to (in this case with the initial value 0.0) and leave those that we do not wish to give an initial value:

```
// Three float variables,
// only the first two are initialised
float max = 0.0, min = 0.0, avg;
```

Apart from the integer types we have seen, so far, there are also so-called *unsigned integers* which occupy the same storage as their signed equivalent but can only contain positive numbers (or zero). The definitions of these types are preceded by the word `unsigned`. Thus a definition:

```
unsigned int x;
```

defines a variable `x` that can typically hold values in the range 0 to 65535 (compare this range with that of an `int` in Table 1.2).

## Constants

All the data items that we have encountered so far have been variables. Another useful item is the constant. This is defined in a similar way to a variable, except that the definition is preceded by the word `const`, and it must always be given an initial value, e.g.

```
const float incomeTax = 24.0;
```

In this example the constant `incomeTax` can be used throughout the program in a similar way to a variable. Thus if we need to update our program because the `incomeTax` rate has changed, we need only change the constant definition. If we had used the numeric constant, `24.0`, throughout the program, we would have to find all those occurrences of `24.0` which correspond to income tax and change them.

## Exercises

1.1 Can you think of any types of computer system that have unusual peripheral devices attached to them (i.e. not simply keyboards and screens)?

1.2 What would be the effect of writing a program all on the same line?

1.3 Try to think of any types of data that we might want to use that have not already been mentioned in this chapter.

1.4 Can you think of a use for the modulus operator (i.e. `%`)?

1.5 Can you think of a program that might use an unsigned integer variable and why we might prefer to use unsigned integers rather than signed ones?

1.6 What do you think is the main difference between a constant and a variable?

1.7 Write programs that will perform the following (you should make the programs user-friendly by displaying prompts and explanations of the data that is displayed):

a. read in two numbers, subtract one from the other, and then display the result.
b. read in an integer, divide it by two, and display the result.
c. read in a real number (i.e. one with a decimal part), divide it by two, and display the result.
d. read in a number and increase its value by 25%.

1.8 Write a program that will accept a temperature in degrees Celsius and output the equivalent in degrees Fahrenheit. The formula for the conversion is F = (C * 9.0/5.0) + 32. You should make the variables that you use of type `float`.

1.9 Find as many syntactic errors as you can in the following program

```
#include <iostream.h>

MAIN()
{
   int i,j ;
   characters p,q;
   float a and b;
   char c

cin >> i ;
cout I+1;

cin << j ;
cout << "Some message to the user ;

// This is a comment
/ This is another comment

++i ;
cout << i;

// This code performs some calculations
```

```
i = i + j ;
j = j- ;

cout < j ;
cout << i ;

}
```

# 2

# Making Decisions

## Aims

This chapter introduces the idea of control statements in programming and goes on to explain the way decisions are made in a `C++` program.

After reading this chapter you should be able to:

- understand the need for decision making in a program
- understand the concept of a *logical expression* and the use of *relational* and *boolean* operators
- use the `if` statement in a `C++` program
- construct a program using nested `if` statements
- use the `switch` statement in a program
- lay out a `C++` program in a readable manner

## Introduction

The addition program in Figure 1.2 of Chapter 1 was straightforward; it consisted of a simple sequence: it took some data, performed addition and displayed the result. Most useful programs need to be more complex than this. For example, a payroll program needs to be able to distinguish between normal working hours and overtime in order to calculate the overtime pay at a premium rate. It may need also to perform different income tax calculations depending on an employee's overall salary. So under different conditions, the program will need to perform different actions.

We cannot carry out these sorts of task using a simple sequence of programming statements; we need to be able to change the statements that are executed depending on the particular circumstances. *Control statements* are the mechanism by which we can achieve this. A control statement determines the *flow of control* through a program, i.e. it decides which statements are to be executed and which are not.

The first control statements that we are going to discuss are *selection* statements. This will allow our programs to make decisions and, consequently, choose different courses of action depending on a particular condition.

## The `if` statement

The simplest way of making a decision in C++ is to use the `if` statement. This allows the program to follow one of two paths through a program depending on a specified condition (e.g. whether a variable has a particular value or not). The general form of the statement is:

```
if (condition)
            // statement for a true condition
else
            // statement for a false condition
```

where `condition` represents a *logical expression* that can be either true or false, and the comments are replaced with normal C++ statements. Notice that such a logical expression is an expression like the arithmetic ones we have encountered so far, because it is evaluated by the computer to yield a value. All expressions share the property that they are evaluated to yield some value.

Suppose we want to write a program that distinguishes between negative numbers and ones that are not negative (i.e. positive or zero) and maintains a count of the two different types. Part of the program would need to check if the number typed was less than zero, and if it was, increment the count of negative numbers by one. Similarly, if the number was positive or zero, it would need to increment the count of non-negative numbers by one.

Here is how that fragment of program might look in C++:

```
if (number < 0)
            negativeNumbers++;
else
            otherNumbers++;
```

Within the parentheses, following the word `if`, is the logical expression,

```
number < 0
```

which is true if the variable `number` is less than the value `0`, and false, otherwise. The statement following `if (number < 0)`, is only executed if the logical expression is true. The statement following the word `else` is only executed if the logical expression is false.

If we only wanted to count the number of negative numbers and ignore the others, then the `else` part of the `if` statement, above, would be redundant. In fact, in an `if` statement, the `else` part is optional, so if we were only interested in negative numbers, we could simply write:

```
if (number < 0)
      negativeNumbers++;
```

leaving out the `else` part altogether. The statement following the `if` part of the statement, however, is not optional, so if we were only interested in positive numbers we would need to change the condition.

It is important to note that you can only put one statement in either the `if` of the `else` part of the `if` statement. This is a restriction that is easily overcome, however, as we shall explain later in this chapter.

Look at the layout of the code in the two examples above: the statements that are controlled by the `if` or `else` are indented; this clearly shows the structure of the `if` statement. This sort of layout is highly recommended as it makes your programs easier to read.

## An exam marks program

The program in Figure 2.1 simply decides whether an exam mark represents a pass or a fail: 40 or more represents a pass; anything else is a fail. The first thing to note about the program is the output of character strings to tell the user what to do. So in the C++ line:

```
cout << "Please enter the exam mark: ";
```

the text "Please enter the exam mark: ", is sent to the output stream, and so displayed on the computer's screen. This is done before the cin statement that gets the value for examMark so as to prompt the user to enter the appropriate value.

After the exam mark has been entered, we encounter an if... else... statement. This allows us to decide to take one of two actions depending on the value of the condition: if the condition in the brackets following the word if, is true, then the next statement is executed but the one following the word else is skipped. If the condition is not true, then the statement following the word if is skipped and the one following else is executed.

In the program in Figure 2.1, if the value of variable examMark is less than 40 then "This is a fail" is displayed, otherwise "This is a pass" is displayed.

```
//
// Input an integer and display the grade
// (pass or fail) according to the mark
//
#include <iostream.h>
void main()
{
      int examMark;

      // Prompt the user to enter the mark
      cout << "Please enter the exam mark: ";
      cin >> examMark;
      // Now work out the grade
      if (examMark < 40)
         cout << "That is a fail";
      else
         cout << "That is a pass";
}
```

**Figure 2.1** A simple exam grades program

## Relational operators

So far, we have only seen the use of the *less than* operator in our if statements. This is only one of a set of *relational operators* that are available in C++. They are known as relational operators as they test whether a relationship between two values exists (e.g. whether one value is equal to another, or whether a value is less than another). The combination of these operators and the two values being tested is called a *relational expression* and, as we have already seen in Chapter 1, all expressions must yield a value. The value of a relational expression is always either *true* or *false*.

The complete set of relational operators are shown in Table 2.1.

It is very important that you notice that the equality operator consists of two equals signs together (i.e. ==), the single equals means something quite different.

The program in Figure 2.2 illustrates the use of some of the operators shown in the table.

**Table 2.1** Relational operators

| Operator | Meaning | Example C++ expression | The expression is true if... |
|---|---|---|---|
| > | Greater than | `A > B` | A is greater than B |
| < | Less than | `A < B` | A is less than B |
| == | Equal to | `A == B` | A is equal to B |
| >= | Greater than or equal to | `A >= B` | A is greater than B or A is equal to B |
| <= | Less than or equal to | `A <= B` | A is less than B or A is equal to B |
| != | Not equal to | `A != B` | A is not equal to B |

```
//
// A program to illustrate
// some relational operators
//
#include <iostream.h>
void main()
{
        float num;

        cout << "Enter a number: ";
        cin >> num;

        cout << "The number is...";
        cout << endl;

        // Check if it is zero
        if (num != 0.0)
                cout << "not zero";
        else
                cout << "zero";
        cout << endl;

        //Check if it is 100 or more
        if (num >= 100.0)
                cout << "100 or more";
        else
```

```
            cout << "less than 100";
        cout << endl;

        // Check if it is 10
        if (num == 10.0)
            cout << "equal to 10";
        else
            cout << "not 10";
        cout << endl;
}
```

**Figure 2.2** An illustration of the use of relational operators in `if` statements

We have referred, quite rightly, to the value of a relational expression as being either true or false. However, C++ (unlike some other languages) does not have such values. Instead, a relational expression will yield the value 1 if it is true, or 0 if it is false. The `if` statement simply looks for a zero (false) or non-zero (true) value from the expression in the brackets.

Consequently, whether or not it makes sense in the terms of the program that we are writing, we can use *any* expression that can yield a numeric value for the condition part of an `if` statement. For example, the following statements do not do anything useful, but are quite legal in C++:

```
        // An if statement that always
        // gives a true result

        if (2 + 2)
            cout << "2 + 2 is true!";

        // An if statement that always
        // gives a false result

        if (7 + 3 - 10)
            cout << "This will never appear";
        else
            cout << "But this always will";
```

It may seem strange that the design of the C++ language allows this sort of odd usage. Indeed, some compilers offer a type `bool`, and define values for `true` and `false`. We have not assumed such definitions in this book as they are not yet standard.

The philosophy behind C++ is that programmers should be trusted to know what they are doing. For the beginner, this means that programs will often not behave as expected and that the reasons for this unexpected behaviour may not be immediately obvious. In this book we shall try to highlight some of the most common pitfalls to help you understand why your program does not do what you expect. It may be comforting to know that all programming languages have their own, peculiar, pitfalls.

## A common programming error

One of the most common programming errors in C++ arises because of the way in which logical values are denoted by integers. Consider the following program:

```
#include <iostream.h>
void main()
{
      int age;

      cout << "Please enter your age: ";
      cin >> age;
      if (age = 40)
            cout << "Life begins now!";
}
```

It appears that the programmer intends that the message should be displayed if the age entered is 40. However, there is an error here that means that the message will be displayed no matter what age is entered. The programmer has put an *assignment* statement in the brackets not a *relational expression*! The `if` statement should read

```
if (age == 40)
      cout << "Life begins now!";
```

The original program is perfectly legal (even though it does not do what the programmer wanted) because assignment is an expression too, and so it has a value. Its value is the one that it is assigned to the variable on the left of the assignment operator, in this case it is the value 40. So you can see that the condition in the original `if` statement would always evaluate to 40, a non-zero value (i.e. true), and so the message would always be displayed.

There is a trick that will avoid this sort of error. The boolean expression

```
(x == 40)
```

could just as easily be written as

```
(40 == x)
```

Although it may not seem natural to write this, the two expressions mean the same thing and if you always write relational expressions that test for equality in this way, you will never fall into the trap of writing an assignment by mistake. Reversing an assignment (e.g. 40 = x) produces a nonsense statement that will be found by the C++ compiler. This is because we cannot assign the value of a variable to a number. Logical expressions are also, often, called boolean expressions. It is common to find many words for the same thing in computing. Getting used to and becoming comfortable with this jargon is therefore sadly inevitable.

## Boolean operators

Relational expressions can be made richer by the use of *boolean* operators. There are three such operators as shown in Table 2.2.

**Table 2.2** Boolean operators

| Boolean Operator | Example C++ expression | The expression is true if... |
|---|---|---|
| `&&` | `A&&B` | A is true and B is true |
| `\|\|` | `A\|\|B` | A is true or B is true |
| `!` | `!A` | A is not true |

These operators can be combined with relational expressions and used to construct more complex conditions than could be done with a simple relational expression. Here is an example of the use of the `&&` operator:

```
if ((examScore >= 80) && (courseWork >= 80))
      cout << "Award Distinction!";
```

The condition in this `if` statement says that, if the value `examScore` is greater than or equal to 80 *and* the value of `courseWork` is greater than or equal to 80, then display the message. In other words, the `&&` operator means that the relational expressions on each side of the boolean operator must *both* be true for the entire boolean expression to be true.

The `||` operator is used in a similar way, e.g.

```
if ((ch == 'c') || (ch == 'C'))
      cout << "The letter is a C";
```

The condition here is saying that if `ch` has the value `'c'` (a lower case c) or `ch` has the value `'C'` (an upper case c) then the message will be displayed. In other words the `||` operator means that either one expression *or* the other must be true for the entire expression to be true.

The `!` operator is probably less frequently used than the other two. What it does is to negate the expression that follows it. So if it precedes an expression that evaluates to *true*, then the entire expression is *false*, and if it precedes an expression that evaluates to *false* then the entire expression will be *true*.

Here is a trivial example:

```
if (!(ch == 'C'))
      cout << "The letter is not a C";
```

The expression inside the inner parentheses is *true* if the variable ch has the value 'C' and *false* if it has any other value. So the entire condition is *false* if the value is 'C' and *true* if ch has any other value. In other words, the message will be printed if the value is *not* 'C'.

In these examples, the brackets around the relational expressions, e.g. (ch == 'C'), are not strictly necessary, since the relational operators have a higher precedence than the logical operators and so will be executed first. However, they can aid readability and are included here for that reason.

## Compound statements

A compound statement is usually a group of C++ statements, enclosed in braces, that can be used anywhere that a single statement can be used. (We say 'usually' because strictly, a compound statement in C++ can contain zero or more statements.) Compound statements are also called 'block statements'. They look like this:

```
{
        statement 1
        statement 2
        ...
        statement n
}
```

We can use compound statements to extend the power of the if statement. The program in Figure 2.3 is a complete program using compound statements inside an if statement. The program reads a number from the keyboard and then decides whether it is positive or negative.

The layout of the program, in Figure 2.1, is similar to previous ones, in that the whole of the compound statement is indented. The braces that enclose these statements are, however, in the same column as the words if and else. This is the style that we adopt in this book as we find it very clear to read. Other programmers have their own, similar, styles. It does not matter greatly which style you adopt, as long as it is clear and you are consistent in its use.

---

```
#include <iostream.h>
void main()
{
        float num;
        cout << "Please enter a number: ";
        cin >> num;
```

```
        if (num < 0.0)
        {
                cout << "That was negative:";
                cout << num;
        }
        else
        {
                cout << "That was positive:";
                cout << num;
        }
}
```

**Figure 2.3** A program showing the use of compound statements

## More complex decisions

So far, we have only considered simple decisions but what if you need to distinguish between more than two categories? One way is to use *nested* `if` statements. This means using an `if` statement as the statement to be executed within another `if` statement.

The next example will display the exam grade (A, B, C, D, E or F) for a mark that is typed on the keyboard. Before we can write the program we must know what the grading rules are. Here they are:

*A: 80 or over*
*B: 70 to 79*
*C: 60 to 69*
*D: 50 to 59*
*E: 40 to 49*
*F: below 40*

So we need to write a program that performs the following:

*If the number is 80 or over, then display 'A',*
*otherwise, if the number is 70 or over, then display 'B',*
*otherwise, if the number is 60 or over, then display 'C',*
*otherwise, if the number is 50 or over, then display 'D',*
*otherwise, if the number is 40 or over, then display 'E',*
*otherwise, the number must be below 40 so display 'F'.*

By the way, what we have just done is first to state the problem to be solved before working out how we are going to solve it. This first step is known as program specification and is an essential prerequisite to writing a program.

Take a look at the program in Figure 2.4 and try and see what is happening. You might notice that the variable `grade` is not of type `int`; it is of type `char`. This type of variable is one that can take a character as a value. In C++ a character is an alphabetic, numeral or other special character enclosed in single quotation marks, e.g. `'a'`, `'%'`, `'C'` and `' '` (this last character is a space).

```
//
// Exam grades program 2:
// Input an integer and display the
// grade appropriate to the mark
//
#include <iostream.h>

void main()
{
      int examMark;          // this is the variable to
                             // hold the mark

      char grade;            // this one will
                             // hold the grade

      // Prompt the user to enter the mark
      cout << "Please enter the exam mark: ";
      cin >> examMark;

      // Now work out the grade

      if (examMark >= 80)
            grade = 'A';
      else if (examMark >= 70)
            grade = 'B';
      else if (examMark >= 60)
            grade = 'C';
      else if (examMark >= 50)
            grade = 'D';
      else if (examMark >= 40)
            grade = 'E';
      else
            grade = 'F';

      // Now display the grade

      cout << endl;
      cout << "The grade for that mark is: ";
      cout << grade;
      cout << endl;
}
```

**Figure 2.4** Nested `if` statements

You should also notice that one `if` statement is contained inside the other, or in programming terms, they are *nested*. So, only if the exam mark is not greater than or equal to 80 will the next `if` statement be executed (to check if the mark is greater than or equal to 70).

The chaining of `if` statements, in this way, is a common construction, used in very many programs, so it is worth getting to grips with it. It is also worth looking at the layout of the program in Figure 2.4. We have abandoned our conventional indentation rule for a layout that is more suited to nested `if` statements.

Figure 2.5 shows another example of the use of nested `if` statements. The program calculates the interest for a year on a sum invested with a bank; the interest rate depends on the length of the investment.

Note the use of constants for the different interest rates and periods of investment. Using constant definitions at the beginning of a program allows the program to be easily updated if these values change. If *literal constants* (i.e. the actual numbers, 40, 50, etc.) were used, the programmer would have to find each and every occurrence throughout the program and, if one were missed, the program would be incorrect. Using constants, as in the program in Figure 2.5, the updates would be restricted to one place in the program, thus making the change less error prone.

You should also note the way the `cout` statements have been constructed. Take, for example, the line:

```
cout << "The amount deposited is " << sum;
```

Here we are displaying two different pieces of data in the same statement. The first piece is a string constant that describes to the user what is coming next, and the second piece of data is a variable called `sum`. Each piece of data is separated from the next by a set of chevrons (<<). This is a convenient way of writing several outputs in a single statement and, in this case, is equivalent to:

```
cout << "The amount deposited is ";
cout << sum;
```

We use this technique a great deal in the program in Figure 2.5 for two reasons. The first reason is to allow us to output more than one item in a single statement and the second is to make the program more readable. This is important as programs will be read on media with limited widths. The layout of a program is known to be an important factor in determining how long it takes to read and understand it. The line:

```
cout << "Welcome to the Extremely Generous"
     << " Banking Corporation";
```

is more easily readable than one that is not split into two parts but, due to its length, will extend beyond the edge of the computer screen.

```
//
// The interest rate depends on the length
// of the investment.
// The program prompts for the amount on
// deposit and the length of the investment
//
#include <iostream.h>
void main()
{
      float sum, time, rate;

     // Specify the investment periods
      const int highBand = 10; // 10 or more years
      const int medBand = 5;   // 5 or more years
      const int lowBand = 3;   // 3 or more years

      // The rates that go with the periods
      const int highRate = 40;
      const int medRate = 30;
      const int lowRate = 20;
      const int minRate = 15;  // default rate

      cout << "Welcome to the Extremely Generous"
           << " Banking Corporation" << endl << endl;

      cout << "Enter the sum on deposit: ";
      cin >> sum;
      cout << "And the years on deposit: ";
      cin >> time;

      if (time >= highBand)
            rate = highRate;
      else if (time >= medBand)
            rate = medRate;
      else if (time >= lowBand)
            rate = lowRate;
      else // less than lowBand
            rate = minRate;

      cout << "Your interest rate is " << rate << "%";
      cout << endl;
      cout << "The amount deposited is " << sum;
      cout << endl;
      cout << "The interest for the year is "
           << sum*(rate/100);
      cout << endl << endl;
      cout << "Thank you for your custom";
      cout << endl;
}
```

**Figure 2.5** Interest calculation using nested `if` statements

## The `switch` statement

There is another mechanism for making multiple choices in C++ and that is the switch statement. This allows you to make a decision depending on the value of an expression or variable like the if statement. However, with the switch statement you can check for a number of different values and define different outcomes for each of them.

The general form of the switch statement is:

```
switch (expression)
{
        case value 1:
                statement 1;
        case value 2:
                statement 2;
        .
        .
        .
        case value n:
                statement n;
}
```

The switch statement begins with the word switch followed by an expression in brackets that must evaluate to an integral value (i.e. any form of int or, as in this case, a char). Following this, within braces, are a number of case statements that enumerate the values of the expression that we are interested in. Following the colon of the case statement is the program code required to perform the operations that we want for that particular value.

The program in Figure 2.6 shows an example of the use of the switch statement. It provides the opposite information to that in Figure 2.4. If you enter the grade that you have received in an examination, it will give you the range within which your mark will have fallen. So, for example, if the grade entered was 'A' then the statement following the 'A' case would be executed. (This program checks only for upper case letters. If a lower case letter is entered, e.g. 'c', then none of the cases 'A' to 'F' will match it.) Notice that the code is laid out in a way that shows the relationships between the various parts of the switch statement.

There are two more things to notice about the switch example in Figure 2.6. The first is the default case. This matches any value that does not match any of the specified cases; in this program any character that is not in the range 'A' to 'F' will match the default case. The inclusion of the default case is optional in a switch statement. If it is not present and none of the specified cases match, then the program will continue with the next statement after the switch statement and none of the code in the switch statement will have been executed.

The second thing to take note of is how each message that outputs the range of marks is followed by the word `break`. The effect of `break` is to stop executing the `switch` statement and continue program execution with the statement immediately after it.

If `break` was not included after the code for each case then the statements for each of the following cases would be executed until either `break` was encountered or the end of the `switch` statement was reached. In most programs, each case of the `switch` statement is terminated with the word `break`, but there are situations where this is not so.

In the following piece of code, the *same* operation is required for each of the cases, `'A'` to `'E'`; only `'F'` and the `default` case are treated differently. If the value of grade is `'A'`, `'B'`, `'C'` or `'D'`, the effect is to *fall through* to the code in the `'E'` case. Thus here it would not be correct to include `break`s after every case.

```
switch (grade)
{
        case 'A':
        case 'B':
        case 'C':
        case 'D':
        case 'E':
                cout << "You passed";
                break;

        case 'F':
                cout << "You failed";
                break;

        default:
                cout << "Invalid grade!";
}
```

Notice that there is no code after the colon in each of the cases `'A'`, `'B'`, `'C'` and `'D'`. This is because for each of these cases we simply want to perform the same operation as we do for the case `'E'`. The syntax of C++ allows the programmer not to place any code after a case, but clearly there is no point in having a case unless there is an associated action to be performed when it is encountered. The ability to 'leave a case blank' in this way is therefore a mechanism which should be used to 'collect cases together' as we have done in the exam grades example.

We can make use of this aspect of the `switch` statement to fix the program in Figure 2.6 so that it will accept lower case letters as well as capitals. Figure 2.7 shows a new version of the program that specifies cases for all the relevant upper and lower case letters. The two figures are very similar. Figure 2.7 simply has an extra case for each grade, showing that the same instructions are to be executed whether the grade is entered as an upper or lower case character.

```
//
// Exam grades program showing the
// use of the switch statement
//
// Input the grades that you have received
// and the program will print the range in
// which your mark will have fallen
//
#include <iostream.h>

void main()
{
      char grade;

      // Prompt the user for the grade
      // Note that it must be entered as
      // a CAPITAL letter
      cout << "Please enter your grade (A to F): ";
      cin >> grade;

      // The start of the output message
      cout << "Your mark was between ";

      switch (grade)
      {
            case 'A':
                  cout << "80 and 100" << endl;
                  break;
            case 'B':
                  cout << "70 and 79" << endl;
                  break;
            case 'C':
                  cout << "60 and 69" << endl;
                  break;
            case 'D':
                  cout << "50 and 59" << endl;
                  break;
            case 'E':
                  cout << "40 and 49" << endl;
                  break;
            case 'F':
                  cout << "0 and 39" << endl;
                  break;
            default:
                  cout << "? and ?" << endl;
                  cout << "Unknown grade!" << endl;
      }
}
```

**Figure 2.6** Reverse exam grades

```
//
// Input the grades that you have received
// and the program will print the range in
// which your mark will have fallen
//
#include <iostream.h>
void main()
{
	char grade;

	// Prompt the user for the grade
	cout << "Please enter your grade (A to F): ";
	cin >> grade;

	// The start of the output message
	cout << "Your mark was between ";
	switch (grade)
	{
		case 'A':
		case 'a':
			cout << "80 and 100" << endl;
			break;
		case 'B':
		case 'b':
			cout << "70 and 79" << endl;
			break;
		case 'C':
		case 'c':
			cout << "60 and 69" << endl;
			break;
		case 'D':
		case 'd':
			cout << "50 and 59" << endl;
			break;
		case 'E':
		case 'e':
			cout << "40 and 49" << endl;
			break;
		case 'F':
		case 'f':
			cout << "0 and 39" << endl;
			break;
		default:
			cout << "? and ?" << endl;
			cout << "Unknown grade!" << endl;
	}
}
```

**Figure 2.7** Reverse exam grades allowing for lower case entries

## Exercises

2.1 Are there any circumstances where you would need a statement in the `else` part of an `if... else...` statement but not in the `if` part? How would you write this and how might you re-write it without an `else` part?

2.2 In Figure 2.4, which conditions will be evaluated by the program when the numbers 27, 62 and 60 are entered?

2.3 Again, in Figure 2.4, how would the behaviour of the program change if the >= symbols were replaced with > ?

2.4 Given that the following assignments have just been executed:

```
a = 1;
b = 2;
c = 3;
d = 4;
```

what are the results of the following code fragments?

a)
```
if (a == 1)
        cout << "A is 1";
```

b)
```
if (!(a == 1))
        cout << "True";
else
        cout << "False";
```

c)
```
if (a == b || c == d)
        cout << "True";
else
        cout << "False";
```

d)
```
if (a < b && d > c)
        cout << "True";
else
        cout << "False";
```

2.5 Write a program that will test whether a character entered is a vowel or not and will display an appropriate message as a result.

# 3

# Repetition

## Aims

The aim of this chapter is to describe how various forms of repetition can be achieved in `C++`, and to what use these may be put.

After studying this chapter you should be able to:

- understand the forms of repetition and why they are necessary
- construct `while` and `do ... while ...` loops
- apply the repetitive constructs to various programming problems, including input validation
- understand the concept of nested loops and their use

# Introduction

In this chapter we are going to learn about repetition in C++ programs. The need for repetition may not seem immediately obvious but some form of repetition is present in most, if not all, useful programs.

A major use of repetition is to run the whole program a number of times. The programs in the previous chapter would benefit from this. The user could continue to use the program for any number of grades, without having to run the program over and over. There are other uses for repetition, too, as we shall see in the following examples.

Some problems cannot be solved without using repetition. Consider the following program specification:

**Specification 1**: Write a program to display a line of ten characters on the display screen. The character to be displayed should be chosen by the user.

The solution to this could simply be:

*Get the character from the keyboard,*
*Display the character,*
*Display the character,*
*Display the character,*
*Display the character,*
*Display the character,*
*Display the character,*
*Display the character,*
*Display the character,*
*Display the character,*
*Display the character,*
*Send an end of line character to the display.*

Here we get the character to be displayed from the keyboard and then display it ten times. An experienced programmer would probably think this inefficient, but it is a perfectly good solution to the problem that could easily be coded in C++.

For the problem illustrated by Specification 1 above, we know when we write the program precisely how many times we shall need to print out the character we have read in. This means that we can simply repeat the code to print out the character the required number of times. The reason this would be an unattractive solution to a more seasoned programmer lies in the inelegance and inflexibility of simply repeating code a fixed number of times. For more realistic problems we may not know the number of times to repeat a section of code. Consider, for example, Specification 2 below:

**Specification 2**: Write a program to display a line of characters on the display. The character to be displayed, and the length of the line, should be chosen by the user.

Here is the solution:

> *Get the character from the keyboard,*
> *Get the length of line from the keyboard*
> *Store the length in a variable called counter,*
> *Repeat the following until the value of counter is zero:*
>
> > *Display the character,*
> > *Subtract 1 from counter,*
>
> *End of the repeated section,*
> *Send an end of line character to the display.*

In this case, again we get the character to be displayed from the keyboard and we also get the length of the line in the same way. Then, we assign this last value to a variable called `counter`; this will be used to control the number of times the character is displayed. The next four lines form the repeated section: we execute the two indented actions repeatedly until the value of the variable `counter` is equal to zero. Since one of the statements in the loop decrements the variable, the number of times that the loop is executed is equal to the initial value of `counter`, and since the other statement is to print the character, the character will be printed that many times.

Had we been aware of how to use repetition we could, of course, have designed the first program in the same way as the second, and given that the solution looks simpler, we probably would have done so. (By the way, rather than the word repetition, programmers normally talk of iteration and looping; from now on so shall we.)

You should notice that the approach that we adopted to solve the problem in Specification 1 is not applicable to Specification 2. In fact, we *cannot* solve the problem in Specification 2 without using a loop.

## The `while` loop

We will implement the design for Specification 2, above, in C++ using a *`while`* loop (so called because it is a C++ statement that performs looping, and it starts with the word `while`). The general form of the `while` loop is

```
while (condition)
      statement;
```

The condition in the brackets is formed in exactly the same way as we have seen for the conditions used in the `if` statement. It is typically a relational expression and must yield a non-zero (true) or zero (false) result. Again, this is the same as the conditions used in the `if` statement.

On encountering a `while` loop, the condition is executed. If the value yielded is false, then the `while` loop terminates. If the value is true, then the statement part of the loop is executed and the whole process is repeated. The single statement can, of course, be replaced by a block statement, and usually we shall find that we need to do this.

Figure 3.1 contains the C++ implementation of Specification 2. Having received the character to be displayed and the length of the line, a `while` loop is used to print out the correct number of characters by using the variable `counter` to control the number times the loop is executed. This is an example of a *counter controlled loop* and we shall see another example in the next section.

There are two other types of loop that we shall discuss in the following sections; these are *condition controlled* and *sentinel controlled*. Each of the three types of loop are very common programming constructs and are very useful for solving programming problems. You should familiarise yourself with the way each of them is constructed and the ways in which they are used.

```
//
// Display a line of characters, the length and contents of
// which are read in from the keyboard.
//
#include <iostream.h>

void main()
{
      char character;
      int counter;

      cout << "Enter the length of the line: ";
      cin >> counter;
      cout << "and the character: ";
      cin >> character;

      while (counter > 0)
      {
            cout << character;  // display the character
            counter--;          // decrement the counter
      }

      // The loop terminates when the value of the
      // counter reaches zero.
      // That is the controlling condition becomes false

      cout << endl;
}
```

**Figure 3.1** Display a line of characters with a `while` loop

## Counter controlled loops

A counter controlled loop is one where the number of iterations is determined by the value of a variable which is usually incremented or decremented each time the loop is executed.

Here is another example of a program that uses a counter controlled loop: a multiplication table calculator. The program should print out the multiplication table for a number between one and nine, that has been entered by the user. Here is a solution to the problem:

> *Set the last multiplier to 10*
> *Set the counter to 1*
> *Get the number*
> *While the counter is less than or equal to the last multiplier*
>         *Print counter * number*
>         *Increment the counter*
> *End of repeated section*

A counter controlled loop prints the table using the counter value itself, as the multiplier. In the previous program, the counter was decremented each time the loop was executed and the loop terminated when the counter reached zero. In the multiplication program, the counter is incremented each time the loop is executed and the loop terminates when it reaches the limit value. The `C++` program for this solution is shown in Figure 3.2.

## Condition controlled loops

Although all `while` loops continue until the controlling condition becomes false, there is a class of loop that is termed *condition controlled* to distinguish it from the other two types (counter and sentinel controlled).

In a counter controlled loop, the loop is executed a number of times determined by a counter. The starting value for the counter may be known when the program is written, and therefore it will be the same for every execution of the program (as in the multiplication table program in Figure 3.2) or it may not be known until the program is executed (as in the program in Figure 3.1). Whichever is the case, the number of iterations can be calculated — either by the programmer when the program is written or by statements in the program before the loop is executed.

When using a condition controlled loop, the relationship between the condition and the statements executed within the loop is generally more complex than simply incrementing or decrementing a counter because the number of times that the loop will execute cannot be calculated before the loop starts.

```
//
// The user enters a number and
// the multiplication table for
// this number is displayed
//
#include <iostream.h>

void main()
{
	const int limit = 10;

	// Remember to initialise the counter to the
	// correct value before entering the loop
	int number, count = 1;

	cout << "Multiplication Table Program";
	cout << endl << endl;

	cout << "Please enter an integer number: ";
	cin >> number;

	while (count <= limit)
	{
		// Display the next line of the table
		cout  << count << " times " << number
		      << " = " << count * number
		      << endl;

		count++; // increment the counter
	}
}
```

**Figure 3.2** Multiplication tables implemented with a counter controlled loop

Consider how a program might be written to calculate how long it will take to pay off a loan, given that we know the amount of the original loan, the monthly payment and the interest rate that is applied each month.

One solution would be to calculate how much of the loan would remain after each month and to continue this calculation until the sum owed became less than zero, i.e.

*Get the values for the loan, the payment and the interest rate*
*While the amount owing is greater than zero*
    *Calculate the interest for the month*
    *Add the interest to the amount owing*
    *Subtract the monthly payment from the amount owing*
    *Print the amount owing*
*End of repeated section*

In this solution, the number of times that the loop is executed cannot be calculated until it has finished. In fact the number of times the loop executes *is* the value that we want to calculate.

The program in Figure 3.3 is the C++ implementation of this solution. We have added a counter to count the number of iterations and thus the number of months it will take to pay off the loan. This counter does not *control* the loop, however, it is simply a record of the number of times that the loop was executed.

```
//
// If a loan is paid back at a certain amount per month
// how long will it take to pay back the loan?
//
#include <iostream.h>

void main()
{
	float loan, rate, payment;
	int month = 0;

	cout << "Amount of loan: ";
	cin >> loan;
	cout << "Monthly interest rate: ";
	cin >> rate;
	cout << "Payment per month: ";
	cin >> payment;

	while (loan > 0.0) // one month per loop iteration
	{
		month++; // Increment the month counter

		// Add the interest for the month
		loan = loan + (loan * rate/100);

		// Subtract the monthly payment
		loan = loan - payment;

		// Display the current balance
		cout  << "In month " << month
		      << " the sum remaining is "
		      << loan << endl;
	}

	cout  << "It will take " << month
	      << " months to pay";
}
```

**Figure 3.3** Loan Calculator: an example of a condition controlled loop

## Sentinel controlled loops

In this last type of loop, the number of times that the loop is executed is often determined by the user. The condition that terminates the loop is that of a variable (known as a sentinel) being given a particular value (the sentinel value).

A common use of this type of loop is where a program performs the same task a number of times on different data, supplied by the user. When there is no more data to enter the user enters a value that the program recognises as a signal to stop. This value is the sentinel value.

Our example of a sentinel controlled loop is a program that calculates the average of a set of exam scores. The scores are entered by the user, but the program does not know how many will be entered. In order to signal that there are no more data, the user enters the special value of −1. This is an invalid exam score and so cannot appear in the set of data to be entered; it is, therefore, safe to use it as a sentinel value.

*Set a counter to zero*
*Get the first score*
*While the score is not equal to −1*
    *Add the score to the total*
    *Increment the counter*
    *Get the next score*
*End of the repeated section*

*If the counter is zero then*
    *Print "No scores were entered"*
*Else*
    *Set the average to total/counter*
    *Print the result*
*End of if... else... section*

Notice that the first score is entered before the loop begins. This is done because the while condition uses the score, so it must be given a valid value before the loop is entered. It also has the effect that if there are no scores to enter, and so the first value is −1, the loop will not be executed at all and so will not cause erroneous calculations to be made. The averaging program is shown in Figure 3.4.

## Input validation

Input validation is simply making sure that the user of the program inputs the sort of data that the program expects. For example, we might write a program that only works with a certain range of numbers and so would need to ensure that the user only enters numbers that fall within the valid range.

```
//
// Enter a list of exam scores and the
// program will calculate the total
// and average.
//
// Signal the end of the list by entering
// a score of -1.
//

#include <iostream.h>

void main()
{

      int counter = 0, score, total = 0;

      cout  << "Enter the exam scores as integers"
            << "(-1 to finish)"
            << endl;

      cout << "First score: ";
      cin >> score;

      while (score != -1)
      {
            total = total + score;
            counter++;

            cout << "Score: ";
            cin >> score;
      }

      if (counter == 0)
            cout << "No scores were entered";
      else
            cout  << "Total = " << total
                  << endl
                  << "Average = " << total/counter
                  << endl;
}
```

**Figure 3.4** Exam score average calculator: An example of a sentinel controlled loop

What is the result of dividing any number by zero? In computing terms, the answer is often that the result is an error and the program stops (this is dependent on the compiler being used; some compilers do not produce an error). Of course, this is not an acceptable state of affairs and it is the responsibility of the programmer to write programs in such a way that this sort of error does not occur. Programs that cannot 'crash' when executed are said to be *robust*.

In a program that uses division, we could make sure that a divisor is not zero by using an `if` statement: this would allow us to avoid making a calculation that would cause an error. But this is not a very good solution, as the program would not then be doing the job that it was designed to do. Using a loop, however, we can repeatedly attempt to obtain a new, non-zero, number.

As an example, let us consider a simple program that gets two numbers from the keyboard and divides the first by the second. We want to ensure that the second number is not zero, so as not to cause an error. However, we do not want to abandon the program if the second number is zero; we want to allow the user another chance to enter a valid number. Here is a solution:

*Initialise the variable that will hold the second number to zero*
*Get the first number*
*While the second number is 0*
        *Get the second number*
*End of repeated section*
*Calculate the result as first number / second number*
*Print the result*

Notice the initialisation of the variable that is to hold the second number. This is done to ensure that the loop will be entered and the second number will be obtained from the user. The loop is an example of a condition controlled loop that will continue to execute until a non-zero value is entered for the second number. The program in Figure 3.5 is the C++ implementation of this solution.

## Allowing a range of inputs

We have seen how we can filter out a single value (i.e. zero) from an input, but what do we do if we require the user to enter a number within a certain specified range? Let us imagine that part of a program will only work with the numbers one to ten, inclusive. This is a simple example of a common situation, where a part of a program will give the wrong result if it performs a calculation on a number which is not within a specified range. In such situations we will want to avoid executing the 'fragile' part of the program if the number is not in the specified range. We can ensure that only numbers between one and ten are accepted using the following loop:

```
while ((secondNum < 1) || (secondNum > 10))
{
      // input code goes here
}
```

As we saw in Chapter 2, the `||` means 'or', so the loop continues if the value of `secondNum` is less than one, or it is greater than ten. That is, the loop continues *while* the value of `secondNum` is 'out of range'.

```
//
// An example of input validation.
//
// This is a program that will accept two integer
// numbers, divide the first by the second and
// then display the result.
//
// Entering zero as the second number
// is not allowed
//
#include <iostream.h>

void main()
{
      int firstNum;
      int secondNum = 0;

      // Input the data
      cout << "Enter the first number: ";
      cin >> firstNum;

      while (secondNum == 0)
      {
            cout << "Enter the second number"
                 << "(not zero): ";
            cin >> secondNum;
      }

      // Display the result on the screen (output)
      cout << firstNum / secondNum;
      cout << endl;
}
```

**Figure 3.5** A simple division program

## The `do ... while ...` loop

In the program in Figure 3.5, the variable `secondNum` needed to be initialised to an invalid value (i.e. zero) before the loop started executing, otherwise the loop would refer to an uninitialised variable. Uninitialised variables may have any value that happened to be in the computer's memory at the time that the program started, so you should regard the value as undefined. (In fact, some `C++` compilers do initialise all variables to zero before the program starts. But others do not! So you cannot rely on this being the case.) There is another form of `while` loop that eliminates the need for initialisation; it is the `do ... while ...` loop. It is a simple variation of the `while` loop theme.

The general form of a `do ... while ...` loop is:

```
do
        statement;
while (condition);
```

The `do ... while ...` loop looks quite similar to the `while` loop. But, as you might guess from the layout, there is a significant difference. The plain `while` loop makes the test on the condition before any code in the loop is executed and, if the conditional expression is false, the loop will not be entered. In the `do ... while ...` loop the code in the loop is executed first and *then* the test is made. Therefore, the statement controlled by the `do ... while ...` loop is guaranteed to be executed at least once.

The program in Figure 3.6 shows the use of the `do ... while ...` for input validation. The program itself is trivial: it gets two numbers from the user, adds them together and displays the result. However, both numbers must be in the range one to ten inclusive and the validation required is performed by two `do ... while ...` loops. Notice that the variables `firstNum` and `secondNum` do not need to be initialised because they are each given a value when the statements in the respective loops are executed for the first time.

---

```
//
// This program only accepts input in the range 1 - 10
//
#include <iostream.h>
void main()
{
      int firstNum, secondNum;

      do
      {
            cout << "Enter the first number: ";
            cin >> firstNum;
      } while (firstNum < 1 || firstNum > 10)

      do
      {
            cout << "Enter the second number: ";
            cin >> secondNum;
      } while (secondNum < 1 || secondNum > 10)

      // Now display the sum on the screen
      cout << firstNum + secondNum << endl;
}
```

---

**Figure 3.6** Using the `do ... while ...` loop for input validation

## Nested loops

A nested loop is one which occurs within the body, or statement part, of another loop (similar to the nested `if` statements that we saw earlier in Chapter 2, where one `if` statement is contained in the body of another). Nested loops prove to be a very powerful programming construct. The program below shows how nested loops are constructed:

```
#include <iostream.h>
void main()
{
      int counter1 = 1, counter2;

      while (counter1 <= 10)
      {
            cout << "Counter 1: "
                 << counter1
                 << endl;

            counter2 = 1;
            while (counter2 <= 10)
            {
                  cout << " Counter 2: "
                       << counter2
                       << endl;
                  counter2++;
            }
            counter1++;
      }
}
```

The program consists of two counter controlled loops both of which terminate after ten iterations. The inner loop, which is controlled by the value of the variable `counter1`, is nested inside the outer one, which is controlled by the value of the variable `counter2`. The inner loop is executed ten times, on every occasion when the outer loop is executed. The inner loop is therefore executed 100 times in total because the outer loop is executed ten times in all. In order to see what is happening we have printed out the values of the variables which control each loop on each iteration. By running the program you can see the relationship between the two counters (note that the counter for the inner loop is initialised just before the loop is executed).

The program in Figure 3.7 is another version of the exam average calculator we first saw in Figure 3.4. This time a counter controlled loop reads and calculates the average score over four exams for each student. This loop is nested inside a sentinel controlled loop that is executed once for each student. The user must enter a numeric identifier for each student. This identifier is used to signal that there are no more marks to process when the value entered is the 'special' identifier −1. At the end of the program, the overall average for the whole class is calculated.

```
//
// Exam Average Calculator (2)
//
// First enter a student ID (integer).
// Then enter a list of exam scores for
// that student and the program will
// calculate the total and average
// for that student.
//
// Signal the end of the student list by
// entering a student ID of -1.
// The program will calculate the overall
// average overall score.
//

#include <iostream.h>

void main()
{
      const int NoOfExams = 4;

      int studentID, examCounter, total, score,
          numberOfStudents = 0,
          grandTotal = 0;

      cout  << "Enter the student ID "
            << "(-1 to finish): ";
      cin >> studentID;

      while (studentID != -1)
      {
            examCounter = 1;
            total = 0;

            while (examCounter <= NoOfExams)
            {
                  cout << "Enter the result of exam "
                       << examCounter
                       << " for student "
                       << studentID
                       << endl;

                  cin >> score;
                  total = total + score;
                  examCounter++;
            }

            cout << "The total for student "
                 << studentID
                 << " is "
                 << total
```

```
                    << endl
                    << "and the average per exam is "
                    << total/NoOfExams
                    << endl;

          grandTotal = grandTotal + total;
          numberOfStudents++;

          cout   << "Enter the student ID "
                 << "(-1 to finish): ";
          cin >> studentID;
     }

     if (numberOfStudents == 0)
          cout << "No results were entered";
       else
          cout << "The number of students was "
               << numberOfStudents
                  << endl
               << "and their overall average was "
               << grandTotal/numberOfStudents
               << endl;

}
```

**Figure 3.7** An example of nested loops

# Exercises

3.1 Consider what would happen if the expression that controls the `while` loop, in Figure 3.1, was

```
while (counter != 0)
```

Would the program still work? Can you think of any circumstances when the program would not work?

3.2 How could you write a program, similar to the one in Figure 3.1, but where the counter is incremented rather than decremented ?

3.3 Write a `C++` program that will perform either addition or subtraction on two numbers. The user should be prompted for two integers and then asked whether they should be added or subtracted (since there are only two possible answers to this, the input should be validated).

The program should then perform the appropriate calculation and display the result.

3.4 Study the following program; there are no comments in it. There are two loops, one inside the other, and every time that the first loop is executed, the second is executed ten times. Add appropriate comments to the program and explain what it does.

```
#include <iostream.h>

void main()
{
        int x = 0;
        int y = 0;

        while ( y < 10 )
        {
                x = 0;

                while ( x < 10 )
                {
                        cout << '*';
                        x = x + 1;
                }

                cout << endl;
                y = y + 1;
        }
}
```

3.5 Write a program, similar to the one in Exercise 3.4, but let the user enter the dimensions of the shape that is drawn (they should not be so large that the resulting shape does not fit on the screen).

3.6 How would you design a program to draw a right-angled triangle? Try to work out the method, and if you can, write the program.

3.7 Can you write a loop that never terminates? Can you think of a program in which such a loop would be useful?

3.8 How could you use a loop to make your program pause for a few seconds before printing a result? This might be useful if a lot of output is produced and the user will not have time to see it all as it appears on the screen. The fact that computers are so fast is not always an advantage!

3.9 Adapt the multiplication table program in Figure 3.2 so that it will print the multiplication table for all numbers between 1 and 12. (Hint: use a nested loop.)

3.10 Write a program to test the user on a selected multiplication table, asking them to enter the answer to each of the 12 multiplications and printing the string `"Correct"` or `"Incorrect"` as appropriate.

3.11 Write a program that reads in a sequence of positive numbers and prints out the total and average value. The end of the sequence should be signalled by entering the value –1.

3.12 Write a program to produce a hollow rectangle, i.e. if the user types in 5 and 4, the result would be:

```
*****
*   *
*   *
*****
```

3.13 Find as many syntax errors as you can in the following program:

```
#include iostream.h

void main()
{
      const int NoOfExams = 4;

      int studentID, examCounter, total, score,
          numberOfStudents = 0,
          grandTotal = 0;

      cout  << "Enter the student ID (-1 to finish): ";
      cin >> studentID;

      while studentID != -1
      {
            examCounter = 1;
            total = 0;

            while (examCounter <== NoOfExams)

                  cout << "Enter the result of exam "
                       << examCounter
                       << " for student "
                       << studentID
```

```
                        << endl;

                cin >> score;
                total = total + score;
                examCounter++;
        }

        cout << "The total for student "
             << studentID
             << " is "
             << total
             << endl
             << "and the average per exam is "
             << total/NoOfExams
             << endl;

        grandTotal = grandTotal + total;
        numberOfStudents++;

        cout  << "Enter the student ID "
              << "(-1 to finish): ";
        cin >> studentID
}

if (numberOfStudents == 0)
        cout << No results were entered";
  else
        cout << "The number of students was "
             << numberOfStudents
                 << endl ;
             << "and their overall average was "
             << grandTotal/numberOfStudents
             << endl;
```

# 4

# Data Structures

## Aims

This chapter introduces two types of data structure: the array and the class. Classes are covered in more detail in Chapter 10; this chapter provides merely an introduction. It shows how arrays and classes may be used to structure data, so that several related items of information can be viewed as a single entity.

After reading this chapter you should be able to:

- define and use arrays and classes as data structures
- use a `for` loop
- write programs which manipulate large amounts of data
- design appropriate structures for storing information

## Introduction

We have seen in the preceding three chapters that `C++` programs may use and manipulate various forms of data, each of which has a particular form or *type*. The types that we have encountered so far are the integer (`int`), the character (`char`) and the decimal number (`float`).

In the next two chapters we will explore the way in which several items of data can be stored together, allowing us to model the information from the real world that influences our programs. A data structure is a way of grouping several smaller items of data into one larger item of data. We often want to do this — here are some examples:

- the marks of a class of students are made up of several individuals' marks
- a person's name is made up of several individual characters
- the details of a customer are made up of, at least, name, address and phone number

In this chapter we shall show how simple data types, such as integers, characters and floating point numbers (`ints`, `chars` and `floats`) can be combined into larger data structures. The two data structuring techniques of `C++` which we shall consider are the `array` and the `class`.

## Arrays

An array is a data structure. A data structure is one large data object made up of several smaller data items, grouped together because they are related to one another in some way. For an array data structure, all the smaller, component, data items are of the same type.

A data structure is used in the development of software in order to model some aspect of the real world. Programmers have found that flexibility in the definition and manipulation of data structures is essential. The closer a data structure models the real world, then the easier it is to adapt a program to changes in the world and the easier it is to understand and debug the program.

The array was the first kind of data structure invented during the development of software technology, and it is the simplest. The more recent developments of object-oriented software technology allow for far more elaborate data structures to be created which model both the world and the way humans interact with computers more accurately than does the humble array. In this chapter we will see how the array allows us to group an arbitrary number of similar data items together and how the class structure allows us to store dissimilar data items together.

## The minimum example

To see why we need an array we shall consider a simple programming problem. Suppose we want to write a program to read in two numbers and print out the smallest of the two. A natural way to do this is to declare two integer variables, read in the numbers and compare the two using an `if` statement. A program to do this is given in Figure 4.1 below:

```
#include<iostream.h>

main()
{       int x,y;

        cout << "Please type in two numbers" ;
        cin >> x >> y ;

        cout << "The smallest number is ";
        if (x<y) cout << x;
        else cout << y;
}
```

**Figure 4.1** Finding the smallest of two numbers

This program works fine. We might consider extending the problem to find the smallest number amongst three input values. To do this we have a more involved problem because not only do we require an extra variable, but we require an extra `if` statement. The program to find the smallest amongst three numbers is given in Figure 4.2 below:

```
#include<iostream.h>

main()
{       int x,y,z;

        cout << "Please type in three numbers" ;
        cin >> x >> y >> z;

        cout << "The smallest number is ";
        if ((x<y) && (x<z)) cout << x;
        else if ((y<x) && (y<z)) cout << y;
              else cout << z;
}
```

**Figure 4.2** Finding the smallest of three numbers

The program in Figure 4.2 is slightly larger than that in Figure 4.1, but then the problem has increased in complexity by a similar amount, and so we might now consider the problem of finding and printing out the smallest number in a sequence of 10, 100 or 1,000,000 numbers.

One of the nice aspects of computer programming is the way in which we can write a small program which performs a task that a human would find unimaginably time-consuming and tiresomely boring. Sadly, in this case, we cannot merely adapt the approach we have taken so far since there is an inherent 'scaling up' problem.

> The approach that applies to a simple problem cannot always be extended to apply to larger problems which merely involve more processing of a similar kind.

## An extended minimum example: the need for an array

If we wanted to find the smallest number chosen from a thousand numbers, then, using the approach adopted so far, we would have to define a thousand variables, and we would have a thousand `if` statements. When we start to conceive programs with very many statements, all of which perform a similar task, then we should start to think that we need to use a loop. Loops are fundamental to programming languages because they allow us to avoid writing the same piece of program over and over again.

So we could modify the approach we have taken so far, to use a loop, but we will *still* end up with as many variables as we have numbers to read in. What we need is an *array*.

An array is a collection of data items grouped together in a sequence. When we define an array we must tell the computer two things:

- how many data items we want
- what type of data items we want

If we want an array of 10 integers, and we want to call the array `A`, for example, we write the definition like this:

```
int A[10] ;
```

Notice how similar this is to the definition of a single integer variable called `A`, which would look like this:

```
int A ;
```

The only difference is that we have added the *number* of integers to the definition, so that the computer knows that `A` is to be an array variable, and that it is to have ten elements.

The two pieces of information (size of array and element type) define an array, fixing both its size and the kind of thing which can be stored within it.

- because we have to say how many data items we want, our array will have a *fixed size*, which we must choose when we write the program.
- because we must tell the computer the type of the data items, all must have the same type, which we must also choose when we write the program.

Conceptually we can think of an array of `ints` as a sequence of boxes each of which contains a single integer:

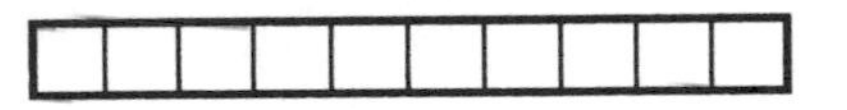

In this case there are ten boxes.

What if we want to print out the value of an integer which is stored as an element of an array? In this situation, we have to tell the computer which element we want.

The elements of an array are numbered, so that we can refer to each individually.

*The first element is numbered 0.*

This means that in an array of 10 elements, the *last* element is number 9. The numbers which tell us which position an element occupies in an array are called indices. The first index is *always zero*, and the last is determined by the size of the array (it is always one less than the size of the array, because we start counting at zero).

An array of 10 elements can be thought of as a sequence of elements. Each element in the sequence is identified by its position in the sequence, which is described by its index number. We can therefore extend our pictorial view of an array to include index numbers like this:

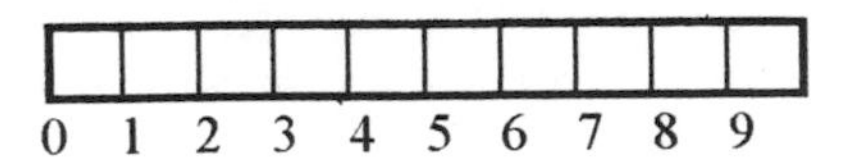


In this case we have 10 indices starting from 0 and ending up at 9. The array consists of 10 numbered boxes.

Now, if we want to print out the value of a *single integer* variable, say x, we can do that like this:

```
cout << x;
```

To print out the value stored in an *element of an array*, we must specify the *index* of the element. For example, to print out the first element of the array A, defined above we would write:

```
cout << A[0];
```

To print out the last element we would write:

```
cout << A[9];
```

You could think of A as one large item of data with 10 boxes which are numbered 0, 1, 2, 3, 4, 5, 6, 7, 8 and 9. Alternatively you could imagine that the definition:

```
int A[10];
```

defines 10 variables called A[0], A[1], A[2], A[3], A[4], A[5], A[6], A[7], A[8] and A[9]. The first view is the better one, however, because, as we shall see, the index can be calculated so we can refer, for example, to

```
A[i+2]
```

meaning the element two positions further towards the end of the array from position i. The next question to address is how we put values into the elements of an array. Fortunately, we use the same notational device of placing the desired index inside square brackets [ ... ]. For example, in order to store 42 in the first element of the array A, we would write:

```
A[0] = 42 ;
```

We are now in a position to write the minimum program again, so that this time the program finds the minimum number in a sequence of numbers. To make the problem seem more impressive, we shall assume that the user is going to type in twenty numbers.

We shall need to define an array of twenty elements. This is as easy as defining an array of ten or a thousand. We shall need to use a loop which executes twenty times. This is as easy as writing a loop which executes ten or a thousand times. The array is to data repetition what the loop is to statement repetition.

The minimum program with an array is given in Figure 4.3. The program reads in 20 integers and works out which is the smallest. This value is printed out at the end of the program.

```
#include<iostream.h>

main()
{
int A[20] ;          // to store the numbers
int i ;              // a loop control variable
int smallest ;       // to store the result

cout << "Type in 20 numbers" ;
i=0 ;
while(i<20)
{      cin >> A[i] ;
       i++;
}
i=0 ;
smallest = 99 ;       // start with a very
                      // large value for smallest
while(i<20)
{      if (A[i] < smallest)
             smallest = A[i] ;
       i++;
}

cout << "The smallest is" ;
cout << smallest ;
}
```

**Figure 4.3** The `minimum` program

Notice that we start by assuming that `smallest` should be set to `99`. This is intended to be a sensible value to start with, because everything in the array will be smaller than it, and so as soon as the loop body is first executed, the value `99` will be lost (replaced by the first element of the array). Notice that we *must* put some value in the variable `smallest` before the loop starts, because before the first assignment to `smallest` in the body of the loop, we test the value of `smallest` using the `if` statement's controlling boolean expression.

## The danger of artificial limits in computer programs

Now if the user types in a set of numbers all of which happen to be larger than `99`, for example a list of top peoples' salaries in pounds sterling, then the *smallest* salary will be *larger* than `99`, and the assignment to the variable `smallest` inside the loop will never take place. This means that the program will print out the *wrong* number. It will print out '`the smallest number is 99`'.

We could raise the threshold a little, say storing 9999 in smallest as our initial value, but we can play this 'think of a bigger number' game forever, without being sure that we have made a suitable choice.

A lot of problems which have been discovered in real computer programs are to do with programmers assuming that values will never exceed a preset limit. At the time of writing, the so-called 'Year 2000 problem' is currently worrying very many computer users. What happens to programs which calculate interest payments and other important values which depend upon the date, when the year clicks around to the number 2000? Some old systems were written with a two digit number to store the year — such systems cannot distinguish between the year 1900 and the year 2000. This flaw could cost a great deal of money!

Faced with a situation where we are about to pick an artificial limit when we write a program we have two possibilities:

- look for a way to avoid setting such a limit
- choose the limit, clearly document it, and store the value of the limit at one point alone in the program text (as a constant)

In the first case, we simply take another look to see if there is a way around the problem, so that the limit need not be imposed. This may not always be possible, in which case we are forced to adopt the second, less desirable, approach.

In the second case, we make a choice, entirely arbitrarily, about the limit. Usually, we shall choose a limit which allows as much room for manoeuvre as possible. However, the issue is not to choose a 'good' limit — experience has taught us that there is no such thing. Instead, we seek to make the choice *at one point alone* in the program, and to document this decision as *clearly* as possible. We can do this by defining a constant, in this case to define the value of the 'large number' that we shall use in finding the smallest element of an array. The version of the program with a constant definition is given in Figure 4.4 below:

---

```
#include<iostream.h>

main()
{
const int LargeNumber = 9999 ;
// this integer must be larger than any number
// in the array A. If not the program will
// print that 9999 is the largest number in
// the array A.

int A[20] ;        // to store the numbers
int i ;            // a loop control variable
```

```
int smallest ;   // to store the result

cout << "Type in 20 numbers" ;
i=0 ;
while(i<20)
{      cin >> A[i] ;
       i++;
}

i=0 ;
smallest = LargeNumber ;
           // start with a very
           // large value for smallest

while(i<20)
{ if (A[i] < smallest)
       smallest = A[i] ;
  i++;
}

cout << "The smallest is" ;
cout << smallest ;
}
```

**Figure 4.4** The `minimum` program with a large constant definition

Fortunately, a superior approach is available. We can write the program so that it does not require an artificial limit. The improved program, without an artificial limit, is given in Figure 4.5 below.

We know that the smallest number in the array will be *one* of its elements, so the initial value for the smallest might as well be the *first* element of the array. Notice that this improvement in the program also allows us to start the loop counting from the number one, in place of the number zero, thus making the program slightly more efficient.

```
#include<iostream.h>

main()
{
int A[20] ;      // to store the numbers
int i ;          // a loop control variable
int smallest ;   // to store the result

cout << "Type in 20 numbers" ;
i=0 ;
while(i<20)
```

```
{       cin >> A[i] ;
        i++;
}

i=1 ;
smallest = A[0] ;   // start with the first
while(i<20)
{       if (A[i] < smallest)
                smallest = A[i] ;
        i++;
}

cout << "The smallest is" ;
cout << smallest ;
}
```

**Figure 4.5** A better version of the `minimum` program

## Reversing the input

In the previous example we attempted to demonstrate the necessity for an array. We did this by showing that it would be impossible to write a program to find the smallest number in a sequence of numbers input from the keyboard without an array.

This is not strictly true. We showed that declaring a large number of variables would make it *hard* to write such a program without an array, but not *impossible*. We could, however, have written a program to solve the problem without an array at all. This version of the program is given in Figure 4.6 below:

```
#include<iostream.h>

main()
{
int Anumber ;     // to store the numbers
int i ;           // a loop variable
int smallest ;    // to store the result

cout << "Type in 20 numbers" ;
cin >> smallest  ;      // start with the first
cin >> Anumber ;        // set up the 'current'
                        // number
i=0;
while(i<18)
{       if (Anumber < smallest) smallest = Anumber ;
        i++;
        cin >> Anumber ;
}
```

```
cout << "The smallest is" ;
cout << smallest ;
}
```

**Figure 4.6** The `minimum` program without an array

All we have done is to move the reading in of numbers into the loop. As we need only to remember one number (the smallest) outside the loop, we need only one variable to store it — there is no need to store all the other numbers.

We now turn to a problem where arrays *are* required to avoid an explosion in the number of variables needed to solve a problem.

Suppose we want to write a program to read in a set of numbers and print out the sequence in reverse. We shall need an array to store the input as it is read in because the last number to be read in is the first to be printed out. We shall suppose that we want to read in ten numbers. The program which reverses the order of the input is given in Figure 4.7 below:

```
#include<iostream.h>

main()
{
int A[10] ;        // to store the numbers
int i ;            // a loop control variable

cout << "Type in 10 numbers" ;

i=0;
while(i<10)
{       cin >> A[i] ;
        i++;
}

cout << "In reverse order that is" ;
i=9;
while(i>=0)
{       cout << A[i] ;
        i--;
}
}
```

**Figure 4.7** Program to reverse ten numbers read in from the keyboard

We use two loops, one after the other. The first reads in the input from the user. Notice that once we have the input stored in an array we can access the elements of the input in *any order* we choose, using the indices of the array. In this case, we use the second loop to start at the end of the array and print out the elements of the array in reverse order.

Notice that to print in reverse order we start at the end of the array (element 9) and finish at element 0.

## The `for` loop and the array

There is a common pattern emerging in the use of an array and a loop together. We often find ourselves processing the elements of an array using a loop to apply the same operation to each element of the array. In this situation we have to use a loop which requires a control variable to *count* the iterations of the loop and act as an index into the array. This variable is initialised at the outset of the loop, making it refer to the first element we wish to process, and then on each iteration of the loop we adjust the control variable to access the next element of the array. The controlling expression of the loop decides when we have reached the last element we wish to process (usually the end of the array).

For example, suppose we want to add one to all the elements of an array called `Num`, which contains one thousand numbers. We could do that with a `while` loop, like this:

```
i=0;
while(i<1000)
{       Num[i]  = Num[i]  + 1;
        i++;
}
```

This loop pattern occurs so often in C++ that we have a special loop, which allows us to express the whole concept of initialising the control variable, testing it, repeating and altering the control variable.

This loop is called a `for` loop, and it is merely a shorthand notation for a `while` loop together with some initialisation. Using a `for` loop, we could rewrite the fragment of code above like this:

```
for(i=0;  i<1000;  i++)  Num[i]  = Num[i]  + 1;
```

The body of the loop is

```
Num[i]  = Num[i]  + 1;
```

If the body contains more than one statement it must be written between a { and a }.

Before the loop starts executing the assignment

```
i=0;
```

is performed. Next the test

```
i<1000
```

is performed and if true, the body of the loop is executed. On each iteration of the loop, just before the test is recalculated, the assignment

```
i++;
```

is performed.

Any `for` loop can be rewritten as a `while` loop. Consider the `for` loop below (in which *e1*, *e2* and *e3* stand for any expression and *s* stands for any statement):

```
for(e1;e2;e3) s
```

This loop can be rewritten as a `while` loop like this:

```
e1;
while(e2) { s; e3; }
```

For example, in the loop:

```
for(i=0; i<1000; i++) Num[i] = Num[i] + 1;
```

| | | |
|---|---|---|
| *s* | is | `Num[i] = Num[i] + 1;` |
| *e1* | is | `i=0` |
| *e2* | is | `i<1000` |
| *e3* | is | `i++` |

Notice how the use of a `for` loop shortens the program. Many of the features of C++, inherited from its predecessor, C, are designed to allow such shorthand notations. Used carefully, they lead to simpler programs, which execute faster, and which are easier to understand. However, if the concept is pushed to the limit, the result is code of the most unreadable form, which is potentially very dangerous as it is difficult to maintain.

Using a `for` loop, we can rewrite the two programs which we used to solve the 'minimum' problem and the 'reverse' problem. The program in Figure 4.6 to find the smallest element of the input using a `for` loop is given in Figure 4.8. Notice how the structure of the loop in Figure 4.6 is preserved in the `for` loop in Figure 4.8. The initialisation of the variable `i` and its increment after each loop iteration is made a part of the loop structure in the `for` loop of Figure 4.8.

```
#include<iostream.h>

main()
{
int Anumber ;      // to store the numbers
int i ;            // a loop control variable
int smallest ;     // to store the result

cout << "Type in 20 numbers" ;

cin >> smallest   ;    // start with the first
cin >> Anumber ;       // set up the 'current'
                       // number

for(i=0; i<18; i++)
{     if (Anumber < smallest) smallest = Anumber ;
      cin >> Anumber ;
}

cout << "The smallest is" ;
cout << smallest ;
}
```

**Figure 4.8** The `minimum` program using a `for` loop

The `reverse` program of Figure 4.7 can also be written using a `for` loop. This version of the `reverse` program is given in Figure 4.9. Notice that the use of the `for` loop makes the structure of the `reverse` program much clearer — as two loops, one 'ascending' and one 'descending'.

```
#include<iostream.h>

main()
{
int A[10] ;       // to store the numbers
int i ;           // a loop variable

cout << "Type in 10 numbers" ;
for(i=0; i<10; i++) cin >> A[i] ;

cout << "In reverse order that is" ;
for(i=9; i>=0; i--) cout << A[i] ;
}
```

**Figure 4.9** The `reverse` program using a `for` loop

## Indices out of range

At this point, a natural question to ask is: 'What happens if we write:

```
cout << A[219];
```

in a program where the array A is defined to contain 10 elements?'

We are thereby attempting to print out an element of the array which is not 'valid' because we only asked for an array of ten elements, and the index value we have used is outside the range 0 to 9. This is an example of a run-time error. Run-time errors manifest themselves when the program is run. By contrast, compile-time errors manifest themselves when the programmer attempts to compile the program. The compiler cannot check that an index to an array will always be in range, as the value of the index will, in general, depend upon the input to the program. The compiler will therefore compile the `cout` statement above adding machine code to check, at run time, to see if the value of the index is in range. If this check reveals that the index value is out of range then the program will be terminated with an appropriate error message.

As well as referring to an invalid element of an array there is also the problem of using an invalid array index to store a value in an array. Suppose we write a statement like

```
A[21] = x;
```

for an array A, which has a maximum index of 20. Then we are attempting to store a value, x, in some part of memory that we have not told the computer we intend to use for that purpose. If we write a statement like this the run-time machine code check added by the compiler will cause the program to be terminated with an error message.

A natural question to ask at this point is: 'Why can the compiler not tell us that we are accessing an element out of range?' Well, the answer is that, in this case, it can. However, the general problem of whether or not an array index is in or out of range is not a question that the compiler can answer. Consider the program fragment below:

```
cin << y ;
A[y] = 42 ;
```

Clearly the element of the array which is affected by the second statement *depends* upon the value read into the variable y when the first statement is executed. The compiler has to create a program that can handle any possible execution, and cannot therefore decide when it compiles the program whether or not the index used in the second line is in range.

Many compilers do not check for *any* form of array indexing at compile-time, as the value used for the index will often depend upon the input to the program. This is a shame, as we should like compilers to warn us of *any* potential foreseeable problems.

Gradually, compilers are getting better at warning us of potential problems in our programs. The development of source code analysis techniques and improvements in the performance of machine code generated by compilers is the subject of on-going research. Of course, there will never be a time when the compiler tells us about every pitfall in our program because the computer cannot be programmed to work out what ideas are in our head. What we *tell* the computer to do and what we *want* the computer to do are sometimes two different things. There is no such thing as 'computer error', there is only 'programmer error' in our inability to express what we *want* the computer to do correctly. Anyone who blames bad service or shoddy work on a 'computer error' is a fraud.

## Initialisation of arrays

When we declare an array we can initialise it with a value in the same way that we initialise a numeric or character value. With a numeric value we might write:

```
int answer = 42;
```

or

```
float pi = 3.14156 ;
```

and with a character value we might write:

```
char specification = 'Z' ;
```

However, with an array, we have a slight problem: How do we write a constant to represent the entire contents of an array?

The answer is that we use curly brackets (also known as 'braces'). For example, to represent an array of five numbers, all of which are set to zero, we would write:

```
{0,0,0,0,0}
```

To represent an array containing, in ascending order, the first seven positive, odd numbers we would write:

```
{1,3,5,7,9,11,13}
```

So, in order to initialise an array we would write, for example:

```
int A[10] = {2,4,6,8,10,12,14,16,18,20} ;
```

This tells the compiler that the array `A` is to be 10 integers long and that its contents are to be the first 10 positive even numbers when the program starts executing.

A question arises: 'What happens if we write an initialisation in which there are too few or too many elements in the constant array?'

Well, if, for example, we write:

```
int A[10] = {2,4,6,8,10,12,14} ;
```

then we simply initialise only the first seven elements of the array A, leaving the last three elements uninitialised.

On the other hand, if we write:

```
int A[10] = {2,4,6,8,10,12,14,16,18,20,22};
```

then the extra element, 22, is simply ignored.

## Example: payroll program

Using what we have learnt so far about arrays, we can write a simple program to work out the amount of pay an employee should receive. A simple solution to this problem is given in the payroll program of Figure 4.10 below:

---

```
// A simple payroll program
// Input the number of hours worked for each day
// and work out the pay due.
// Saturdays and Sundays are paid at a
// premium rate.
//
//
#include <iostream.h>

void main()
{
const float normalRate = 5.00;
const float overTimePremium = 1.5;

float hours[7];     // This will hold the
                    // hours for each day
int i = 0;
float pay = 0.0;

cout << "Enter the hours for each day"
     << endl
     << "(day 0 is Monday, "
     << "1 is Tuesday, etc.)"
```

```
      << endl;

// Get the hours into each array element
while (i < 7)
{
      cout << "Enter the hours for day "
           << i << ": " ;
      cin >> hours[i];
      i++;
}

// Work out basic pay for Monday to Friday
i = 0;
while (i < 5)
{
      pay = pay + (hours[i] * normalRate);
      i++;
}

// Now add the pay for the weekend
// We left the variable i at 5.
// i.e. Saturday
// but just in case the program gets changed
// in the future we will set to the
// value we want here.

i = 5;       // Saturday
while (i < 7)
{
      pay = pay+(hours[i]*(normalRate*overTimePremium));
      i++;
}

cout << "Your total pay is: " << pay << endl;
}
```

**Figure 4.10** A simple payroll program

## The class as a data structure

When we declare an array, we choose the size of the array and the type shared by the elements that occupy the array. The elements of the array all have the *same* type. This is just what we want for many applications, since we want to perform the same form of processing upon each element of a large data structure which is made up of identical individuals. However, there are many occasions when we shall want to store related pieces of information together even though they are *not* of the same type. For example, we might want to store a character together with the number of times that it occurs in a sentence. In order to do this we shall use the `class` structure.

## Example: representing the date

Suppose we want to represent the current date, as years, months and days. We could use an array with three elements, all of which are `int` types. With such an array we can use the first element for the day of the month, the second for the month of the year and the third for the year.

However, instead, we might use a `char` type for the day and month because these will not exceed the range storable in the `char` type (remember that a `char` can be used to store small integer values as well as character values). We will not be able to use a `char` type for the year, however, as this value is ultimately unlimited. We could use an `int` type for the year as this will give us a wide range of possible values for the year. Using an array will, therefore, require us to choose an `int` type for all three values we want to store, because the type of thing we store must be the same for all elements of the array.

Another possibility is that we might want to store *four* values for the date: the three letters representing the day of the week and the numbers representing the day of the month, the month of the year and the year. In this situation we cannot use an array at all; the type of the day of the week is fundamentally different from the types for the other three values.

We can define a class data structure to represent the date like this:

```
class date {

public:
      char WeekDay[3] ;
      char DayOfMonth ;
      char MonthOfYear ;
      int  Year ;

} ;
```

*Note that it is a very common programming error to forget the semicolon after a class declaration.*

The word `public` is required because, by default, the elements of a `class` type are private to the class (this will become clearer in Chapter 10, which describes classes in more detail).

Notice that the class contains three different types of data: an array of three characters (used for `WeekDay`), an integer (used for `DayOfMonth` and `MonthOfYear`) and an individual character used for `Year`. All are grouped together under the title of `date` (the word which appears immediately after the word `class`). The elements which are grouped together as elements of the class are defined between the curly brackets `{...}`. Each of these elements is defined using the normal syntax for defining variables, but these definitions do *not* define variables.

Having written the definition above we will not have *any* new variables, we shall have a new *type* (called `date`). We can use the new type `date` in the subsequent declaration of variables. For example, if we write:

```
date TodaysDate;
```

we are declaring that the variable `TodaysDate` is to be of type `date`. The variable `TodaysDate` will have four components to it and they are indexed using 'dot' notation like this:

```
TodaysDate.Year
```

This expression represents the last element of the variable `TodaysDate`, which is an integer. To access the first element of the variable `TodaysDate`, we would thus write:

```
TodaysDate.WeekDay
```

This refers to the first element of the variable `TodaysDate`, which (according to the type definition of the class `date`) is an array of three characters. We could therefore print out the three letters making up the day of the week using a mixture of array and class indexing notation like this:

```
cout << TodaysDate.WeekDay[0]
     << TodaysDate.WeekDay[1]
     << TodaysDate.WeekDay[2] ;
```

Notice that the array index goes at the end. This is because the expression `TodaysDate.DayOfWeek` represents an array of characters, which we index in the normal way we have been doing for other arrays. Pictorially, a variable of type `date`, defined like this:

```
class date {

public:
      char WeekDay[3] ;
      char DayOfMonth ;
      char MonthOfYear ;
      int  Year ;

} ;
```

looks like this:

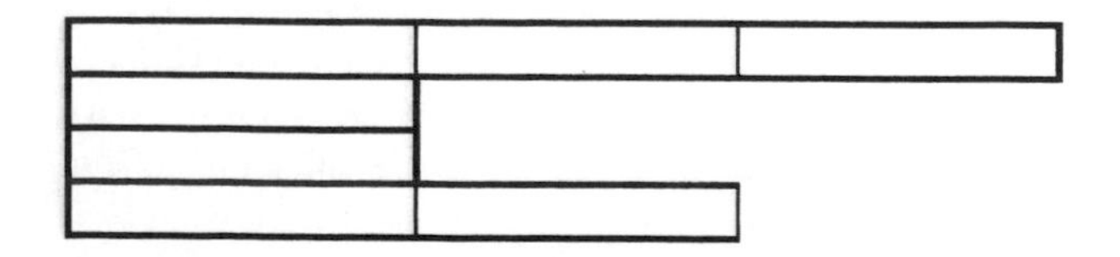

Each box represents one byte of storage on a typical computer. The four rows are the four elements of the variable. The first row is the three bytes which are used to store the three characters in the DayOfWeek part of TodaysDate. The next two rows are the two character elements DayOfMonth and MonthOfYear and finally, the last row is the two bytes used to store the integer value for the element Year.

Using a class allows this unimportant information (about the size of things) to be hidden from us, and we may think of all variables of type date as simply a collection of four relevant pieces of information.

Suppose we want to write a program to store and print out a date stored using the variable TodaysDate. A program which does this is given in Figure 4.11 below:

---

```
#include <iostream.h>

// First define the type
// and declare a variable

class date {

public:
      char WeekDay[3] ;
      int  DayOfMonth ;
      int  MonthOfYear ;
      int  Year ;

} ;

main()
{
date TodaysDate ;

// Store a date
TodaysDate.WeekDay[0] = 'F' ;
TodaysDate.WeekDay[1] = 'r' ;
TodaysDate.WeekDay[2] = 'i' ;
TodaysDate.DayOfMonth = 17 ;
TodaysDate.MonthOfYear = 11 ;
TodaysDate.Year = 1995 ;


// Now print it out again

cout << "The date is: ";

cout << TodaysDate.WeekDay[0]
     << TodaysDate.WeekDay[1]
     << TodaysDate.WeekDay[2] ;
```

```
cout << " the " << TodaysDate.DayOfMonth ;

if ((TodaysDate.DayOfMonth = 11) ||
    (TodaysDate.DayOfMonth = 12) ||
    (TodaysDate.DayOfMonth = 13)) cout << "th" ;
else
if (TodaysDate.DayOfMonth % 10 == 1)
      cout << "st" ;
if (TodaysDate.DayOfMonth % 10 == 2)
      cout << "nd" ;
if (TodaysDate.DayOfMonth % 10 == 3)
      cout << "rd" ;
      else cout << "th." ;

cout << " of " ;

switch(TodaysDate.MonthOfYear)
{
      case 1  : cout << "January"   ; break ;
      case 2  : cout << "February"  ; break ;
      case 3  : cout << "March"     ; break ;
      case 4  : cout << "April"     ; break ;
      case 5  : cout << "May"       ; break ;
      case 6  : cout << "June"      ; break ;
      case 7  : cout << "July"      ; break ;
      case 8  : cout << "August"    ; break ;
      case 9  : cout << "September" ; break ;
      case 10 : cout << "October"   ; break ;
      case 11 : cout << "November"  ; break ;
      case 12 : cout << "December"  ;
}

cout << ", " << TodaysDate.Year ;

}
```

**Figure 4.11** A program to store and print the date using a `class` structure

At this stage we are entitled to think that this is a lot of effort simply to print out the date.

This is because we have made some implicit trade-offs in the way we have stored the date. For example, we have stored the components of the date separately — week day name, day of month, month and year. We could instead have simply stored the date as an array of characters, so that the date 13:8:1995 would be stored as

```
"Sunday the 13th. of August 1995"
```

This would make printing out the date extremely easy — we simply need one cout statement. However, we would not find it at all easy to, for example, increase the month of the year number by one, using this method of storing the information.

We chose to *structure* the information we wanted to store in a logical way that reflected how the information breaks up into smaller units. This makes the information easier to manipulate, but there is an initial overhead in setting up the structure and a separate overhead in reconstructing the information in a form suitable for the user.

Usually we shall want to process the information we store in the computer and therefore, it will usually make sense to use a data structure and to put up with the frustration of setting up the information in the structure and representing it to the user. This frustration will be far outweighed by the ease of manipulation. However, in the very rare cases where there is some data which is merely to be stored and printed out unaltered, then we will not need to structure the data — an array of characters will do.

## Classes of classes

A class can contain elements of any type, including class data structures. Suppose we want to store names and dates associated with historic events. A natural step is to build upon the class structure that we have already defined for the date class.

We could define a bigger class, called event, which contains an array of characters which describes an event and a date, represented using the class date. The definition looks like this:

```
class date {

public:
      char WeekDay[3] ;
      int  DayOfMonth ;
      int  MonthOfYear ;
      int  Year ;

} ;

class event {

public:
      char description[20] ;
      date when ;

} ;
```

If we now declare a variable, JFK, of type event like this:

```
event JFK ;
```

we can assign values to the elements of the event, using the normal class indexing notation. The only difference is that there are two levels of indexing involved in accessing elements of the when part of an event. The following assignments set four fields of the variable JFK:

```
strcpy(JFK.description, "J.F Kennedy is shot") ;
JFK.when.DayOfMonth  = 22   ;
JFK.when.MonthOfYear = 11   ;
JFK.when.Year        = 1963 ;
```

The statement strcpy(x,y) copies the string y into the string x, but in order to use it we must add

```
#include <strings.h>
```

to the beginning of our program (either just before or just after the #include <iostream.h>, which we have become accustomed to including without question).

Notice that the expression:

```
JFK.when
```

results in a class of type date, which has its own structure containing the four components defined by the class date. The field when of the class event is of type date, an example of a class within a class.

## Arrays of classes

As well as defining a class within a class, we may also use a class as a component of an array. Indeed, any type may be used as the type of data to be stored in an array. Suppose we want to store a list of historic events. We could define an array called HistoryList of elements of type event like this:

```
event HistoryList[10] ;
```

To print out the year associated with the third element of the sequence of events we could write a cout statement like this:

```
cout << HistoryList[2].when.year ;
```

Remember that we start counting the elements of an array at *zero*, so the third element of HistoryList is obtained by writing the expression:

```
HistoryList[2]
```

This expression results in a class of type event.

The expression:

```
HistoryList[2].when
```

results in a class of type `date` (since `HistoryList[2]` is a class of type `event`, the `when` component of which is a class of type `date`). The expression:

```
HistoryList[2].when.Year
```

results in an `int` (since `HistoryList[2].when` is a class of type `date`, the `Year` component of which is an `int`). The way in which we have built bigger data structures from smaller ones is a typical example of how the facilities of C++ allow us to construct large complex data structures from smaller simpler ones.

We shall now look at another example of the class data structure, which is at the heart of the data storage mechanisms used in the many databases which store information about us. Using this structure we shall build an array which is, effectively, a simple model of the central data structure in a database.

## Example: personal details

When you take a book out of a library, money out of a bank, book a holiday, join a college course, go to hospital or pay your taxes, your 'personal details' are stored on a computer and used to make decisions about you.

Information about people has always been stored by banks and governments in card indexes. Computers and mass storage provide such organisations with greater speed and flexibility in how they choose to use the information that they possess.

The data structure required to store information about people is essentially a `class` data structure. The only variation between the applications is the type and amount of information stored. Suppose we are storing information about employees in a company. We want to record a person's name, address, telephone number, age, gender and the position of the person on the pay scale. We might start out by defining a class called `PersonDetails`, like this:

```
class PersonDetails {

public:
      char Name[20] ;
      char Address[50] ;
      char PhoneNumber[15] ;
      int  Age ;
      char Gender ;
      int  Grade ;
} ;
```

In defining this data structure we have made several decisions about the limits to the information we will store.

We have limited the sizes of the name, address and phone number elements of the structure. We have chosen an `int` to represent the age. We could equally well have chosen a `char`, as this type has a wide enough range for reasonable lifetimes. We have chosen a `char` type for the gender, although we shall only use two of the possible values: `'F'` for female and `'M'` for male.

We have chosen to store the phone number of the employee as an array of characters because we shall not be performing any processing on the number, and the range of phone numbers may require very many digits. We have chosen an `int` type for the grade, although it is unlikely that a `char` type would be found to be too restrictive.

## Example: the payroll program again

Suppose we want to rewrite the payroll program to take account of the grade of the employee. In order to simplify the program we shall concentrate on the fragment which works out the person's pay, and ignore the parts of the program that establish the database of employees and their personal details. We shall include the data type declarations and variable definition which set up an array of person details which represents the employees in the company. The more elaborate version of the payroll program is given in Figure 4.12 below:

---

```
#include <iostream.h>

void main()
{
   const NumberOfEmployees = 10 ;
   const float overTimePremium = 1.5;
   const float Rate[3] = {4.25,5.00,5.50} ;

   class PersonDetails {

   public:
      char Name[20] ;
      char Address[50] ;
      char PhoneNumber[15] ;
      int  Age ;
      char Gender ;
      int  Grade ;
      float Hours[7] ;
      float Pay ;
   } ;

   PersonDetails DBase[NumberOfEmployees] ;
```

```
// DBase contains the details of the 10
// employees.

int Person = 0 ;
int i;

while (Person < 10)
{
   DBase[Person].Pay = 0.0;
   DBase[Person].Grade = 1;

   cout << "Employee Number:" << Person << endl;
   cout << "Enter the hours for each day"
         << endl
         << "(day 0 is Monday, "
         << "1 is Tuesday, etc.)"
         << endl;

   // Get the hours into each array element
     i = 0;
   while (i < 7)
   {
         cout << "Enter the hours for day "
              << i << ": " ;
         cin >> DBase[Person].Hours[i];
         i++;
   }
     Person++;
}

// Now that we have read in the hours worked
// for each day by each employee

Person = 0 ;

while(Person<10)
{
   i = 0;
   while (i < 5)
   {
         DBase[Person].Pay = DBase[Person].Pay +
   (DBase[Person].Hours[i]*Rate[DBase[Person].Grade]);
   i++;
   }

// Now add the pay for the weekend
// We left the variable i at 5
// i.e. Saturday
// but just in case the program gets changed
// in the future we will set to the correct
// value here.
```

```
      i = 5;       // Saturday
      while (i < 7)
      {
            DBase[Person].Pay = DBase[Person].Pay +
(DBase[Person].Hours[i]*Rate[DBase[Person].Grade]*
                overTimePremium);
            i++;
      }
        Person++;
   }

   // No we go through the database printing out
   // pay slips for each employee

   Person = 0;
   while(Person<10)
   {
      cout << "PAY SLIP" << endl;
      cout << "Number: " << Person << endl;

      cout << "Grade: " << DBase[Person].Grade ;
      cout << endl ;
      cout << "Pay: " << DBase[Person].Pay ;
      cout << endl ;

        Person++;
   }
}
```

**Figure 4.12** A more elaborate payroll program

## Explanation

The statement which works out an employee's pay for the days of the week Monday to Friday is quite complex, and in order to understand how it works we must break it down into its component parts. The whole statement is:

```
DBase[Person].Pay = DBase[Person].Pay +
(DBase[Person].Hours[i]*Rate[DBase[Person].Grade]);
```

The part:

```
DBase[Person].Pay
```

consists of two levels of indexing. `DBase[Person]` uses the loop variable `Person` to index into the array `DBase`. This results in an object of type `PersonDetails`, which allows us to further index using the `Pay` component of the `class PersonDetails` giving us a value of type `float`.

This float represents the amount of pay owed to the employee at location Person in the array DBase.

The value of DBase[Person].Pay starts off at zero before the loop is executed. The whole instruction

```
DBase[Person].Pay = DBase[Person].Pay +
(DBase[Person].Hours[i]*Rate[DBase[Person].Grade]);
```

adds to the current value of DBase[Person].Pay the value of the expression:

```
(DBase[Person].Hours[i]*Rate[DBase[Person].Grade])
```

The variable i tells us the day of the week we are interested in. This variable cycles through the five weekdays (day numbers 0 through 4) as a result of the loop in which the whole instruction is contained. The expression:

```
DBase[Person].Hours
```

yields an array containing the hours worked by the employee given by the variable Person. This array contains seven elements, one for each day potentially worked. The expression:

```
DBase[Person].Hours[i]
```

therefore yields the number of hours worked on day i by employee number Person.

The expression :

```
DBase[Person].Grade
```

yields an integer number between 0 and 2 which represents the grade of the employee number Person in the database. The expression is used to look up the hourly rate for that grade as an index into the 3 element constant array called Rate.

The amount of pay for employee number Person and day number i is thus calculated by multiplying the hourly rate for the employee by the number of hours worked for day i. This is the purpose of the expression:

```
(DBase[Person].Hours[i]*Rate[DBase[Person].Grade])
```

In order to work out the total pay for the employee number Person, the amount for each day must be accumulated by adding it into the current total built up day-by-day in the loop controlled by the variable i. To work out pay for all employees the calculation must be repeated for each employee. This is achieved by performing the same calculation for each employee in the database, using the loop controlled by the variable Person.

Of course, the calculation for pay at weekends is slightly different because there is an overtime premium which increases the hourly rate for work carried out on a Saturday or Sunday. The means that we have worked out the pay for these two days separately, multiplying the hourly rate for the employee by the variable `overTimePremium`.

After we have calculated the pay for each employee, it remains to print out the payslip. This is comparatively straightforward, as all that is required is to go through each employee, printing out the details of their name and address and the amount of pay due to them for the week. The method used to print the name and address of an employee is rather complicated as this information is contained in an array of characters. In the next chapter we will see how a slight modification to the way characters are stored in an array will allow us to store this information in a string, making it very much easier to print it out.

## Exercises

4.1 Write a program which reads 5 numbers into an array and prints out the value of each and every number which has a value less than 10.

4.2 Write the program from Exercise 4.1 without using an array.

4.3 Adapt the program in Exercise 4.1 so that numbers which lie between 0 and 100 inclusive are printed out.

4.4 Write a program to read in 5 people's salaries and work out the tax to be paid (at 25%) for each.

4.5 Adapt the program from Exercise 4.4 so that it takes account of the banding of tax. Tax bands apply to income. Income earned in band one is untaxed. In band two a small percentage of the income is taken in tax, in band three a larger percentage is taken and so on. You may assume that there are four bands of tax in total.

4.6 In Exercise 4.5 you may not have been *aware* of the current rates of tax and the values for each of the bands of tax. Even if you were aware of these values, you know that they are likely to change. This is an example of a situation where we have made an arbitrary decision about a value in our program.

Write the tax program so that it is easy to *find* and *change* the decision that we have made about the range of each tax band and the rate for each band.

4.7 Write a program fragment which reduces by 10% the value stored in each element of an array. What type do you think the array elements should be in this exercise?

4.8 Write a class data type suitable for storing the description of a book. The type should include the title, author, price and publisher, but you should add any other details that you think might be important.

4.9 Write a fragment of code which prints out the details stored in the book data type you defined in Exercise 4.8.

4.10 Consider the program below and find as many syntax errors in it as you can:

```
#include <iostream.h>

void main()
{
   const NumberOfEmployees : 10 ;
   const float overTimePremium = 1.5
   constant float Rate[3] = {4.25,5.00,5.50} ;

   class PersonDetails {

   public:
      char Name[20] ;
      char Address(50) ;
      char PhoneNumber[15] ;
      int  Age ;
      char Gender ;
      int  Grade ;
      float Hours[7] ;
      float Pay ;
   }

   PersonDetails DBase[NumberOfEmployees] ;
   // DBase contains the details of the 10
      employees.

   int Person = 0 ;
   int i, j;

   while Person < 10
   {
```

```
        DBase[Person].Pay = 0.0;
        DBase[Person].Grade = 1;

        cout << "Employee Number:" << Person << endl;
        cout << "Enter the hours for each day"
              << endl
              << "(day 0 is Monday, "
              << "1 is Tuesday, etc.)
              << endl;

        // Get the hours into each array element
          i = 0;
        while (i < 7)
        {
              cout << "Enter the hours for day "
                   << i << ": " ;
              cin >> DBase[Person].Hours[i];
              i++;
        }
          Person++;
    }

    // Now that we have read in the hours worked
    // for each day by each employee

    Person = 0 ;

    while(Person<10)
    {
       i = 0;
       while (i < 5)
       {
              DBase[Person].Pay = Pay +
       (DBase[Person].Hours[i]*Rate[DBase[Person].Grade]);
       i++;
       }
    }
}
```

# 5

# Strings and Pointers

## Aims

This chapter shows how varying length strings may be implemented using the null character to terminate a string and introduces the concept of dynamically allocated memory (creating variables as the program is running).

After reading this chapter you should be able to:

- write programs which manipulate strings
- write programs which allocate memory as the program executes

## Introduction

In Chapter 4 we saw how more complex forms of data can be represented in structures. There was a recurrent problem in the way we defined and used these data structures; we had to decide when we defined the structure how much space it should occupy. This limitation forced us to decide, for example, how long the longest name we would store should be. For many applications the restriction is unacceptable.

The problem is that we tell the *compiler* about the size of the data we intend to use in our program. This means that we decide the amount of storage *at the time we write the program*. This kind of storage allocation is called *static* because it is decided at the time the program is compiled and remains unchanged throughout the execution of the program[1].

The alternative is to write our programs so that they use up a varying amount of storage space as they execute. The program will therefore need to allocate storage space using an *instruction*, and to give up this storage space when it is no longer needed.

In this chapter we shall look at the problem of fixed size and varying sizes of data structure. First we shall look at a compromise, in which the amount of store for an array is decided at compile time (that is, statically), but where the amount of the array which we actually use may vary. In the section headed 'Pointers', we shall take a brief look at the way in which a program may allocate and deallocate its own storage space as it executes. The subject of pointers is a very important one for C++ programmers. In this chapter we shall provide only an introduction.

## Arrays of characters: checking for a palindrome

Arrays can contain *any* type of data we please. For example, in Chapter 4, we saw how to define arrays of integers and arrays of classes. In this section we shall look at a particularly important type of array element — the character.

An array of characters can be used to represent a word, a car registration number, a date, a piece of prose, even, if we choose, a number (as an array of characters which make up its digits).

As an example of the use of an array, consider the problem of working out whether or not a word is a palindrome. A palindrome is a word that is spelt the same forwards as it does backwards, for example 'noon' and 'madam' are palindromes whilst the words 'push' and 'shove' are not.

---

[1]In general, aspects of a program which are decided at compile time (and therefore remain unchanged throughout execution) are called static, whilst those decided as the program executes (and which may, therefore, change during the execution of the program) are called dynamic.

As so often happens in computing, there is an obviously correct and straightforward way to write this program, which is not particularly efficient (i.e. that is slow), and there is a faster version, which is more efficient (i.e. comparatively fast), but which is, perhaps, not the approach that immediately springs to mind.

We shall consider the easy way first. A palindrome is spelt the same backwards and forwards, so we could read in an array of characters, work out the reverse, and then test the reversed version against the original to see if they are identical. This 'simpleminded' version of the palindrome program is given in Figure 5.1 below:

```
#include <iostream.h>

main()
{
int i ;
char Input[5] ;      // To store the original
                     // word
char Reversed[5] ;  // for the reverse of
                     // the original word
int IsNotPalindrome ;          // will store 0 if the
                               // Input is a palindrome,
                               // and 1 if it is not

cout << "Type in a word of five letters" ;
for(i=0; i<5; i++) cin >> Input[i];

for(i=0; i<5; i++) Reversed[i] = Input[4-i] ;

IsNotPalindrome = 0;
for(i=0; i<5; i++)
  if (Input[i] != Reversed[i]) IsNotPalindrome = 1;

if (IsNotPalindrome)
      cout << "The word is not a palindrome";
else cout << "The word is a palindrome";
}
```

**Figure 5.1** A simpleminded version of the palindrome program

Notice that in storing the reversed version of the array, we used the expression `4-i` to allow us to 'count down' from 4 to 0, while the value of `i` was 'counting up' from 0 to 4. We can use any *expression* to index an array, provided the expression returns an integer value.

The variable `IsNotPalindrome` is used to record the decision made about whether or not the input word is a palindrome.

We start comparing the elements of the input word with those of its reversed version having set the value of `IsNotPalindrome` to `0`. The value zero indicates that the word *is* a palindrome. As soon as we find a letter in the input word which does not agree with the corresponding character of the reversed version, we set `IsNotPalindrome` to `1`, indicating that the word is not a palindrome.

Notice that the value of `IsNotPalindrome` can only change from zero to one, but never from one to zero. We can use this observation to improve upon the efficiency of the execution of the loop which sets the value of `IsNotPalindrome`: if the value becomes one we may as well finish the execution of the loop. We can cause the loop to terminate by testing the value of `IsNotPalindrome` during the progress of the loop as well as the condition we already have (which stops the loop when the characters of the input word have been exhausted). The new version of the loop looks like this:

```
IsNotPalindrome = 0;
  for(i=0; (i<5) && !IsNotPalindrome; i++)
    if (Input[i] != Reversed[i])
       IsNotPalindrome = 1;
```

Notice that the only way that the value of `IsNotPalindrome` remains at zero is if the loop finishes having exhausted all elements of the arrays `Input` and `Reversed`. This observation can be used to remove the need for the variable `IsNotPalindrome`. We can simply finish the loop if we find a letter in `Input` which is not the same as the corresponding character in `Reversed`. We can then use the value of the loop control variable as an indicator of whether or not the word was a palindrome — if `i` is less than the length of the input word (i.e. less than 5), then the word cannot be a palindrome. The improved version of the palindrome program is given in Figure 5.2 below:

```
#include <iostream.h>

main()
{
int i ;
char Input[5] ;     // To store the original word
char Reversed[5] ; // for the reverse of the original

cout << "Type in a word of five letters" ;
for(i=0; i<5; i++) cin >> Input[i];
for(i=0; i<5; i++) Reversed[i] = Input[4-i] ;
for(i=0; (i<5) && (Input[i] == Reversed[i]); i++) ;
if (i==5) cout << "The word is a palindrome";
else cout << "The word is not a palindrome";
}
```

**Figure 5.2** The palindrome program without the variable `IsNotPalindrome`

Notice that this change means that the body of the second `for` loop is empty — all that is required in each iteration of the loop is to increase the value of the loop control variable, which is achieved by the `i++`.

As we said earlier, this version of the program represents the 'easy' solution to the problem, which is inefficient because it requires two arrays.

The first thing we should do when we have got a small fragment of code that works as we intend, is to see if we can find a simpler way of writing it. This is not just an academic exercise. Simpler versions of programs are often more efficient and easier to understand and maintain.

In this case we see that the first two loops of the program have an identical initialisation, increment and upper bound and so we may coalesce them into a single loop, creating the faster and simpler program given in Figure 5.3 below:

```
#include <iostream.h>

main()
{
int i ;
char Input[5] ;      // To store the original
                     // word
char Reversed[5] ;   // for the reverse of the
                     // original word
int IsNotPalindrome ;   // will store 0 if the
                        // original word is
                        // a palindrome,
                        // and 1 if it is not

cout << "Type in a word of five letters" ;

for(i=0; i<5; i++)
{      cin >> Input[i];
       Reversed[i] = Input[4-i] ;
}

IsNotPalindrome = 0;
for(i=0; i<5; i++)
       if (Input[i] != Reversed[i]) IsNotPalindrome = 1;

if (IsNotPalindrome)
       cout << "The word is not a palindrome";
else cout << "The word is a palindrome";
}
```

**Figure 5.3** A simplified palindrome program with two loops coalesced

The next step is to try to eliminate the need for *two* arrays. We should be able to work out whether or not a word is a palindrome from a single array alone, as it will contain all the information we could need. The key is to use the expression `4-i`, to allow us to 'reverse the direction of counting' embodied by the loop control variable, `i`. This will allow us to check the last element of the array against the first, the second last against the second and so on. This leads us to the further simplified version of the palindrome program with only one array given in Figure 5.4 below:

```
#include <iostream.h>

main()
{
int i ;
char Input[5] ;        // To store the original
                       // word
int IsNotPalindrome ; // will store 0 if the
                      // original word is
                      // a palindrome,
                      // and 1 if it is not

cout << "Type in a word of five letters" ;
for(i=0; i<5; i++) cin >> Input[i];

IsNotPalindrome = 0;
for(i=0; i<5; i++)
      if (Input[i] != Input[4-i]) IsNotPalindrome = 1;

if (IsNotPalindrome)
      cout << "The word is not a palindrome";
else cout << "The word is a palindrome";
}
```

**Figure 5.4** The palindrome program with only one array

Now this program works, but it is still inefficient because there is no need to complete 5 iterations of the second `for` loop. Once we have compared the first element with the last, there is no need to compare the last with the first. We should stop the loop once it reaches the middle of the word, in this case we stop when the variable `i` has the value 2. To do this we simply have to replace the 5 in the controlling expression of the second loop with a 2.

Perhaps a final simplification would be to realise that a loop which iterates only twice is not worth having, and so we replace the second loop with two tests to check the first and last elements of the array and the second and second last elements. However, there is something more deeply wrong with the program: it is far too specific — why should we, the programmer, decide how long the user's input word is to be?

Surely working out that 'ada' is a palindrome ought to involve a similar process to working out that 'madam' is a palindrome? We should be able to handle a word of *any* size (perhaps up to a maximum, which we shall have to fix, because we have to decide on the size of the array when we write the program). In order to deal with words of any length, we shall use a special version of the array of characters known as a *string*.

## The string

A string is an array of characters, where the array may be of any length, but where a special character, the 'null' character, is *guaranteed* to occur somewhere in the array.

The 'null' character has the ASCII value `0`, which is not one of the printable characters. That is, if we do print the null character, then what actually appears as output will vary from one system to another. Its role is to indicate the 'end' of the string. That is, the characters leading up to the null character form part of the string, the characters in the array after the null character do not form part of the string and should be ignored in any processing effort.

We usually denote the null character like this:

```
'\0'
```

The backslash character, \, when used in a character constant, as in `'\0'`, indicates that the character's ASCII value is being supplied. The number after the backslash is the ASCII value of the character. This is sometimes necessary when there is no key on the keyboard which represents the character that we want. The null character is an example of this as there is no null character key on the keyboard. Of course the character `'\0'` could simply be written as the integer `0`, but we prefer to write `'\0'`, because this makes it clear to the reader of the program that the value zero is being used as the null character to signify the end of a string.

The use of a null character allows us to define a large enough array to store any and all of the words we intend to use, and we use the null character as a sentinel, to indicate where each word ends.

Suppose we decide that 10 characters are enough to store any word. In that case we should declare an array of 11 characters (10 for the word and one extra for the null character). Conceptually, the word 'adam' would look like this:

and the word 'madam' looks like this:

| m | a | d | a | m | \0 | | | | | |
|---|---|---|---|---|---|---|---|---|---|---|

The characters which appear after the null character (the 0) are not part of the string, and could be any characters — we should never attempt to use them.

## The constant string

When we write a constant string in double quotes like this " ... ", we are defining an array of characters just big enough to store the sequence of characters *and* the terminating null character. So the string "hello" is in fact an array of characters that looks precisely like this:

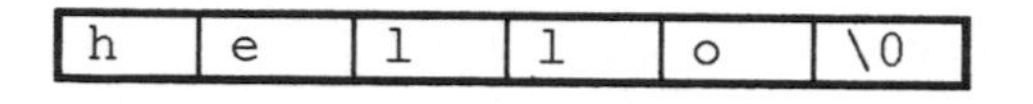

We have been using strings ever since we wrote the first program to print 'hello' on the screen as

```
cout << "hello" ;
```

but we were simply not aware of it.

## Input and output of strings

Having defined an array of characters we shall often want to read in a sequence of characters from the keyboard. Fortunately, we do not have to do this using a loop, we can merely read the array of characters using `cin`. Suppose we have declared the array A, to contain 10 characters. We can read in a string into this array using `cin` like this:

```
cin >> A;
```

The computer will read in characters into A until the user types in a return character, at which point the computer will put the null character into the array and carry on with the next statement. We could thus write a program to read in a person's name and print it out in reverse like this:

```
cin >> A;
for(i=0; a[i]!='\0'; i++) ;
for(i--; i>=0; i--) cout << A[i] ;
```

Notice that the first `for` loop has no body. This is because the increment part:

```
i++;
```

is all that we require to set the value of the variable `i` to the end of the string (the null character). The second `for` loop requires the initialisation

```
i--;
```

because the first `for` loop leaves `i` at the index of the null character, which we do not want to print.

## Initialisation of strings

To initialise a string at the time it is declared we could use the notation we saw in Chapter 4, which addressed the general problem of writing a value for a constant array. In this fashion, we would write:

```
char N[10] = {'K','a','t','h','y','\0'} ;
```

Notice that we have to add the null character ourselves. Also notice that there is no need to supply all the elements of the array on initialisation, and that this is not an issue, since we have the null character to indicate the end of the 'real' part of the string.

Although this initialisation syntax works, it is rather tiresome to have to write so many single quote and comma characters when we typically write a constant string like `"Kathy"` in double quotes. We can use this form of syntax as an alternative to the longer curly bracket form. We could write the initialisation above like this:

```
char N[10] = "Kathy" ;
```

Notice that, as usual, the compiler adds in the null character as the end of the string for us. We therefore have to be careful not to write:

```
char OhDear[5] = "happy" ;
```

In this situation we have not allowed enough space for the null character, and so the compiler will truncate our word so that there is room to fit a null character and to make a proper string. The string we shall get will therefore be `"happ"` and not `"happy"` as we had intended.

Notice that this solution to the problem of an overlarge constant in an initialisation definition is preferable to the alternative — leaving out the termination character altogether.

## Pointers

An address is a number which identifies a byte of the computer's memory. At each memory address, a value will be stored. Often addresses are referred to as 'locations'. Each variable that we declare thus has an address associated with it. The address at which we shall find the first byte of information is used to represent the value stored in the variable.

A pointer is a variable which contains an *address* as its value. That is, instead of a pointer containing the value of interest, it contains the address of the value. There is thus a level of indirection involved in finding the value of interest; first the address of the pointer variable is used to find its content. The content of the pointer variable is, however, itself an address, which is used to find the value of interest.

We say that a pointer 'points to' the elements whose address is stored in the pointer variable. Figure 5.5 shows this situation pictorially for a pointer variable, `p`, which points to the value 42. The value 42 happens to be stored at address 20566.

| Variable name | Address | Value |
|---|---|---|
| p | 20500 | 20566 |
| | | |
| | | |
| | | |
| x | 20566 | 42 |

**Figure 5.5** Addressing memory using a pointer variable

This situation could arise, for example, after the execution of the following code sequence:

```
int *p ;
int x = 42;
p= &x;
```

The declaration `int *p;` declares that the variable `p` is to be a pointer to an integer. The declaration `int x = 42;` declares that the variable `x` is to be an integer and that it is to be initialised to contain the value `42`. The third line of the fragment is an assignment, which stores the address of the variable `x` in the pointer variable `p`. Given any variable name, `v`, we may write `&v` to obtain the address of the variable `v`.

In order to print out the value pointed to by a variable such as `p` in the example fragment above, we use the asterisk symbol to indicate that a pointer variable is to be de-referenced. De-referencing a pointer variable means looking up the value that it points to.

If p is a pointer variable then *p is an expression whose value is the contents of the address stored in p. Thus writing:

```
int *p ;
int x = 42;
p= &x;
cout << *p;
```

will cause the value 42 (the value pointed to by p) to be printed.

Pointers are required when we allocate memory at execution time, that is, when storage space is allocated dynamically. Because the storage is allocated as the program executes, the particular address of the allocated storage will vary from one execution to the next. A variable is therefore required to contain the address of any dynamically allocated storage space — this is the purpose of pointer variables.

Pointers are used extensively in C++ programs, because without them the amount of memory used by a program would be fixed, which would be unrealistic for many applications where the amount of storage required by a program will depend upon the input to the program.

In this section we shall show how pointers are related to arrays, and how they may be used together with the new instruction to allocate storage for arrays dynamically.

## The new instruction

Hitherto, when we defined an array we decided, *at compile time*, how large the array should be. For example, to read in 10 numbers into an array we would write:

```
int Numbers[10] ;
int i = 0;
while(i<10)
{      cout << "Type in a number" ;
       cin >> Numbers[i] ;
       i = i + 1;
}
```

We could re-write this program fragment like this:

```
int* Numbers ;
int i = 0;
Numbers = new int [10] ;
while(i<10)
{      cout << "Type in a number" ;
       cin >> Numbers[i] ;
       i = i + 1;
}
```

In the second version, notice that the type of the variable `Numbers` is

```
int*
```

This type is pronounced 'pointer to an integer'. In general, we can write the asterisk (*) after any type and this transforms the type into a 'pointer to' type.

If a variable is a pointer to an integer this means that the variable does not contain an integer, but the address of an integer. Thus, the variable `Numbers` contains the address of an integer, rather than the actual integer itself.

In all the examples where we have been using arrays, the name of the array is also, in fact, an address, in precisely the same way that `Numbers` is in the program fragment above. When we write the declaration:

```
char Fred[100] ;
```

we obtain a variable, `Fred`, which points to a character. The `100` in square brackets at the end of the declaration tells the compiler that a sequence of continuous storage must be set aside for 100 characters and that the variable `Fred` is to contain the address of the first in this sequence of characters. `Fred` is the address of the first element of the array we call `Fred`, thus, in fact `Fred` is equal to `&Fred[0]`.

Now, when we write an expression like this:

```
Fred[7]
```

we are referring to the eighth element of the array `Fred` (remember that we start counting at zero). What this means in practice, for the computer, is that the address of the eighth element is obtained by adding seven to the address stored in the variable `Fred`. We write `Fred[7]`, rather than telling the compiler to add seven to the address stored in `Fred`, because it is conceptually easier for us to think of `Fred` as the name of the whole sequence of the array.

Now if we want a sequence of 10 `ints` we can either write the definition:

```
int Numbers[10] ;
```

or

```
int* Numbers ;
```

Both definitions tell the compiler that `Numbers` is a variable which contains the address of an `int`. There is a difference though. In the first example, we tell the compiler that we want 10 `ints` and in the second we do not. How does the compiler know that we want to store 10 `ints` in the variable `Numbers` when we present it with a definition in the second form?

Well, the answer is that the compiler *does not know* how many `int`s we want in this case, it merely knows that we want `Numbers` to be a pointer to an `int`.

The instruction:

```
Numbers = new int [10] ;
```

tells the computer that we want 10 `int`s of storage space for the array `Numbers`. Notice that there is a crucial difference between the two storage allocation techniques below:

```
int Numbers[10] ;
```

and

```
int* Numbers ;
Numbers = new int [10] ;
```

In the first example, we tell the compiler (statically) that we want 10 integers. In the second we ask the computer (dynamically, at execution time) to provide us with 10 integers. To make the distinction clearer, consider the program in Figure 5.6 below, which uses the dynamic storage allocation technique:

```
#include<iostream.h>

main()
{
int* Numbers ;
int length ;
int i ;

// Ask the user how many numbers they will
// type in.
cout<< "How many numbers do you need?";
cin >> length ;
// Ask the computer for enough space for
// the numbers that the user will type in.
Numbers = new int [length] ;
// Read in the user's numbers.
i=0 ;
while(i<length)
{      cin >> Numbers[i] ;
       i++;
}
}
```

**Figure 5.6** A program which uses dynamic storage

Notice that the *user of the program* decides how big the array `Numbers` should be, when they type in the first number in response to the question:

```
How many numbers do you need?
```

The number typed in by the user is stored in the variable `length`, which is used as the part of the `new` instruction which tells the computer how many `int`s are required. The *compiler cannot calculate* how much space will be required when the program is executed. Indeed, from one execution of the program to the next *different* amounts of memory will be used by the program depending upon what the user types as the first input to the program.

Using static memory allocation, we cannot write such a program. We might try to write the program using static memory, attempting to define the limit of the array used to store the numbers typed in, *after* we have established how many numbers there are to be.

This incorrect program is given in Figure 5.7 below:

```
#include<iostream.h>

main()
{
int length ;
int i ;

// Ask the user how many numbers they will
// type in.

cout<< "How many numbers do you need?";
cin >> length ;

// Now we know how big the array is, we
// can define it
int Numbers[length] ;   // this will not work


// Read in the user's numbers.
i=0 ;
while(i<length)
{
      cin >> Numbers[i] ;
      i++;
}
}
```

**Figure 5.7** An incorrect program that attempts to dynamically allocate static memory

However, the compiler will not accept this program, because the definition

```
int Numbers[length] ;
```

is not one to which the compiler can respond. The compiler must set aside space for the array `Numbers` *as it compiles the program*. However, as `length` is a variable, the compiler cannot decide how much space to set aside and will produce an error message saying that `Numbers` is not properly defined. When we write

```
int v[e] ;
```

for some expression `e` and variable name `v`, we are asking the compiler to allocate storage as a fixed part of the program, so the compiler must be able to work out the value of `e`. Therefore the value of `e` must be constant (since a constant cannot alter as the program executes).

## The `delete` instruction

When we allocate storage space with the new instruction we use up some of the computer's resources. Often we do not need the resource — the storage allocated — for the entire duration of the program. In this situation it is important to release the resource so that it can be recycled, and used by some other part of the program.

When we no longer need storage space allocated by the `new` instruction, we can release it using the `delete` instruction. Suppose we have allocated storage space for a pointer to a single integer like this:

```
int* p;
p = new int ;
```

When we no longer need the storage space taken up by the integer, we simply execute the instruction

```
delete p;
```

We should not use the pointer `p` in any subsequently executed statement, as the storage space it once pointed to is no longer available to us.

If we have allocated space for a whole sequence of integers, using a `new` instruction like this:

```
int* p;
p = new int[22];
```

then we should deallocate (release) the storage space using the delete instruction followed by empty array brackets.

For example, to deallocate an array of elements pointed to by the pointer variable p, we would write:

```
delete [] p;
```

The storage allocation mechanism records the amount of space it has allocated when the new instruction is executed and so when an instruction like

```
delete [] p;
```

is executed, the amount of storage space to reclaim can be calculated.

## Exercises

5.1 Write a program to read in a word and print out the number of times the character 'a' appears in the word.

5.2 Write a program to read in a word and a letter and print out the number of time the letter occurs in the word.

5.3 Write a program that reads in a word and a letter and prints the positions in the word at which the letter occurs.

5.4 Write a program 'fragment' to merge the contents of one word and another, so that letters are taken alternately from one word and then from the other. (Do not forget to account for the null character correctly, and you will have to decide what to do if the strings are of unequal length.)

5.5 Write an encryption program which reads in a string and encrypts it into a 'secret code'. The coding technique consists of replacing space characters with an asterisk (*), replacing an 'a' with a 'b', a 'b' with a 'c' and so on up to 'z' which is replaced by an 'a'. You will have to read the characters one at a time using a loop; if you attempt to read the string with a single cin statement then it will be truncated at the first space character, as cin treats this as signifying the end of the user's string.

5.6 Write a decryption program which unscrambles the coded strings produced by the program you wrote in answer to Exercise 5.5.

If you feed the result of the encryption program into the decryption program then you should get back the string you started with. On many computers, you can verify that your decryption program does the opposite of the encryption program by writing

```
encrypt < file | decrypt
```

where file is the name of some file of characters and `encrypt` and `decrypt` are the names of your two programs. The file should be unaffected by this command. It is not recommended that you initially try this out on an important file!

5.7 Combine the two programs from Exercises 5.5 and 5.6 so that you have a program for encryption and decryption. The program should allow the user to decide whether to encrypt or decrypt a word and to process as many words as they please until they choose to terminate the program.

5.8 The encryption program that we have developed is rather poor — it is not too difficult to break the code! Design and implement an improved program and see if your friends can break the code.

5.9 Write a program to read in a person's name and print out the number of letters in their name. Try to write the program so that invalid names are not allowed. A valid name can contain letters, but remember that some names have hyphens and apostrophes in them.

5.10 Write a program which reads in two words and prints 'substring' on the screen if the second word occurs anywhere in the first word.

5.11 Find as many syntax errors as you can in the program below:

```
#include <iostream.h>

main()
{
int i ;
char Input(5) ;          // To store the original
                         // word
int IsNotPalindrome      // will store 0 if the
                         // original word is
                         // a palindrome,
                         // and 1 if it is not
```

```
cout << "Type in a word of five letters" ;
for(i=0, i<5, i++) cin >> Input[];

IsNotPalindrome = 0;
for(i=0; i<5; i++)
      if (Input[i] !  = Input[4-i])
            IsNotPalindrome = 1;

if IsNotPalindrome
      cout << "The word is not a palindrome";
else "The word is a palindrome";
}
```

# 6

# Introduction to Functions

## Aims

This chapter introduces the concept of a function as a named block of code with a local scope. It introduces the concepts of local and global variable, explaining when and where each should be used.

After reading this chapter you should be able to:

- write programs which define and call functions
- decide whether variables should be local to a function or global to the entire program
- use scope rules to decide whether a variable is local or global

# Introduction

A function is a block of program statements to which we give a name so that we can refer to the whole block, using the name we have given them. In addition to this, functions provide a facility for parameters to be provided when we use the name of the function. These parameters provide an initial environment in which the block of statements associated with the function's name are executed. The use of parameters will be discussed in Chapters 7 and 8.

Functions (also called 'procedures', 'routines' or 'subroutines' in other languages) are extremely important. The mechanisms provided by functions are found throughout computing. Functions involve the crucial idea of *abstraction* and *parameter passing*. In this context, abstraction means capturing the essence of a process (or data structure) by avoiding irrelevant detail. The encapsulation that this involves makes it easier to test parts of a large system in isolation. It also makes it possible to reuse components of one system in another.

The idea of parameter passing is also central to many successful approaches to computer science and software engineering. Parameters allow us to *modify* the way a component behaves each time we use it.

In the next four chapters the idea of functions and parameter passing will be introduced gradually. We start with a very simple idea of a function (with no parameters) and then we shall extend our idea of a function to see how parameters allow us to make our functions more flexible (thereby increasing the potential for reuse).

Throughout Chapters 6 and 7 we shall use the same function as an example, adapting it to incorporate new features as they are introduced. This example is, of necessity, rather small, and so some of the aspects of functions which we shall be looking at will appear a little unnecessary. The use of functions really comes into its own when larger programs are constructed. In such situations the task of designing, implementing and verifying a program would be unrealistic without the use of functions.

# A simple function

We shall write some code in `C++` to print a row of 80 dashes on the screen. We could do this with a `while` loop, counting from 1 to 80 and printing out a dash each time around the loop.

```
{
        int i; // a loop control variable
        for(i=1; i<=80; i++) cout << '-';
}
```

This fragment of code could be used to break up separate sections of a stream of output (or perhaps to underline a title in the output, *if* it happened to be 80 characters long).

Since we may want to use this fragment of code several times, it would be nice if we could simply give it a name and then call it up by name each time we want a line of 80 dashes. The function definition is contained in Figure 6.1.

```
int i;

void line() ;
//
// prints out 80 dashes
//

void line()
{
      for(i=1; i<=80; i++) cout << '-';
}
```

**Figure 6.1** A simple line drawing function

The part which says

```
void line();
```

is called a 'function prototype' (in this case it is a prototype for the function called `line`). A prototype is used to tell the C++ compiler that we intend to use the name `line` and how the name is to be used. In this case we say that we intend to use a parameterless function, called `line`, and this function does not return a value. The empty parentheses (round brackets, like those surrounding this aside) indicate that the function called `line` has no parameters.

We shall return to this topic in Chapters 7 and 8, where we will consider parameters in some detail. In this chapter, all function names will be followed by empty parentheses. The word `void` at the start of the prototype says that our function *does not* compute a value to be returned. We shall return to this topic in Chapter 9. In this chapter, and in Chapters 7 and 8, all our prototypes will start with the word `void`.

After the prototype comes the function proper. The first thing we write is a repeat of the prototype (notice there is no semicolon this time, if there was then how would the compiler know that this is the 'real' function coming up and not just a prototype?). After repeating the prototype (without the semicolon), we can write any C++ code we like (with the exception of a function definition, which is disallowed as we are not allowed to nest one function definition inside another in C++). This code, the *body* of the function, is enclosed in braces — the curly brackets { and this }.

To call the function we simply refer to it by its name (we need the open and closed parentheses with our `line` function to say there are no parameters for the call). So to call our function `line`, we simply write

```
line();
```

A call to a function like `line`, is therefore simply another statement in C++. However, it is a *new* statement that we have *added* to the original language, by defining the effect of the statement in the function body for `line`.

The program in Figure 6.2 prints a line of dashes on the screen using the function `line`.

```
#include<iostream.h>

int i;

void line() ;

void line()
{
        for(i=1; i<=80; i++) cout << '-' ;
}

void main()
{
        line();
}
```

**Figure 6.2** A simple call to the line drawing function

Where there is more than one function in a program, the function prototypes may be collected together and placed at the top of the program. This allows the reader of the program code to see immediately what functions are in our program, and is good practice, although the definition of the C++ programming language does not insist upon it.

Later we will see how more information about the function can be expressed by the prototype. Ultimately, with suitable comments, all the information required to understand the way a function behaves will be available in the prototype. Thus putting all the prototypes together at the start of the program provides the programmer with an excellent way of describing functions to the reader of the program without them becoming immersed in the irrelevant details contained in the function bodies.

Notice that the `main` function contains only one statement.

This is the function call:

```
line();
```

which is a call to the function `line`.

Some questions should arise:

- Is `main` a function? It looks like one
- This seems to make a meal out of drawing a line
- If `main` *is* a function, then where is its prototype?

Well, `main` *is* a function, it is the only one that we have not bothered to write a prototype for. Though not required by the C++ compiler[1], prototypes are, however, good practice, because they allow us to say how the function 'interfaces' to the rest of the program. This is an idea which we shall develop more fully in Chapters 7, 8 and 9.

The most important question is 'why bother with all this effort? Drawing a line is easier without functions'. To answer this criticism, we will have to engage in a willing suspension of disbelief for a while, until we have seen some more features of functions.

For the time being, notice that to draw three separate lines we would simply use the function `line` three times, like this:

```
#include<iostream.h>
int i;

void line() ;

void line()
{
        for(i=1; i<=80; i++) cout << '-';
}

void main()
{       line();
        cout << '\n' ;
        line();
        cout << '\n' ;
        line();
        cout << '\n' ;
}
```

[1]Prototypes *are* required if we choose to call a function *before* we have declared it, but we can nearly always arrange our function definitions so that no function is called before it is used. The only time this will not be possible is when we use mutual recursion (see Appendix A for an explanation of recursion).

Also, if we wanted to draw 100 lines of 80 dashes, for example using a loop, then *without* functions we would nest the loop that draws 80 dashes inside another loop to do the whole thing 100 times. As you have probably noticed, as we nest more and more loops inside each other, our programs become harder and harder to read, understand and verify.

Because we have encapsulated the line drawing process in a function, we can make the loop nesting more palatable (see Figure 6.3).

```
#include<iostream.h>

int i,j;

void line() ;

void line()
{
        for(i=1; i<=80; i++) cout << '-' ;
}

void main()
{       for(j=1; j<=100; j++)
        {       line();
                cout << endl;
        }
}
```

**Figure 6.3** Printing 100 lines of 80 dashes

Notice that we know what the function `line` does — it prints 80 dashes. Having worked this out, we do not need to read the body of the function *every time* we encounter a call to it. Instead, when we see a call to `line`, we simply think 'that draws 80 dashes'. The function `line` has encapsulated the task of line drawing. This clearly makes the body of `main` in Figure 6.3 easier to understand since the call to `line` is as easy to understand as, for example, the statement `j++;`.

## How to mentally execute a function

When the computer encounters a call to a function it executes the body of the function and then carries on with the statements after the function call. It is rather as if the computer was happily going along, executing our program, and then, suddenly, we side-tracked it by calling up a function. Having dealt with this side-track, the computer carries on with what it was doing.

In order to see, mentally, the effect of a function call in a piece of program, all you have to do is to substitute the body of the function (the part between the curly brackets) for the piece of code that calls the function. After performing the substitution of function body for function call, we do not need the function definition and we will be left with a program which will behave in exactly the same way as the original with the call.

We shall see how this substitution process allows us to understand the effect of a function call with the example below:

```
#include<iostream.h>
int i,j;

void line() ;

void line()
{       for(i=1; i<=80; i++) cout << '-';
}

void main()
{       for(j=1; j<=100; j++)
        {       line();
                cout << endl;
        }
}
```

In the function `main` we use the function `line`. To see the effect of this, we simply replace the line of code which says `line();` with the body of the function `line`, which is:

```
for(i=1; i<=80; i++) cout << '-';
```

This gives us the program below (we have thrown away the function `line`, because it is not used now that we have 'substituted it out'). We call this process of substituting the body of a function for its call 'unfolding'. In Figure 6.4 we have 'unfolded' the call (in `main`) to the function `line`.

```
#include<iostream.h>
void main()
{       int i,j;
        for(j=1; j<=100; j++)
        {       for(i=1; i<=80; i++) cout << '-' ;
                cout << endl;
        }
}
```

**Figure 6.4** Unfolding the call to `line` in `main`

Notice how this substitution reveals the *implicit nesting* of the loops controlled by the variables `i` and `j` in the original program.

Also notice that the original is easier to read because the function `line` can be understood in *isolation*. Having understood `line`, we can treat it as an 'atomic' action, forgetting the details of all loops and variables in its function body.

The `main` function in Figure 6.3 is shorter and easier to understand than the `main` function in Figure 6.4, because we have broken the problem up into two separate parts. One part draws a line of 80 dashes and the other part (`main`) draws 100 lines of 80 dashes.

## Functions are language extensions

When we write a function like `line`, what we are really doing is *enriching* the programming language `C++`. We could have started this chapter by saying that there was a part of `C++` called a '`line`' statement which draws dashes on the screen. This would have been no different from writing it ourselves. The point is that by writing functions like `line` we are *extending* the language to suit our needs. For example, when we are going to want to perform complicated graphical operations, we would extend the language by defining functions which plot points, draw boxes, triangles, ellipses and so on. After we have written several of these functions, we will effectively have a language which we could *think* of as having 'built-in' graphics facilities. Or, to put it another way, we would have enriched the programming language by providing new statements for performing the graphical operations in which we were interested.

## The function's prototype

The prototype of a function provides the compiler (and other programmers reading our programs) with information about the way the function is to be called. So far we have not seen very much of prototypes, because we have not discussed parameters and returned values (which we shall describe in Chapters 7, 8 and 9).

However, one point worth making at this stage is that the prototype provides a useful way of alerting other programmers to the particular features of our function. For this reason it is advisable to include comments with the prototype of a function, specifically aimed at other programmers, which describe the effect of the function. The prototypes of functions, together with associated comments, act as the documentation of the program we have written. This documentation will be used by other programmers who may want to use the functions which we have defined. The documentation will also be useful to the programmer writing the functions as it will focus attention upon the operations performed by the functions.

## Local variables

Local variables are variables declared *inside* the body of the function. The variables can be used to store values inside the function, but *do not exist* outside the function.

By contrast, variables declared before a function (and outside the body of any other functions in the text of the program) are called global variables, and can be accessed inside *any function* which follows the variable declaration.

Consider the simple example below, in which we have used the variable name `global` for a global variable and the name `local` for a local variable:

```
int global;

void fun() ;

void fun()
{
        int local;

        local = 1;
        global = 2;
}

main()
{
        fun();
}
```

After the call to the function `fun`, in the function `main`, we shall be able to print out the value of the variable called `global`, and if we did so, we would see that it had the value 2, as assigned in the function `fun`.

However, if we attempted to print out the value of the variable `local`, then we would find that we could not. In fact, if we try to refer to the variable `local` outside the function `fun`, we shall find that the compiler will reject our program with a message like:

```
'local' is an undeclared identifier
```

This is because `local` is not declared inside the body of `main` (where we would be using it), neither is it declared before the function `main`, as a global variable (that is, outside any other function body).

A question which naturally arises at this point is why we would *want* to have a variable which we cannot access outside of the function in which it is declared. The answer to this question revolves around the use of several different functions within the same program.

In such a situation, it would be highly likely that each function uses a loop, and requires a variable to control the number of iterations in the loop. Each of these loop control variables is unimportant outside the function in which it is used. It would be irritating if we had to think up a different name for each loop control variable, often we shall want to use the same name (for example `count` or `i`) in each of the functions.

Furthermore, if we use a global variable for each of the loop control variables, then we shall very quickly run up a large list of global variables. This would present a problem to another programmer, who may be trying to understand the workings of our program. In order to understand a program with a large number of global variables, we have to keep all the global variables in mind *throughout* the consideration of each and every function of the program.

The central idea behind the use of functions is that of *encapsulation*. That is, we want to capture all the details of the task carried out by a function in the function's definition. This means that the function can be treated as a single unit, which can be used without the worry that it may have some hidden effect upon some global variable. Such a global variable will affect the rest of the program, depending upon the point at which the function is called. Local variables are provided to help us achieve encapsulation in our function definitions.

Consider the function `line`, which we defined in Figure 6.2. The variable `i`, used to control the loop which prints out the dashes should be defined as a local variable, because it has no use outside the function. We would thus re-write the function like this:

```
void line() ;
//
// line prints 80 dashes on the screen
//

void line()
{
int i;
for(i=1; i<=80; i++) cout << '-';
}
```

Now, when we call the function `line`, we can be sure that it has *no effect*, other than printing out 80 dashes on the screen. If we had defined the variable `i` outside the body of the function `line`, then it would be a global variable and this would have meant that when we called the function, it would not only print 80 dashes, but *also* would have stored 81 in the global variable `i`. By storing the value of the loop control variable in a local variable we allow the programmer to understand the function `line` in isolation from the program in which it is used. The function will have the same effect no matter what program it is used in, because it affects the value of no variables declared outside its body.

## Scope

Another question arises at this point to do with the choice of local and global variables. We might have a local variable which has the *same name* as a global variable, in which case the compiler will surely not know whether the use of such a variable is a use of the local version or the global version.

The compiler resolves this potential ambiguity by consulting rules which define the portion of code for which the definition of a variable is applicable. The rules which describe the range of applicability of a variable definition are called '*scope rules*', and we often speak of the '*scope* of a variable', by which we mean the portion of code in which the variable can be used.

Consider the example below, in which the variable `i` is defined as both global *and* local to the function `fun1` (but not defined locally within the function `fun2`):

```
int i ;

// Prototypes :-

void fun1() ;

void fun2() ;

// Functions Proper :-

void fun1()
{
        int i ;
}

void fun2()
{

}
```

**Figure 6.5** Scope rules

In Figure 6.5, we are not interested in the bodies of the functions `fun1` and `fun2`, we are concerned only with the variables which may or may not be used in these bodies, according to the scope rules of C++.

Inside `fun1` the variable `i` is declared local, and so any reference to the variable `i` is a reference to this local version of `i`, and any assignments to `i` within the function `fun1` will *not* have an effect upon the global variable `i`.

Thus nothing that `fun1` does to the variable called `i` will be observable outside the body of the function `fun1`.

The function `fun2` does *not* contain a local declaration of the variable `i`, and so any reference to the variable `i` within the body of `fun2` will be a reference to the global version of the variable. Any effect that the function `fun2` has upon the variable called `i` *will* be observable outside the body of the function.

The general rule is:

Local declarations take precedence over global declarations

If we declare a local variable, called `i`, inside a function called `f`, then the global version of the variable `i`, if there is one, is not accessible within the body of the function `f`. We say that there is a 'hole' in the scope of the global variable `i`. The hole, in this case, is the body of `f`.

Giving local declarations priority over global declarations makes sense because a local variable *only* means anything *inside* the function in which it is declared. If the rule operated in reverse, with global declarations taking precedence over local ones, then a local definition *may* have no effect. We would not be able to understand a function in isolation. Wherever possible, a function should be treated as a single, indivisible unit, and a function should mean the same thing, even if it is used in different programs.

## Exercises

6.1 Change `line` so that it draws 100 equals signs.

6.2 Change `line` so that it draws 25 dashes.

6.3 Work out the effect of three consecutive calls to the function you defined in Exercise 6.2 by the substitution method introduced in this chapter.

6.4 Write a function `ClearScreen`, which clears the screen or window in which the program is executed (by printing sufficient new lines).

6.5 Consider the functions defined on the following pages. Decide whether the variables used in the functions should be local or global, based on what you have read in this chapter.

```
void Indent() ;
//
// prints n space characters on the screen
//

void Indent()
{
      i=0;
      do
      {
            cout << ' ' ;
            i++;
      } while (i < n);
}

void AdditionTest() ;
//
// Tests the user's arithmetic
//

void AdditionTest()
{
      x = 42 ;
      y = 17 ;
      cout << "What is " << x << "+" << y << "?" ;
      cout << endl ;

      cin >> answer ;

      if (answer == x+y)
            cout << "Correct" ;
      else
      {
            cout << "No." ;
            cout << x "+" << y "=" << x+y << endl ;
      }
}

void Calc() ;
//
// Calculates the answer to a simple sum
//

void Calc()
{
      cout << "Enter two numbers" ;
      cin >> num1 ;
      cin >> num2 ;

      cout << num1 << "+" << num2 << "=" ;
      cout << num1 + num2 << endl ;
}
```

```
void Init() ;
//
// Sets the elements of the array A to zero
//

void Init()
{
      i = 0;
      do
      {
            A[i] = 0 ;
            i++;
      } while (i <= 10);
}
```

6.6 How could you use the 25-dash version of `line` to define a 100-dash version?

6.7 Work out the scope rules that apply to the following set of functions:

```
int i ;

void f();

void g();

void f()
{
      int i,j ;
}

void g()
{
      int j;
}
```

6.8 Work out the scope rules that apply to the following set of functions:

```
void fun1() ;

int i,j ;
float r;

void fun2() ;
```

```
void fun3() ;

void fun1()
{
        int i ;
        int k ;
        float r;
}

void fun2() ;
{
        int k ;
        float r1 ;
}

int k;

void fun3() ;
{
        int i,j,p,q ;
        float f,r1;
}
```

6.9 Find as many syntax errors as you can in the following program:

```
#include <iostream.h>

void f()
{
        int i,j ;

        i=v;
        v++;
}

int v;

void g();

void g()
{
        void h();

        char c;
        int t;

        t = 1;
        while (t<10)
        {
                cin << c;
                t++;
```

```
        }
}

main()
{
        int ;

        g(); f()
        if (f()) cout << "f is true";
}
```

# 7

# Value Parameters

## Aims

This chapter introduces the concept of parameter passing to functions. Functions with value parameters are described with examples showing how a human can understand a function call by mentally executing it. The chapter shows how more parameters make a function more flexible and introduces the concept of an open array parameter.

After reading this chapter you should be able to:

- write functions which have several parameters
- understand the scope rules for the various names which may be used in a function
- mentally execute functions with parameters
- use open array parameters

## Introduction

In this chapter we will see how parameters make our functions much more useful, by making them more flexible.

There are two kinds of parameter in C++: reference parameters and value parameters. In this chapter we shall describe value parameters. In Chapter 8 we shall introduce reference parameters. Throughout this chapter, where we use the word 'parameter' we mean a 'value parameter'.

## Making `line` more flexible

Looking at the `line` function defined in Chapter 6, we can see that it *is not* very flexible — it always draws a line of the same length. Why cannot we draw lines of varying length, deciding the length of each when we use the function? This is what *parameters* will allow us to do.

We would like to be able to say `line(10)` to draw a line of `10` dashes, `line(1000)` to draw one of one thousand dashes and `line(1)` to draw simply one dash. The numbers `10`, `1000` and `1` in the parentheses are called *parameters* to the function `line`. Notice how the essential process is drawing a line, but that the parameters allow us to modify the *kind* of line drawn each time we call up the function.

In order to be able to give a parameter each time we call `line`, we shall have to change the way we have written it. It will now look like this:

```
void line(int HowMany) ;
//
// Draws a line of dashes on the screen.
// The number of dashes is given in the
// parameter HowMany.
//

void line(int HowMany)
{
      for(i=1; i<=HowMany; i++) cout << '-';
}
```

Compare this new definition of `line` with the parameterless version defined in Chapter 6. Notice that the *only* change to the body of the function is to replace the constant `80` with the word `HowMany`. This word is also the one we have added to the prototype. Its purpose is to *stand in* for any value that we put in parentheses when we call up the function.

To draw a line of `100` dashes, we now have to say that we want `100` when we call the function. The parameterised version of `line` and a program which uses it are given in Figure 7.1.

```
#include<iostream.h>

int i,j;

void line(int HowMany) ;
//
// Draws a line of dashes on the screen.
// The number of dashes is given in the
// parameter HowMany.
//

void line(int HowMany)
{
	for(i=1; i<=HowMany; i++) cout << '-' ;
}

void main()
{
	line(100) ;
}
```

**Figure 7.1** `line` parameterised by the number of dashes to be drawn

## Some terminology

The program above contains two kinds of value parameter; *a formal parameter* — `HowMany` and *an actual parameter* — the number `100`.

The formal parameter is used in the *definition* of the function. It is a name which allows us to refer to the value specified when we call the function. The formal parameter is *always* a name.

When we call up the function and specify that we want 100 dashes, we are supplying an *actual* parameter. The actual parameter can be *any* value, so long as it has the right type declared for the formal parameter in the function prototype. This means that we can write any *expression* which gives us the correct type of value for the actual parameter. In the case of the `line` function that means any value which is an integer (because we said that the parameter was to be an integer when we wrote the prototype of `line` with an `int` in front of the formal parameter `HowMany`). All the following calls to `line` supply valid parameters:

```
line(1);
line(1000);
line(2+9*7);
line(j+1);
line(j*2+1000);
line(x);
```

that is, assuming that we have defined the variable `j` and the variable `x` in our program to be integers. If we were to call the function `line` like this:

```
line("hello line try taking this");
```

then this would not be a sensible call, because the string of characters:

```
"hello line try taking this"
```

is not an integer.

The words 'call', 'formal parameter', 'actual parameter' and 'passing' are standard terminology used in descriptions of C++ and other languages to describe functions and the way that they are used. When we call a function we pass an actual parameter which corresponds to the formal parameter declared as part of the function's prototype. The formal parameter is the name used in the body of the function to refer to the value of the actual parameter. From one call to the next we may pass different actual parameters to a function, and therefore the value of a formal parameter inside the body of a function will depend upon which call of the function is being executed. Parameters therefore make the use of functions more flexible.

When we call the function `line` like this:

```
line(20)
```

the actual parameter is `20`. It is passed to `line` for the formal parameter `HowMany`. During the execution of the body of the function `line` for the call `line(20)`, the name `HowMany` could be thought of as a local variable whose value is initialised to `20` at the start of the function.

When we call the function `line` like this:

```
line(13)
```

the actual parameter is `13` and is passed to `line` for the formal parameter `HowMany`. During the execution of this call of the function `line` the name `HowMany` could be thought of as a local variable whose value is initialised to `13` at the start of the function. This observation allows us to define a method for understanding the way function calls are executed with actual parameters being passed for formal parameters. This is the subject to which we now turn.

## Mentally executing functions with parameters

Recall how we have talked about how to understand a function call by substituting the body of the function for the call to it. When functions have parameters we can still understand a function call in this way, but we shall have to do more than simply substituting the body of the function for the point at which it is called. Consider the following example:

```
#include<iostream.h>

void fun(int x) ;

void fun(int x)
{
        cout << x+1 ;
}

void main()
{
        fun(10);
        fun(9) ;
}
```

If we want to understand the effect of the two calls to the function `fun`, then we copy the body each time we encounter a call as normal, but we also add an initialised declaration for the formal parameter `x`. As there are two calls to the function, we will require two copies of the body of the function, but the first copy will have `x` initialised to `10` and the second to `9`. This gives us the equivalent program below:

```
#include<iostream.h>

void main()
{
        { int x = 10;
         cout << x+1;}

        { int x = 9 ;
         cout << x+1;}
}
```

Notice that this program contains nested curly bracketing. This is perfectly valid in C++. It allows us to introduce a new local scope which commences with the `{` and finishes at the `}`. For example, consider the execution of the statements below:

```
{
int v = 2;
{ int v = 4; }
cout << v ;
}
```

When these statements are executed, the number `2` will appear as the output because the initialiser `int v = 4;` occurs in a local scope.

The computer does *not* execute function calls by substituting the bodies of functions for calls in the manner we have described because it would be far too costly in computation time. Instead the compiler creates code to store the values of actual parameters and the address of the point in the program to which the program must return when the function's body has been executed. You do not need to know about these implementation details, however, in order to understand and use functions. For the purpose of understanding a call to a function, the substitution method we have been using will work fine. In fact, there is no reason, other than speed of execution, why function calling should not be executed by the computer in this manner.

This substitution method also tells us what a call to a function passing an actual parameter means: it means that the function's body is executed in a local scope in which the formal parameter is initialised at the start of the body with the value of the actual parameter.

## The client–server concept

It is often helpful to think of writing and using functions in terms of a relationship between a client (who wants to be provided with some service) and a server, who supplies that service.

The client is the person who calls the function. The server is the person who defines the function. Often these two people are one and the same person, but in a team of programmers working on a large system they may not be. Even where client and server *are* one and the same person, it is still helpful to think of them as two individuals with different requirements. At one time, when writing the function, a programmer takes on the rôle of the server. At another time, when calling the function, the same programmer will be taking on the rôle of the client.

To illustrate, we shall look at line drawing as a client–server relationship. The server sets out what they are prepared to do — they will draw a line of dashes on the screen. The function prototype acts as a *contract* between the server and client. In this case the contract dictates that the client must specify how long they want the line to be. To do this the client must keep *their* side of the bargain and specify exactly how long they want the line to be by passing an actual parameter which contains this value.

Like all contracts there should be some *small print*. In programming terms, this is provided by the server, in the form of *comments*. The server will say what kind of actual parameters are acceptable. The following code fragment contains the prototype for the function line together with the comments which form the small print details of the contract offered by the client.

```
void line(int HowMany) ;
//
// This function draws a line of
// length 'HowMany'.
// If 'HowMany' is less than 1 then no output
// will occur.
//
```

Notice that the client does not need to see the *body* of the function at all in order to know what it does and how to use it. This is what is meant by the word 'abstraction', which occurs frequently in computing textbooks; 'achieving the correct level of abstraction' means that it is important to be able to 'ignore irrelevant detail'. The details of how the function carries out its task — the nitty-gritty of loops and variables — are irrelevant at the client's level of abstraction.

This idea of an appropriate level of abstraction occurs frequently in everyday life. For example, you do not need to be an electrician to use a light switch, and that is how things should be. When you switch on the light you are the client. The electrician who installed your lighting is the server. The server guarantees that the light will come on when the switch is pressed. There is a lot of hidden effort required to ensure that this guarantee is satisfied, but the client need not be aware of it. The workings of the light switch are the 'irrelevant detail'.

If you happen to install your own lighting, then you are both the client and the server, just as if you were both the author of a function and the person who writes a program which calls it. Even if you *do* install your own lighting, you will not think of the installation details when you press the switch, apart for, perhaps, the first time you press the switch, having installed the light. At this time, you are testing your installation. It is exactly the same with functions. As programmers we swap roles from client to server when we define and call functions.

This idea of 'small print' has been developed considerably in the literature and practice of computing. We have used comments to write the small print, but some languages *enforce* special syntax for prescribing *exactly* what actual parameters are acceptable to a function and how it will behave when supplied with valid (and, indeed, invalid) parameters. C++ does not enforce any form of client-server concept, indeed, our programs will be valid even if they contain *no* comments whatsoever. However, experience has taught us that it is very important to add detailed commentary to our program code if we hope it to remain useful and adaptable.

The client–server relationship idea is useful because it forces us to think about precisely how our functions will behave when they are called. It also forms a framework within which we could test and verify that our function does what we claim it will. The idea was first used in computing the context in which we have presented it here, that is, as a method of specifying what a function does in terms of its parameters. The idea can be found in a wide variety of guises throughout programming and design theory and practice.

## More parameters make for more flexible functions

Our `line` function is still quite inflexible — why should it always draw *dash* characters? We might, in some cases, want to draw stars, equals signs or exclamation marks.

When we added the formal parameter `HowMany` to `line`, we recognised that the line drawing process was 'parameterised' by the number of dashes to be drawn. We had 'abstracted' the number of dashes to be drawn from the process of line drawing. Now we want to abstract the concept of precisely what character is to be drawn on each call to the function. To do this we use another formal parameter, which will stand for the character to be drawn. This version of the function `line` is given in Figure 7.2 below:

```
int i;

void line(int HowMany, char WhichCharacter) ;
//
// Prints out a line of characters.
// The number of characters is given by the
// parameter HowMany.
// The character to be printed is given by the
// parameter WhichCharacter.
//

void line(int HowMany, char WhichCharacter)
{
      for(i=1; i<=HowMany; i++) cout << WhichCharacter ;
}
```

**Figure 7.2** `line` parameterised by the type and number of characters to be drawn

Now when the client calls this function, they must specify the length of the line (the actual parameter corresponding to the formal parameter `HowMany`) *and* the character to be printed (the actual parameter corresponding to the formal parameter `WhichCharacter`). In return we (in the rôle of server) shall guarantee to draw a line of `WhichCharacter` characters and of length `HowMany`.

To draw a line of `80` dashes the client will now call the function like this:

```
line(80,'-');
```

Notice that adding parameters has *not* prevented us from doing anything that we could do without them. The function `line`, in its original parameterless form, as defined in Chapter 6, draws 80 dashes on the screen.

By choosing 80, and '-', for the parameters to the version of the function line defined in Figure 7.2, we can obtain the same effect. This, however, is only one of the many possibilities opened up by the incorporation into line of the extra of parameter. The actual parameters 80 and '-' are only two of an almost limitless selection of possible actual parameters.

## Building up new functions from old

As we described earlier, a function can be thought of as an extension to the programming language. One of the pleasing things about using functions is the way in which we can build up complex functions using simple ones. In the same way that a child uses toy bricks to build a wall and then proceeds to build a model house from several walls and then uses the house as part of a street, we can use simple functions like line to build up more complex functions.

Suppose we want to display a message in a title box. We can write a function, using line, to display a message. The function heading is defined in Figure 7.3 does just this.

```
void heading(char TheMessage[20]) ;
//
// TheMessage is an array of 20 characters.
// The message is written out in a box like
// heading, made up of | and - characters.
//

void heading(char TheMessage[20])
{
      line(23,'-');
      cout << endl << "|  " << TheMessage << "  |" << endl;
      line(23,'-') ;
      cout << endl;
}
```

**Figure 7.3** A function to print a heading

The function heading takes, as a parameter, the message to be printed and uses two calls to the function line to create a top and bottom border for the message.

The function heading is not very flexible, because it must take an array of 20 characters. In the next section we shall consider an extra parameter for the heading function — an open array parameter.

# Open arrays

As we have seen, passing arrays to functions allows us to perform string processing. There has been a significant draw-back to the way we have been using arrays so far — we have had to say exactly how long the array is to be in the function prototype.

C++ provides a way of getting around this difficulty. What we do is we say what *type* of thing is to be contained in the array, but leave unspecified the *length* of the array. This means that the client merely needs to pass any array which contains the right type of values. For example, for string processing (where strings often come in varying lengths) the type of data stored in the array is `char`.

An array parameter for which no length is specified is sometimes called an 'open array', because its length is left 'open'. This does mean that we shall have to find some way of indicating when we have come to the end of the array. This is achieved, for strings in C++, by terminating a string with a 'zero' (or null) character, written '\0', as we saw in Chapter 5.

We can work out the length of a string terminated by a null character by counting the number of characters in the string which precede the null character. The function `PrintLength` defined below works out and prints the length of a string `A` passed to it as an open array.

```
void PrintLength(char A[]) ;
// This function prints out the length of the
// string A.
//
// That is the number of characters in the array
// A which occur prior to the NULL character.
// If no NULL character is present, the function
// will not behave correctly.
//
// PrintLength provides an example of the use of
// open array parameters.
//

void PrintLength(char A[])
{ int i;

for(i=0; A[i]!='\0'; i++) ;
      cout << "The string is of length " << i;
}
```

Notice that the `for` loop needs no body, since all that is required is to increment the value of the variable `i` at each iteration, until we reach the null character. In simple loops such as this it is common to find that the loop requires no body. The use of the open array parameter for the array passed to the function `PrintLength` allows the client to pass any string to the function.

## Scope again

Now that we know about parameters, we can see that an occurrence of an identifier within the body of a function may be one of three kinds:

- a global variable
- a local variable
- a formal parameter

Consider the example fragment below, in which the bodies of the functions `fun1` and `fun2` have been replaced by comments as we are only concerned with scope rules:

```
int x ;

void fun1(int y) ;

void fun2(int y) ;

void fun1(int y)
{
        int z;

        // Body of fun1 goes here
}

int a;

void fun2(int y)
{
        int b;

        // Body of fun2 goes here
}
```

In this fragment of C++, the variable `x` is global to both the function `fun1` and the function `fun2`. The variable `z` is local to the function `fun1` (which means that it cannot be accessed inside any other function). Similarly, the variable `b` is local to the function `fun2` and can only be accessed inside `fun2`.

The variable `a` is global to the function `fun2` (and any which follow it as we go down the page) but is not accessible inside the body of the function `fun1` (since the definition of `fun1` precedes the definition of `a`).

The formal parameter, `y`, is local to the function `fun1`. The function `fun2` also has a formal parameter, called `y`, which is local to `fun2` and has no connection with `fun1`'s formal parameter of the same name.

Notice that the formal parameter to `fun1` seems to share a lot of similarities with local variables. A question therefore arises:

> 'What is the difference between local variables and formal parameters?'

There is only *one* difference:

> A local variable has *no value* when the computer starts executing the body of the function.
> By contrast, a formal parameter *always* has a value, which must be passed to it by the caller as an actual parameter.

This raises the question of what happens if we define a function which contains a formal parameter and a local variable with the same name. Consider the function `fun`, defined in Figure 7.4.

```
void fun(int i) ;

void fun(int i)
{
        int i;
}
```

**Figure 7.4** A function with a name clash

Figure 7.4 is an example of a very badly written function. If we are lucky the definition of the local variable:

```
        int i;
```

will have no effect. If we are unlucky it will overwrite the formal parameter `i`. There is *no* program for which it makes sense to have the same name for a local variable and a formal parameter. Many compilers will treat such an abuse as an error.

## Local variables again

Often we want to use a loop to achieve some goal and this means having a variable to 'count' the number of times the computer has executed the loop body. Such a loop control variable should be made *local* to the function (thus adhering to the idea that a function should be an abstraction, with all 'irrelevant' detail hidden). Ideally, we want the person who calls the function to be able to look *only* at the prototype in order to decide what the function does.

Looking at our `line` function defined in Figures 7.1 and 7.2, it seems silly that we have made the variable `i` a global variable. It would have been better to 'hide it away' inside the body of `line` as we did in Chapter 6. Figure 7.5 shows the new version of the function `line` with the variable `i` as a local variable.

```
void line(int HowMany, char WhichCharacter) ;
//
// Prints out a line of characters.
// The number of characters is given by the
// parameter HowMany.
//
// The character to be printed is given by the
// parameter WhichCharacter.
//

void line(int HowMany, char WhichCharacter)
{
      int i;
      // local loop control variable

      for(i=1; i<=HowMany; i++)
            cout << WhichCharacter ;
}
```

**Figure 7.5** `line` with a local variable

Notice that when we call the function `line` defined in Figure 7.5, it has *no effect* other than to draw the line. The versions of the function `line` in Figures 7.1 and 7.2 had `i` declared as a global variable, there was a sneaky side-effect: as well as drawing a line on the screen, the variable `i` was set to the value of

```
HowMany + 1
```

This happened because `i` was global, and was therefore *shared* with the rest of the program. This sneaky side-effect might have disrupted some other (completely unrelated) bit of the program that happened to use the global variable `i`.

Having made `i` local to the function `line`, the function becomes entirely self-contained. After `line` has been called we know that we can be sure that *all* that will have happened to the state of the computer is that the screen will contain the line of characters that we 'asked for' in the actual parameters we passed as part of the call.

It is clearly important to ensure that no undocumented side-effects occur when a function is executed if we are to respect the idea of function definitions as a contract between client and server.

## An example showing the use of local variables

Suppose that we want to write a function which indents the printing of a character string on the screen. We could write a function which takes an array of characters and an integer saying by how much to indent the string. Then we simply print some space characters before printing the string.

We shall call this function `indent`. It will need a variable to count the number of spaces to be printed. It is often hard to think up new names for variables, particularly trivial ones, like loop control variables. We tend[1] to call loop-control variables `i` and `j`. Having local variables allows us to reuse the same names for similar tasks in different functions. We can thus provide two functions, `line` and `indent` to make formatting output easier, and in each we can use the *local* variable `i`, as our loop-control variable. The two functions `line` and `indent` are given in Figure 7.6.

```
void line(int HowMany, char WhichCharacter) ;
//
// Prints a line of characters of length 'HowMany'
// containing the character given 'WhichCharacter'.
//

void indent(int SizeOfIndent, char message[]) ;
//
// Prints a string passed in the array 'message'
// The message is indented by 'SizeOfIndent' characters
//

void line(int HowMany, char WhichCharacter)
{
      int i; // local loop control variable

      for(i=1; i<=HowMany; i++) cout << WhichCharacter ;
}

void indent(int SizeOfIndent, char message[])
{
      int i; // local loop control variable

      for(i=1; i<=SizeOfIndent; i++) cout << ' ';
      cout << message ;
}
```

**Figure 7.6** The functions `line` and `indent`

[1]This is a throw-back to the very first high level language, FORTRAN, invented in the 1950s, where variables starting with any of the letters, I, J, K, L, M and N were treated as integers. Programmers using FORTRAN soon adopted the convention of using these letters as the names of loop-control variables, and these conventions have survived to this day.

Notice how the use of local variables has allowed us to hide away all the details of how line drawing and indentation are carried out. All the client has to do is to read the prototypes and accompanying comments.

## Default parameters

Suppose we write a program, using a function like `indent` above, in which 90% of the calls to `indent` pass the actual parameter value zero for the formal parameter `SizeOfIndent`. In such cases it would be rather convenient if we could *omit* the actual parameter from the call in cases where its value is zero. This is an example of a *default* parameter. That is a parameter which has an *assumed* value, used when no actual parameter is supplied.

We can re-write the `indent` function, so that a default value is used for the parameter `SizeOfIndent` as follows:

```
void indent(char message[], int SizeOfIndent = 0);
//
// indent prints the array of characters
// in the parameter message on the screen.
//
// The message is indented by SizeOfIndent
// characters.
//
// If no value is supplied for SizeOfIndent
// then the default zero is used.
//

void indent(char message[], int SizeOfIndent)
{
      int i; // local loop control variable

      for(i=1; i<=SizeOfIndent; i++)
            cout << ' ';
      cout << message ;
}
```

In this version of `indent`, the parameter `SizeOfIndent` is defined to have the default value zero. The definition of a default parameter is placed in the prototype of the function. This is a natural place to put default parameter information, because it is the prototype which is used by the client to see what actual parameter information they are required to supply.

Notice that we have reversed the order of the parameters `message` and `SizeOfIndent` in the prototype for the function `indent`. This is because any parameter which occurs after a default parameter in a function prototype must also be a default parameter.

We now have even more choice in the manner in which we call the function `indent`. We can now choose the number of actual parameters we shall supply when we call the function. We must always supply an actual parameter for the formal parameter `message`, as this parameter has no default value. However, we may choose whether or not we shall supply an actual parameter value for the formal parameter `SizeOfIndent`. We could call the function `indent` like this:

```
indent("Spain",10) ;
```

in which case the message:

```
          Spain
```

will be printed on the screen, preceded by 10 space characters. Alternatively, we call the function `indent` like this:

```
indent("France");
```

in which case the message:

```
France
```

will be printed on the screen, preceded by *no* characters.

We may decide to provide default values for as many of a function's parameters as we choose, but we must remember that all the default parameters must come at the end of the parameter list in a function's prototype.

If we have a function of three parameters, for example, then we may decide that all three should have default values. When we call the function we may therefore supply zero, one, two or three parameters. However, we will not be able to supply an actual parameter value for only the first and third parameters, as the compiler will assume (as normal) that actual parameters are supplied to a function in the same order to that in which they are defined in the formal parameter list. If we supply two parameters to a function which has three parameters then the compiler will therefore decide that the third parameter is the one which has been omitted.

As we have seen, parameters can be used to make the use of functions more flexible. The function is defined by a programmer who assumes the rôle of a server. The comment syntax of C++ can be used by the server to document the actions which the function performs in terms of its parameters.

Providing more parameters to functions makes the functions more flexible as the client (the programmer who write the code which calls the function) has a wider choice as to how the function will be executed. Clearly, we should be careful not to push this flexibility too far. It is possible to have too much of a good thing.

# Exercises

7.1 Use five calls to `line` defined in Figure 7.2 to draw this:

```
-----
-----
-----
-----
-----
```

7.2 Now draw the same shape, but with only one call to the function `line` defined in Figure 7.2.

**Hint**
Use a loop.

7.3 Verify that the function `line` defined in Figure 7.2 obeys the small print. (The terminology for this 'small print' is the 'specification' of the function.)

7.4 Try writing some simple functions which take an integer parameter and print out some value which depends upon the value of the actual parameter passed.

7.5 For the functions you have written, try mentally executing various calls to these functions.

7.6 Write down five valid calls to the function `line` defined in Figure 7.2.

7.7 Write down 3 invalid calls to the function `line` defined in Figure 7.2.

7.8 Write a program that reads in a number and draws a line of that many dashes on the screen using the `line` function defined in Figure 7.2.

7.9 Write a program that reads in a character and draws a triangle shape using the character read in. For example, in order to draw a triangle of dash characters, we may start by drawing a line containing a single dash. On the following line we draw a line containing two dash characters and so on. For a triangle of depth five, five lines will be drawn, each containing one more dash character than the line preceding it.

Thus the shape should look like this:

```
-
--
---
----
-----
```

7.10 Sometimes, we might want a carriage return after the line of characters printed by `line`, sometimes not. How could you add an extra parameter to the function `line` defined in Figure 7.2 to cater for this?

7.11 The function `indent` defined in Figure 7.6 're-invents the wheel'. We already have a function for drawing lines of characters on the screen, and a space is simply a character. Adapt the function `indent` to make good use of the function `line` defined in Figure 7.2.

7.12 Work out the scope of each variable in the following code fragment:

```
int x,y ;

void fun1(int y) ;
void fun2(int a) ;
void fun3(int y, int a) ;

void fun1(int y)
{
        int x;

        // body of fun1
}

char a,b;

void fun2(int a)
{
        int y;

        // body of fun2
}

void fun3(int y, int a)
{
        int b;

        // body of fun3
}
```

7.13 What is wrong with the following function definition?

```
void fun1(int x) ;

void fun1(int x)
{
      int x;

      ...
}
```

7.14 Why might we want to have the same name for a local variable in several different functions?

7.15 What kinds of variable make good candidates for local variables?

7.16 What kinds of variable make good candidates for global variables?

7.17 Adapt the function `heading` defined in Figure 7.3 so that it uses an open array parameter for the message passed to it.

7.18 Think of a suitable default value for the formal parameter `message` in the function `indent` defined in Figure 7.6.

7.19 Find as many syntax errors as you can in the program fragment below:

```
void line(int, char WhichCharacter) ;
//
// Prints a line of characters of length 'HowMany'
// containing the character given 'WhichCharacter'.
//

void indent(SizeOfIndent; char message[]) ;
//
// Prints a string passed in the array 'message'
// The message is indented by 'SizeOfIndent'
// characters
//

void line(int HowMany, char WhichCharacter);
{
      int i; // local loop control variable
      for(i=1; i<=HowMany; i++)
```

```
                cout << WhichCharacter ;
}
indent(int SizeOfIndent, char message[])

        int i; // local loop control variable

        for(i=1; i<=SizeOfIndent; i++) cout << ' ';
        cout << message ;
}
```

# 8

# Reference Parameters

## Aims

This chapter introduces the concept of reference parameter passing. It explains the way in which reference parameters allow results to be returned from functions and explains the danger of aliasing which can arise when reference parameters are used. The chapter also introduces the concept of pre- and post-conditions in describing the effect of a function.

After reading this chapter you should be able to:

- use reference parameter passing to return results from functions
- divide a large monolithic program into a small main function and several simple functions which capture individual tasks
- write pre- and post-conditions as comments which accompany your function prototypes

## Introduction

So far we have looked at the way in which a function can be used to name a block of related code (Chapter 6) and how a function can receive values from the code which calls it as parameters, affecting the way the function is to behave (Chapter 7).

The idea of a function is to represent (in program code) a *task*. This may require information *from* the part of the program that calls it, which we achieve by passing parameters, but it may also involve returning the result of calculations *to* the part of the program that calls it.

In this chapter we will show how reference parameters are used by functions to return the results of a function to the parts of the program that call the function.

## The need for reference parameters

Suppose we wish to capture the task of finding the biggest element of an array in a function. The first step would be to write a fragment of code which finds the biggest element of an array. We might write something like this:

```
int Source[100];
int i, biggest ;

// Some code goes here to fill the contents of the
array

biggest = Source[0];

for(i=1; i<=99; i++)
      if (biggest < Source[i]) biggest = Source[i];
```

Notice that we have made an arbitrary choice that the array name shall be `Source`, and that it shall contain 100 elements. Remember that the index of an array starts at zero, so counting from zero, we reach 99 as the maximum index for the array. This explains the controlling boolean expression of the `while` loop. We start off by assuming that the biggest element in the array is the first element (hence the assignment `biggest = Source[0];`), and then, in the loop, we check the 'current' value of `biggest` against one of the elements of the array `Source`, to see if a 'new' biggest value has been found.

Now, suppose that we want to make this fragment of code into a function. The array in which we shall search for the biggest element is a natural candidate for a parameter, since the process of finding the biggest element is the same regardless of the array concerned. The loop control variable, `i`, on the other hand, is not suitable as a parameter.

Were the loop control variable, `i` to be turned into a formal parameter, then the fragment of code would immediately over-write it with the number `1` (this is the initialiser of the `for` loop). We shall make the variable `i` a local variable, by defining it *inside* the body of the function. We shall call the function 'FindBiggest'. It is given in Figure 8.1 below:

```
void FindBiggest(int Source[10]);
//
// Finds the biggest element in the array Source
//

void FindBiggest(int Source[10])
{
      int i, biggest ;

      biggest = Source[0];
      for(i=1; i<=99; i++)
            if (biggest < Source[i]) biggest = Source[i];
}
```

**Figure 8.1** Function to find the biggest element of an array

Now what happens when we execute this function? Well, the answer is, very little. Suppose we want to find the biggest value in an array read in from the keyboard. We might write something like this:

```
      int Numbers[10] ;
      int count ;

      cout << "Please type in 10 numbers" ;

      for(count=0; count<=9; count++)
            cin >> Numbers[count] ;
      FindBiggest(Numbers) ;
```

The problem with the way we have written the function `FindBiggest` is that the result is stored in the variable `biggest`, which is a *local* variable, and we want to be able to print out this value after calling the function. We *cannot* print out the value of the variable `biggest`, however, because it is local to the function `FindBiggest`, and thus, it is *not accessible* outside the body of the function.

It might seem natural to change the function `FindBiggest` so that it *prints out* the biggest number in the array passed to it as a parameter. We could re-write `FindBiggest` to print out the value of the biggest number. This version of `FindBiggest` is given in Figure 8.2.

```
void FindBiggest(int Source[10]);
//
// Prints the biggest element in the array Source
// This function would be better with an open array
// parameter - this is an exercise for the reader
//

void FindBiggest(int Source[10])
{
      int i, biggest ;

      biggest = Source[0];

      for(i=1; i<=9; i++)
            if (biggest < Source[i]) biggest = Source[i] ;

      cout << biggest ;
}
```

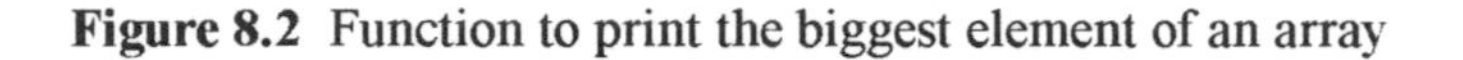

**Figure 8.2** Function to print the biggest element of an array

This will allow us to achieve our goal of reading in the user's list of 100 numbers and printing out the biggest number, but there is still a problem. The idea of a function is that its captures a task, in this case finding the biggest number in some array. We should be entitled to use this function in any larger task that involves finding the biggest element of an array as a sub-task. One such 'larger task' is the problem of printing out all the array indexes at which the biggest number is stored. This might be useful, because the biggest element in an array may occur several times (if the array is allowed to contain duplicate elements).

For example, if the biggest number in the array is 3 and the first part of the array looks like this:

then we would (at least) print out the values 1, 4 and 6 as the indices of the array at which the biggest number is stored. If we had previously worked out the index of *one* of the occurrences of the biggest number in the array, and stored the result in a variable called `biggest`, then we could achieve this output for an array called `Numbers`, using the code fragment in Figure 8.3.

Sadly, we cannot use the version of the `FindBiggest` function given in Figure 8.2, because it prints out the value of the biggest element but does not *store* it in a variable that we can access outside the function. The version of `FindBiggest` given in Figure 8.1, is of no use either, as this does not print the value of the biggest element *neither* does it store the value in a variable that we can access outside the function.

```
int count ;

cout << "The biggest number is " << biggest ;
cout << "." << endl;
cout << "It occurs at indices: " ;
cout << endl;

for(count=0; count<=99; count++)
if (Numbers[count] == biggest) cout << count ;

cout << endl ;
```

**Figure 8.3** Code fragment to locate occurrences of the biggest array element

The natural solution that springs to mind, given the C++ features that we have learnt so far, is to store the value of the biggest element of the array in a *global* variable. This way, we shall be able to access the value outside the function, and we shall have the choice over when and where this value is printed (if we want to print it), and we shall also be able to use the value in subsequent computations.

We could re-write the function `FindBiggest` using a global variable called `biggest`. This version of the function `FindBiggest` is given in Figure 8.4 below:

```
void FindBiggest(int Source[100]);
//
// Finds the biggest element in the array Source.
// The result is stored in the global variable
// biggest
//

void FindBiggest(int Source[100])
{
      int i ;

      biggest = Source[0];
      for(i=1; i<=99; i++)
            if (biggest < Source[i]) biggest = Source[i] ;
}
```

**Figure 8.4** Find the biggest element of an array and store it in a global variable

Notice that the body of this function is almost identical to that given in Figure 8.2, which finds the biggest element and stores the result in a local variable. The only change is that we have deleted the local variable `biggest`.

The fragment of code given in Figure 8.3 will now work as we expected, if preceded by a call to the version of `FindBiggest` given in Figure 8.4, passing the parameter `Numbers` as the actual parameter corresponding to the formal parameter `Source`.

## Call by reference parameters

In the next section we discuss why the use of global variables to communicate values to and from functions is a *bad* idea. In this section we shall describe the alternative — using call by reference parameters.

We have seen that a function may have parameters. In order to use a parameter, we define the name and type of a formal parameter in the heading of the function (and in its prototype). The kinds of parameters that we have been using so far are known as 'value' parameters, because the value of the actual parameter is passed to a function and associated with the name of the corresponding formal parameter inside the body of the function.

There is another form of parameter known as a 'reference parameter', which allows us to pass the name of a variable to a function as the actual parameter[1]. Because we are passing a *reference* to a variable (its name), the function can use this reference to alter the value of the variable passed as the actual parameter.

In Figure 8.5 we consider a simple example before moving on to see how we can use a reference parameter in our function `FindBiggest`.

```
#include <iostream.h>

void fun(int x) ;
void fun(int x)
{ x = 42; }

main()
{
      int v ;

      v = 0 ;
      fun(v);
      cout << v;
}
```

**Figure 8.5** A function which does nothing

[1]Strictly speaking, this parameter is also a value; the value is the *address* of the variable. However, it is helpful to think of this kind of value as representing a different form of parameter altogether.

When we run this program the number 0 will appear as the output. This might not be what you expected. We passed the variable v as the actual parameter to the function fun, corresponding to the formal parameter x. The body of fun says that x is to be given the value 42, so surely the variable v should be 42 after the call to fun?

Well, no. Remember that the parameter *only* has a meaning inside the function. So the assignment of 42 to x inside the function fun happens *not* to the variable v, but to the *local copy* of v, held inside the parameter x. It would not make sense for the assignment

```
x = 42;
```

inside the body of the function fun to act upon anything *other* than fun's local copy of the value passed to it.

If we want assignments to the variable x inside the body of the function fun to affect the value of a variable that we pass as an actual parameter then we must declare the formal parameter x to be a *reference parameter*. The reference parameter version of the function fun is given in Figure 8.6.

```
#include <iostream.h>

void fun(int& x) ;

void fun(int& x)
{ x = 42; }

main()
{
      int v ;

      v = 0 ;
      fun(v);
      cout << v;
}
```

**Figure 8.6** A function which does something

Notice that the only difference between this version of function and the one in Figure 8.5 is that the formal parameter x of the function fun has a different type. We have written int&, instead of int. Any formal parameter which does not have an & before its parameter name is a value parameter. Putting an & between the type name and the formal parameter name tells the compiler that the formal parameter is a reference parameter. When we run this program we *shall* see the number 42 appear on the output.

The &, which makes a parameter a reference parameter, has two important consequences:

- we may pass *only* a variable's *name* as the actual parameter
- any assignment to the formal parameter in the body of fun is *also* an assignment to the actual parameter that we pass to it

A reference parameter is so-called because the formal parameter is a *reference* to the actual parameter; that is, the formal parameter *refers* to the name of some variable.

In this simple example, the effect that the function fun has upon its reference parameter is rather pointless. If we want to assign 42 to a variable, there is no need to call up a function in order to do it. However, now that we have seen how reference parameters work, we may return to the FindBiggest function and re-write the function so that it uses a reference parameter to store the biggest number in the array passed to it. The reference parameter version of the function FindBiggest is given in Figure 8.7.

```
void FindBiggest(int Source[100], int& result);
//
// Finds the biggest element in the array Source.
// The biggest number is stored in the
// reference parameter, result.
// It is an exercise to make Source an open array.
//

void FindBiggest(int Source[100], int& result)
{
      int i ;

      result = Source[0];
      for(i=1; i<=99; i++)
            if (result < Source[i])
                  result = Source[i] ;
}
```

**Figure 8.7** Find the biggest element of an array, using a reference parameter

When we call the function FindBiggest, we will be able to choose in which variable we should store the result. Suppose we want to use the function to find the four best marks in four different classes. We will store the marks for each class in an array. We shall use the array names English, Maths, French and Chemistry, for the four classes. We shall use the variables TopEnglish, TopMaths, TopFrench and TopChemistry for the best marks in each class.

Also, suppose that there is a special 'Kurt Gödel Prize', which is awarded to the top Mathematics student *if* the mark obtained in mathematics is *better* than that obtained by the best students in the other three disciplines. We shall also write our program so that it decides whether or not the Gödel Prize is to be awarded.

Suppose we have already read in the marks for the students into the four arrays `English`, `Maths`, `French` and `Chemistry`, and that we have defined the function `FindBiggest`, as in Figure 8.7 above. The rest of the code to find the best marks in each class is given in Figure 8.8 below:

```
//
// Fragment of code to print out the best
// students in four classes.
//

FindBiggest(English,TopEnglish) ;
FindBiggest(Maths,TopMaths) ;
FindBiggest(French,TopFrench) ;
FindBiggest(Chemistry,TopChemistry) ;

cout << "The best mark in Mathematics was: " ;
cout << TopMaths << endl ;
cout << "The best mark in Chemistry was: " ;
cout << TopChemistry << endl ;
cout << "The best mark in French was: " ;
cout << TopFrench << endl ;
cout << "The best mark in English was: " ;
cout << TopEnglish << endl ;

if ((TopMaths > TopFrench)  &&
    (TopMaths > TopEnglish) &&
    (TopMaths > TopChemistry))
      cout << "The Godel Prize will be awarded";
else cout << "No Godel Prize this year";
```

**Figure 8.8** Top four marks and Gödel Prize fragment

Notice how this problem highlights the shortcomings of approaches to defining the `FindBiggest` function which do not use reference parameters.

The version of `FindBiggest` in Figure 8.2 *prints out* the biggest number in the array passed to it. This means that we shall only be able to print out the four best marks provided we call the function `FindBiggest`, at the *exact* point in the execution of the program where we wish each of the four numbers to appear on the output device. Using the 'printing' version of `FindBiggest` in Figure 8.2 we would write the fragment of code to print the four best marks as follows:

```
cout << "The best mark in Mathematics was: " ;
FindBiggest(Maths) ;
cout << endl ;
cout << "The best mark in Chemistry was: " ;
FindBiggest(Chemistry) ;
cout << endl ;
cout << "The best mark in French was: " ;
FindBiggest(French) ;
cout << endl ;
cout << "The best mark in English was: " ;
FindBiggest(English) ;
cout << endl ;
```

You may think that this is just as good as the solution with the reference parameter version of FindBiggest. We would argue that it is better to be able to *choose* where the function FindBiggest is called, giving us the freedom to structure the program in a way that we think best reflects our intentions.

However, a deeper problem with the 'printing' version of FindBiggest given in Figure 8.2 becomes clear when we try to work out whether or not the Gödel Prize is to be awarded. We *cannot* do this. This is because the 'printing' version of FindBiggest does not *store* the value of the biggest number in the array passed to it, which we will need for comparison between each of the four top marks.

Clearly then, the decision to print out the results of functions inside the function is a bad one, because this does not allow the person calling the function to *choose* how to use the results of the function. For example, the client may not want the result printed out at all.

The 'global variable' version of FindBiggest given in Figure 8.4 does not *prevent* us from solving the problem of finding the top four marks. It also allows us to decide whether or not to award the Gödel Prize. This version of the function *does* store the result of the function in a variable, so we shall be able to use this value in any way we choose. However, we shall find that using this version of the function is rather more irritating than using the 'reference parameter' version given in Figure 8.7. This is because we cannot *choose* the variable in which the result is stored when we call the function, so we shall have to follow each call by an assignment to 'preserve the result of the call'.

The four calls to FindBiggest in Figure 8.8 would thus have to be replaced by the code fragment below (if we use the 'global variable' version of FindBiggest defined in Figure 8.4). The result would look like this:

```
FindBiggest(English) ;    TopEnglish = biggest ;
FindBiggest(Maths) ;      TopMaths = biggest ;
FindBiggest(French) ;     TopFrench = biggest ;
FindBiggest(Chemistry) ; TopChemistry = biggest ;
```

## Global variables versus parameter passing

If we chose to, we could *always* use global variables to communicate the result of a function to the client. We could also use global variables to supply to a function the values of its value parameters. We could therefore *always* use parameterless functions in our programs. Whilst this is true, it is also true that we could dispense with functions altogether, and write our programs as one monolithic function.

Most of the features of programming languages are not *essential*, in the sense that we can write our programs in a very simple language, without features such as `for` loops, arrays, functions and `classes`. If we wanted to be perverse, we could write our programs in binary. After all, the C++ compiler translates a program into a single (very large) binary number. The very first computers *were* programmed in binary, but very quickly programmers designed software tools to make their lives a lot easier. Object Oriented Programming is one step in a path that began with the first Hexadecimal[2] Loader, which allowed a programmer to write a program in hexadecimal rather than binary.

In order to use the features of a programming language to best effect, it is often important to understand why they were invented. The best way to do this is to imagine how programs would look *without* such features. Suppose, for example, that we decided *not* to have parameters for our functions, but to use global variables instead. This would have some advantages:

- we would not have to write parameters when we call a function
- in the body of a function we would be able to access any variable, so we would not have to worry about scope rules

These advantages, however, are outweighed by the disadvantages, especially when we consider the problem of *understanding* the behaviour of a *large* program, perhaps developed by *several* programmers. In this situation the advantages of parameters become overwhelming:

- parameters can be used to delimit each programmer's part of the program
- parameters can be used to define the effect of a function (the client–server concept)
- parameters allow us to view a function as a language extension
- parameters make it easier to reuse a function

---

[2]Hexadecimal means hex (6) and decimal (10), which is the number base 16. There are sixteen digits in base sixteen, starting with 0 up to 9 and then continuing with A, B, C, D, E and F. One hexadecimal digit corresponds to four binary digits, making hexadecimal a convenient way of representing the contents of memory. For example, two hexadecimal digits denote precisely the range of numbers which can be stored in a single byte.

Furthermore, without parameters:

- we would have to maintain a mental note of the purpose of a large list of global variables
- we would have to think of *every* function as potentially affecting the value of *any* variable
- we would find that the effect of calling one function might affect the behaviour of another, due to their sharing a global variable
- calling a function at a different point in the program would give different effects, due to the current values of global variables at each point

## Examples of the use of reference parameters

In this section we shall illustrate the use of reference parameters with several examples. We shall also use this section to illustrate some of the criteria which should be considered when deciding which aspects of a function's behaviour should be parameterised, and those which should be fixed every time the function is called.

Suppose we want to swap the values stored in two variables. This is a natural task to perform with a function, and we shall need reference parameters to allow us to choose the variables whose contents are to be swapped. The function which does this is called `swap`, and it is defined in Figure 8.9 below:

```
void swap(int& x, int& y) ;
//
// The final value of x is the
// initial value of y.
// The final value of y is the
// initial value of x.
//

void swap(int& x, int& y)
{
      int temp;

      temp = x;
      x = y ;
      y = temp ;
}
```

**Figure 8.9** A function to swap the contents of two variables

Another common task we shall want to perform is to read in data and validate the data before it is passed on to the part of the program that uses it. For example, suppose that we want to read in a valid percentage, that is, a `float` which must be in the range 0.0 to 100.0. We may want to call this function from several points in the program, and may want to store the valid percentage in any one of several variables. This is a natural candidate for a function (since it is a well-defined task) and it is also a natural candidate for a reference parameter (since we want to calculate a result and store it somewhere). The function to read in a valid percentage is given in Figure 8.10 below:

```
void GetPercentage(float& pc) ;
//
// The value stored in pc is read
// from the keyboard.
// pc is guaranteed to be in the range
// 0.0 to 100.0 inclusive.
//

void GetPercentage(float& pc)
{
      do
      {
            cout << "Enter a number between "
                 << "0 and 100" ;
            cin >> pc ;
      } while ((pc < 0.0) || (pc > 100.0));
}
```

**Figure 8.10** A function to read in a valid percentage

Notice that we use a `do ... while ...` loop, which is preferable to a `while` loop because we *first* want to read in a number, *then* continue reading the number until it is in range.

Also, notice that the guarantee mentioned in the comments can be *proved* to be correct, since we know from the behaviour of a `do ... while ...` loop that the value of the boolean expression after the word `while` is *false* at the point in the program immediately after the execution of the loop. Thus, in this case, we know that the boolean expression :

```
( pc < 0.0) || (pc > 100.0)
```

is false at the point at which the function terminates. That is, the following boolean expression will be true at the point at which the function terminates:

```
!(( pc < 0.0) || (pc > 100.0))
```

Using the rules of boolean logic we can re-write this expression as:

```
(pc >= 0.0) && (pc <=100.0)
```

which precisely captures (in the language of C++) the guarantee (written in English in the comments).

## Abstraction

As we have already seen, the best functions are those which are most general, and we make a function more general by increasing the number of parameters it has. This process is called 'abstraction'. Of course, we can take abstraction too far. We would not want to add any parameters to the function `swap`, as its task is already as general as it 'should be'. This 'should be' is a matter of judgement. A balance has to be arrived at which weighs flexibility against a ridiculous proliferation in parameters.

If we turn our attention to the function `GetPercentage`, we can see that the task of reading in a valid `float` depends upon the range of numbers within which the `float` is considered to be valid. A percentage is a *special case* of this process. We could define a more general function `GetValidFloat`, which we do in Figure 8.11 below:

```
void GetValidFloat(float bottom, float top,
                   float& result);
//
// Reads a float from the keyboard into result.
// The value of result is guaranteed to be
// no smaller than bottom, and no larger than
// top.
//

void GetValidFloat(float  bottom, float top,
                   float& result)
{
      do
      {
            cout << "Type a number in the range ";
            cout << bottom << " to " << top;
            cout << " (inclusive)" ;
            cin >> result ;
      } while ((result < bottom) || (result > top)) ;
}
```

**Figure 8.11** Generalised input validation function

We can now re-define the function `GetPercentage` *in terms* of the function `GetValidFloat`, like this:

```
void GetPercentage(float& result) ;
//
// Reads in a valid percentage.
// That is, a float in the range
// 0 to 100 (inclusive).
//

void GetPercentage(float& result)
{
        GetValidFloat(0.0,100.0,result) ;
}
```

## Arrays are implicit reference parameters

A natural question to ask at this point is whether or not it makes sense to write a function to read in the elements of an array using a reference parameter for the array. It may come as some surprise to realise that we can write such a function like `ReadArray` defined in Figure 8.12 below:

```
void ReadArray(int result[10]) ;
//
// reads in elements into the array result
//

void ReadArray(int result[10])
{
      int i ;

      i = 0 ;
      do
      {
            cin >> result[i] ;
            i++ ;
      } while (i <= 9);
}
```

**Figure 8.12** Function to read into an array

You will have noticed that the function `ReadArray` takes a *value* parameter `result`, and yet it claims (correctly) that it reads elements into the array. It might seem that we should have used a reference parameter.

Arrays are a 'special case' of value parameter passing. Remember that the name of an array is, in fact, the address of the first element of the array (see Chapter 5). The *value* passed when we pass an array parameter to a function is therefore effectively a reference to the array's contents (via the first element of the array). We can think of passing an array to a function as an exception to the rule that all parameters are value parameters unless we indicate otherwise with an `&`. Array parameters should therefore *always* be considered to be reference parameters.

We can therefore write a program to sort an array, *returning* the sorted version, simply by virtue of the fact that the array is a parameter to the function. The function `Sort` in Figure 8.13 does just this.

```
void Sort(int result[10]) ;
//
// sorts the elements of the array result into
// descending order.
//
// It is an exercise to make result an open array.
//

void Sort(int result[10])
{
	int i,j ;

	for(i=0; i<9; i++)
		for(j=i+1; j<10; j++)
			if (result[i] < result[j])
				swap(result[i],result[j]) ;
}
```

**Figure 8.13** A function to sort the contents of an array

Notice that this function uses nested loops. The outer loop controlled by the variable `i` moves through the array from the first element to the last but one. The inner loop runs from the current value of `i` in the outer loop to the end of the array. The inner loop uses the same algorithm as `FindBiggest` to put the biggest element from the current value of `i` to the end of the array at the index `i` within the array.

Initially we assume that the element `result[i]` is the biggest element from index `i` to the end of the array, whilst the body of the loop checks each element it finds against the value of `result[i]`, and updates `result[i]` (using a call to the `swap` function) if another element of the array is found to be bigger. Notice that the inner loop need not start at the beginning of the array, since each traversal of the outer loop ensures that the element `i` of the array result is the `i`$^{th}$ biggest element of the array result, and so is in the correct place.

We may not want to alter the values of an array, but, may instead, want to pass an array as a *call by value* parameter. In order to do this we shall have to *mimic* the effect of call by value parameter passing. We can do this by *copying* the contents of one array into another. The function `CopyArray` does this — it is defined in Figure 8.14.

```
void CopyArray(int from[10], int to[10]) ;
//
// Copies the array 'from' to the array 'to'.
//

void CopyArray(int from [10], int to[10])
{
      int i ;

      for(i=0; i<=9; i++) to[i] = from[i] ;
}
```

**Figure 8.14** Function to copy the contents of on array to another

Now suppose we return to the problem of finding the biggest element of an array. We could do this (in a rather inefficient way), by first sorting the array into descending order, and then returning the first value. However, we shall *not* want to sort the array as a by-product of finding its biggest element, and so we shall have to preserve the unsorted version of the array before sorting it.

We can re-write `FindBiggest`, using the functions we have defined so far, giving the correct (but inefficient) version of `FindBiggest` in Figure 8.15.

```
void FindBiggest(int  Numbers[10], int& result);
//
// Finds the biggest element of the array Numbers.
// The biggest value in Numbers is stored in result.
//

void FindBiggest(int Numbers[10], int& result)
{
      int CopyOfNumbers[10] ;

      CopyArray(Numbers,CopyOfNumbers) ;
      Sort(CopyOfNumbers) ;
      result = CopyOfNumbers[0] ;
}
```

**Figure 8.15** The inefficient version of the `FindBiggest` function

## Mentally executing functions with reference parameters

We have described the way in which we can mentally execute a function by substituting the body of a function for each call to the function. This allows us to work out the effect of any call to a function in an automatic way. Having performed the substitution, we can then look at the body we have created, to work out what the call to the function means.

We can apply this idea to understanding the effect of a function which has reference parameters also. Where a function has a reference parameter, we shall have to substitute all occurrences of the formal parameter name with the actual parameter (which is the name of a variable).

Consider the function `ReadArray`, defined in Figure 8.12. We might call this function with the actual parameter `AnnArray`. We can work out the effect of this call by replacing occurrences of the formal parameter `result` with the actual parameter `AnnArray`, giving the code fragment below:

```
{
        int i ;

        for(i=0; i<=99; i++)
                cin >> AnnArray[i];
}
```

Similarly, we could work out the effect of calls to the function `GetValidFloat`, defined in Figure 8.11. Suppose we call the function like this:

```
GetValidFloat(17.5,20.04,x);
```

The effect of this call can be obtained by replacing the formal parameter `result` with the actual parameter `x`, and by adding initialised declarations for the two value parameters `bottom` and `top`. The result of the substitution gives the code fragment below:

```
{
        int bottom = 17.5;
        int top = 20.04 ;

        do
        {
                cout << "Type a number in the range ";
                cout << bottom << " to " << top;
                cout << " (inclusive)" ;

                cin >> x ;
        } while ((x < bottom) || (x > top)) ;
}
```

The body of the function after the substitution is valid C++, and it is what will be executed when the function is called with the actual parameters 17.5, 20.04 and x for the formal parameters bottom, top and result respectively.

Notice that occurrences of the reference parameter result on the left-hand side of an assignment in the body of GetValidFloat are replaced by the actual parameter x. By contrast, value parameters are treated as local variables which are given an initial value because any assignment to a value parameter has *no effect outside the body of the function*.

We can also see the effect of valid calls to the function, which nonetheless, result in erroneous behaviour. Suppose we call the function like this:

```
GetValidFloat(20.1,10.5,y);
```

This call to the function yields the substitution below:

```
{
        int bottom = 20.1 ;
        int top = 10.5 ;

        do
        {
                cout << "Type a number in the range ";
                cout << bottom << " to " << top;
                cout << " (inclusive)" ;

                cin >> y ;
        } while ((y < bottom) || (y > top)) ;
}
```

The trouble with this call is in the boolean expression which controls the termination of the loop. That is the expression:

```
((y < bottom) || (y > top))
```

By substituting the values assigned to the variables bottom and top at the start of the fragment of code, we can see that this expression means the same thing as the expression below:

```
((y < 20.1) || (y > 10.5))
```

This will always be true (try thinking of a number which is neither less than 20.1 nor greater than 10.5 nor both). Since the boolean expression controlling the do ... while ... loop is *always* true, the loop will *never* terminate regardless of what the user types at the keyboard. So the hapless user would be required to supply an *infinite* number of float's to the greedy function GetValidFloat.

# Aliasing

An alias is a reference to a variable which already has another reference. That is, aliasing occurs when there are two references to the same variable, and this situation can arise with call by reference parameter passing. Consider, for example, the function `SumAndProd` in Figure 8.16.

```
void SumAndProd(int x, int y,
                int& res1, int& res2) ;
//
// x+y is stored in res1
// The final value of res2 is the square of its
// initial value.
//

void SumAndProd(int x, int y,
                int& res1, int& res2)
{
      res1 = x+y ;
      res2 = res2*res2 ;
}
```

**Figure 8.16** A simple function with two reference parameters

Notice that the `SumAndProd` function takes two value parameters (`x` and `y`) and two reference parameters (`res1` and `res2`). Also, notice that the *initial* value of the reference parameter `res2` is used in defining its *final* value. In this way a reference parameter may provide an *input* into a function as well as being a receptacle for its *output*.

We shall look at a normal call to the function `SumAndProd`, to see how it works. Suppose we call the function like this:

```
SumAndProd(12+2,8*4,v1,v2);
```

where `v1` and `v2` are global variables. Performing the substitution of actual parameters for formal parameters we obtain the following:

```
{
      int x = 12+2;
      int y = 8*4 ;

      v1 = x+y;
      v2 = v2*v2 ;
}
```

Now, consider what happens with the following call:

```
SumAndProd(3,5,v1,v1);
```

Notice that, in this call, we are passing the *same* variable name as the actual parameter for both of the reference parameters. This leads to aliasing in the body of the function `SumAndProd`, since both `res1` and `res2` will refer to the variable `v1`. That is, `res1` will be an alias for the name `res2` and `res2` will, likewise, be an alias for the name `res1`.

When we perform the substitution of actual for formal parameters we obtain the code fragment below:

```
{
      int x = 3 ;
      int y = 5 ;

      v1 = x+y;
      v1 = v1*v1 ;
}
```

which we can see has the effect of assigning first `8` to `v1` and then assigning `64` to `v1`, *overwriting* the effect of the first assignment.

Now the comments for the function say that :

```
//
// The final value of res2 is the square of its
// initial value.
//
```

but this is *not true*, at least not if there is aliasing of references within the body of `SumAndProd`. If we pass the value *k1* for the value parameter `x` and *k2* for `y`, but pass the *same* variable name, say `z`, for both the reference parameters `res1` *and* `res2`, then we shall find that the result stored in `res2` is $(k1+k2)^2$.

This happens because the first assignment (to `res1`) in the body of `SumAndProd` will also *implicitly* assign a value to the other reference parameter (`res2`), thus affecting the second assignment in `SumAndProd` (which uses the value of `res2`).

This form of implicit effect, where the existence of an alias allows one assignment to a variable to affect the value of another, *apparently unrelated*, statement is a good reason for avoiding aliasing in programs. We cannot think of a sensible use of aliasing in which a problem is inexpressible or woefully inefficient without aliasing. Neither can we think of an example where aliasing makes programs easier to understand. On the contrary, it nearly always makes programs harder to understand because it is unclear which variable is being affected when we encounter an assignment statement which may assign a value to a variable through an alias.

## The client–server contract: pre- and post-conditions

Remember that we described the process of writing a function as an example of the client–server principle. The client is the person calling the function and the server is the person writing the function. In order to make sense of this concept we write comments (that is, the server writes comments for the consumption of the client) describing how the function is to behave.

The description of how the function is to behave is often expressed in terms of pre- and post-conditions, where the pre-conditions express the initial state of the parameters on entry to the function and the post-conditions express the final values (perhaps in terms of the initial values) of reference parameters on exit from the function.

The pre-conditions can be thought of as the guarantee that the client gives the server. The client must ensure that the pre-conditions are met if they expect the post-condition to be met.

The post-condition can be thought of as the guarantee provided by the server to the client. If the client meets the pre-condition, then the server promises to establish the post-condition.

We shall look at an example, to make these abstract ideas more concrete.

Suppose we are to write a function that takes a character and a string, and stores (in a reference parameter) the location in the string at which the character occurs. We might write the function using an open array for the string. This solution is given in Figure 8.17 below:

```
void Locate(char s[], char ch, int& location);
//
// Finds the character ch in the array s.
// The position of ch is stored in location.
//

void Locate(char s[], char ch, int& location)
{
      int i ;

      i = 0 ;
      while (s[i] != ch)
            i++ ;
      location = i ;
}
```

**Figure 8.17** A function to locate a character in an array

This is how we might first write the function. However, having written the function we should not be content until we have satisfied ourselves that it works (first and foremost) and that it could not have been written more elegantly and/or more efficiently (subsequently). The comments are particularly vague, and a skilled programmer would find them irritating for what they *fail* to say; What if `ch` does *not* occur in `s`? What if there is *more* than one occurrence of `ch` in `s`?

Let us see what happens when we call the function passing (for the formal parameter `s`) an array `A` that looks like this:

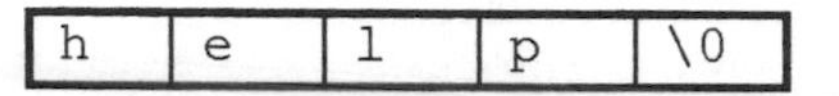

and passing for the formal parameter `ch` the character `'l'`.

The function will execute the loop two times, halting with the local variable `i` set to `2`, which will subsequently be stored in the variable `location`. All is well.

Now, suppose we call the function with an array that looks like this (but still passing `l` for `ch`):

| h | e | l | l | o | \0 |
|---|---|---|---|---|---|

The function will execute the loop two times, halting with the local variable `i` set to `2`, which will subsequently be stored in the variable `location`. The interesting thing in this situation is that the number returned is *a* location of an `l` character within the array, but the array contains *two* `l`s. Clearly our function can only return one integer, and so we must decide how to specify what the function will do if there is more than one character, `ch`, in the array, `s`.

A little consideration will reveal that the function `Locate` will return the *first* location at which the character `ch` occurs in the array `s`. This seems to be as good a result as we could expect, but we shall have to remember to include this fact in the comment associated with the function's prototype.

The next thing to do is to consider what happens if the array passed to the function does *not* contain the character `ch`. In this case we can see that the function will not terminate. That is, a pre-condition of the function is that the array passed to it in the formal parameter `s` *must* contain the character we are looking for. We should therefore write the comments associated with the function like this:

```
void Locate(char s[], char ch, int& location);
//
// pre-condition:  ch occurs in the array s
// post-condition: location is set to the index
// at which ch first occurs in the array s.
//
```

The pre-condition must be satisfied by the client. If it is, then the post-condition will be satisfied by the server, in the sense that `Locate` will set location to the first index at which `ch` occurs in `s`.

We can now consider how the function can be improved. We first notice that the local variable `i` is *not* required, since we can use the reference parameter `location` to index the array `s`. This observation will allow us to re-write the function `Locate`. The improved definition is given in Figure 8.18:

```
void Locate(char s[], char ch, int& location) ;
//
// pre-condition:  ch occurs in the array s
// post-condition: location is set to the index
// at which ch first occurs in the array s.
//

void Locate(char s[], char ch, int& location)
{
        location = 0 ;
        while (s[location] != ch)
        {
                location++ ;
        }
}
```

**Figure 8.18** A better function to locate a character in an array

This version of the function is better because it requires fewer statements and fewer variables. It will thus execute faster and in less memory.

The next aspect of the function to consider is the way it behaves if the pre-condition is not met. In such a situation, in the rôle of server, we might be entitled to say that we are not concerned with the behaviour of a function whose pre-condition is not met, as the responsibility of the client is to satisfy the pre-condition. However, this is not a particularly professional response to the situation. It would be better if the function could 'cope' if the pre-condition is not met, and failing to terminate is not really 'coping' in any meaningful sense.

We shall now re-write the function so that it *does* terminate if the character `ch` is not in the array `s`. This will mean that we have to decide what value to place in the reference parameter `location` when `ch` does not occur in `s`. A sensible approach would be to store `-1` in `location`, as this number is not a valid array index, and the client will therefore have the ability to *test* to see if the character `ch` occurs in `s` using the function `Locate`. In Figure 8.19 we re-write the function `Locate` to make it robust (that is, more able to cope when its pre-condition is not met).

```
void Locate(char s[], char ch, int& location) ;
//
// pre-condition:  s contains a NULL character
// post-condition: location is set to the index
// at which ch first occurs in the array s.
//
// If the pre-condition is not met, the value of
// result will be -1.
//

void Locate(char s[], char ch, int& location)
{
      location = 0 ;
      while ( (s[location] != '\0') &&
              (s[location] != ch) )
            location++ ;

      if (s[location] != ch)
            location = -1 ;
}
```

**Figure 8.19** A robust function to locate a character in an array

Interestingly, in an attempt to understand precisely what our function does, to express it clearly, and to improve upon the behaviour of the function, we have, at no computational cost, produced not only a *better* function, but have *extended* its use. We started out by writing a function to find where a character occurred in a string, and ended up with a function which could also be used to test whether or not a character could be found in a string, as well as locating the character if, indeed, it did occur.

# Exercises

8.1 Consider the function below:

```
void ex1(int x; int &y)
{ y = x+y ; }
```

Use the substitution of actual parameters for formal parameters to work out the effect of the following calls to `ex1`:

```
ex1(10,z);
ex1(z,z);
ex1(z+1,z);
ex1(2*p,q);
```

8.2 Write comments which capture the pre- and post-conditions of the function `ex1` of Exercise 8.1.

8.3 Consider the function below:

```
void ex1(int x; int &y)
{
        x = x+y ;
}
```

Why does this function have no effect?

8.4 The functions `FindBiggest` in this chapter could be improved by allowing them to take arrays of *any* length. Re-write the function `FindBiggest` in Figure 8.7 so that it takes two extra parameters `low` and `high`, and stores the biggest value whose index lies between the indices `low` and `high`.

8.5 Write a function, `Initialise`, that takes an array of characters, terminated by a '`\0`' character, and stores space characters in the array up to the point where the '`\0`' occurs.

8.6 Write the pre- and post-conditions for the function `Initialise` that you wrote in Exercise 8.5.

8.7 Generalise the `Initialise` function so that the client can choose which characters are to be stored in the array.

8.8 Write a function called `Double` which takes an array of integers and doubles its contents. How did you decide what the size of the array passed to `Double` should be?

8.9 Write a function, `Count`, which takes an array, `A`, of integers, and an integer, `i`, and prints the number of occurrences of `i` in `A`. What are the pre- and post-conditions of your function?

8.10 Re-write the functions `ReadArray` (Figure 8.12), `Sort` (Figure 8.13), `CopyArray` (Figure 8.14) and `FindBiggest` (Figure 8.15) using open arrays in place of fixed length array parameters. You will have to think of a suitable sentinel value for integers.

# 9

# Returned Values

## Aims

This chapter introduces value-returning functions and default parameters. It explains when a function should use a reference parameter to return a result from a function and when it should return the result directly (as the value returned by the function).

After reading this chapter you should be able to:

- write functions which return values using the `return` statement
- decide whether a function should return a value or use a reference parameter

## Introduction

In all the functions we have looked at so far, no value is *returned* by the function. This is indicated by the word `void` in the function prototypes. We shall now look at a simple example of a function which *does* return a value:

```
int square(int x) ;

int square(int x)
{
        return x*x;
}
```

The function `square` returns an integer. This is indicated by the word `int` which precedes the name of the function in its prototype. In order to specify the value to be returned we use the `return` statement inside the body of the function. In this case we return the square of the value passed as a parameter to the function.

The call `square(2)` returns the value `4`,
The call `square(4)` returns the value `16`,
The call `square(square(2))` returns the value `16`,
The call `square(3)` returns the value `9`,
The call `square(-3)` returns the value `9`,
The call `square(10)` returns the value `100`.

A question arises:

'Where is this value returned *to*?'

The answer lies in the way we *call* the function. The function `square` returns an integer. If we want to use this integer, we must call the function in a place where an integer is required. For example, we could write:

```
cout << square(4) ;
```

which would cause `16` to appear on the screen.

Notice that it would not make sense to call a function like `line` in the same way. If we wrote:

```
cout << line(100,'-') ;
```

then `100` dashes would appear, because that is what

```
line(100,'-')
```

does.

However, a value will also appear on the screen, the value returned by `line`. The problem is, `line` *does not* return a value, so what will be returned is *not specified*. This is a *silly* way to use `line` and many compilers will warn you that you are using a function which does not return a value in a place where a value is required, or may refuse to compile your program because the use of `line` in this peculiar way is considered to be an error.

The general rule is:

> A function which returns a value should be called in a place where *an expression* is valid.
>
> A function which does not return a value should be used in a place where *a statement* is valid.

An expression is a fragment of code which the computer evaluates, yielding a value. A statement is executed (not evaluated) and has an effect upon the state of the computer, but does not yield a value, hence the use of the word 'execute' rather than 'evaluate'.

When the computer executes an assignment statement like:

```
x = 99+1;
```

the *expression* `99+1` is *evaluated* to yield `100`. This value is stored in the variable `x` as a result of the *execution* of the *statement* `x = 99+1;`. According to the syntactic rules of `C++`, we could write *any expression* which returns a value of the correct type in place of the `99+1`. In this case the 'correct' type is integer. For example, the function `square` which we defined earlier is an integer-returning function, so we could use a call to `square` in place of the expression `99+1`. Furthermore, since the value yielded by the expression `square(10)` is `100` the assignment statement

```
x = square(10);
```

is equivalent to the assignment statement

```
x = 99+1;
```

## Mentally executing functions with returned values

In order to understand the effect of a function which returns a value, we have to do a little more work than we have required for those whose return type is `void`. This is because the function is used in the context of an expression, where a value is required. This means that we cannot simply replace the call to the function by a modified version of its body as we have done until now.

Consider the following program:

```
#include<iostream.h>

int square(int x) ;

int square(int x)
{
        return x*x;
}

void main()
{
        cout << square(2) ;
        cout << square(10) ;
}
```

We shall take the call `square(2)` first. We need to work out the effect of the `return` statement. We cannot substitute the call of the function for its body because the call of the function is used as an *expression* and the body of the function is a *statement*. We have to perform the substitution in a 'work space', that is, on a clean sheet of paper. We use this work space to evaluate the effect of the `return` statement before performing any substitution on the real program.

On the work space sheet of paper we write the call of the function. We then substitute the call of the function by its body (having added initialisers for value parameters and substituted out the reference parameters in the usual way). This will give us a block of code which contains the `return` statement. We work out the value of the expression in the `return` statement and replace the call in the original program with this value.

For example, taking the first call to `square` in the above example we get

```
{       int x = 2;
        return x*x;
}
```

on our work sheet, revealing that the `return` statement is equivalent to

```
return 2*2;
```

or, put simply,

```
return 4;
```

We have executed the function to work out the meaning of the return statement. The execution of the function is only important in so far as it determines this value and we cannot work out this value without mentally executing the body of the function. This is why we require a 'work sheet' on which to perform the execution.

Having worked out the value returned, we can write this value, `4`, in place of the call `square(2)` in the original program giving us the new program:

```
#include<iostream.h>

int square(int x) ;

int square(int x)
{
        return x*x;
}

void main()
{
        cout << 4 ;
        cout << square(10) ;
}
```

Doing the same thing with the call `square(10)`, we get:

```
#include<iostream.h>

int square(int x) ;

int square(int x)
{
        return x*x;
}

void main()
{
        cout << 4 ;
        cout << 100 ;
}
```

This allows us to see that `main` is equivalent to:

```
void main()
{
        cout << 4 ;
        cout << 100 ;
}
```

So we see that the effect of the original program is to print `4` and then `100` on the screen.

As with the mental execution of function which we described in Chapters 6, 7 and 8, it is possible to implement a compiler for C++ that uses this approach to evaluating calls to functions. Although this is a possibility, it is not done in practice as there are far more efficient techniques available.

## Using statements to calculate the returned value

We can write any valid C++ statements inside the body of a function which uses a `return` statement. Suppose we want to add up all the numbers between one and ten, and store the result in the variable `fred`. We could do that like this:

```
int i;   // a loop variable

fred = 0 ;
for(i=1; i<=10; i++) fred = fred + i;
```

At the end of the loop, `fred` will contain

```
0+1+2+3+4+5+6+7+8+9+10
```

or

```
55
```

Now we shall make this code fragment a little more useful: we shall add up all the numbers between one and `n`, where `n` is some variable, which we shall assume has a value before we start off. We can do that like this:

```
int fred,i;   // a loop variable

fred = 0 ;
for(i=1; i<=n; i++) fred = fred + i;
```

Now it would be better if we could make this task into a function which takes `n` as a parameter and returns the value of the summation as its result. We shall *return* the result of the addition as the result of our function, which we shall call `sum`. It is defined in Figure 9.1.

```
int sum(int n) ;

int sum(int n)
{
      int fred,i;   // a loop variable

      fred = 0 ;
      for(i=1; i<=n; i++) fred = fred + i;

      return fred;
}
```

**Figure 9.1** Function to calculate the sum from one to `n`

## When a function should return a value

In Chapter 8 we saw that a reference parameter can be used to return a value from a function, by allowing the client to select a variable, and pass its name as the actual parameter. The result is stored in the variable passed as the actual parameter. A question therefore arises as to the difference between passing a reference parameter to a function to pick up a result, and returning this result as the value returned by the function.

In fact, we can solve any problem which involves calculating a single value with either a value-returning function, or with a single reference parameter. Consider, once again, the problem of calculating the sum of numbers between `1` and `n`, where `n` is a value parameter passed by the user. We can re-write this function using a reference parameter, instead of returning the result as the returned value of the function. The reference parameter version of `sum` is given in Figure 9.2.

```
void sum(int n, int& result) ;
//
// This is a bad way to return the value in result

void sum(int n, int& result)
{
      int i;  // a loop variable

      result = 0 ;
      for(i=1; i<=n; i++) result = result + i;
}
```

**Figure 9.2** Calculate the sum from `1` and `n` using a reference parameter

Notice the difference between the two versions of the function `sum`. In Figure 9.1 `sum` has only one parameter (the limit of the summation), the result is *not* stored in a reference parameter, it *is* the result of the function. The version of the function given in Figure 9.1 contains a `return` statement, which returns the value of a local variable, `fred`. The local variable `fred` is used to accumulate the result to be returned. By contrast, the version in Figure 9.2 does *not* contain a `return` statement (since no value is returned), and does not need a local variable to accumulate the result, since the reference parameter `result` may be used to accumulate the result.

The version in Figure 9.1 has a different return type in the declaration of the function's prototype from that in Figure 9.2. The version in Figure 9.1 returns an integer, whereas the version in Figure 9.2 returns nothing. This difference is crucial to the way in which we use the two versions of the function. The version given in Figure 9.1 may be used in an expression whereas the version given in Figure 9.2 may not.

To see the difference between the two approaches to summation embodied by the two versions of sum given in Figures 9.1 and 9.2, we must consider the various ways in which we may wish to use the result of the function.

Suppose we want to read in a number from the keyboard and print out the result of adding together all the numbers between 1 and this number read in. Using the version of `sum` given in Figure 9.1 we would write a code fragment something like this:

```
cout << "Type in a number" ;
cin >> UpperLimit ;
cout << "The sum from 1 to " << UpperLimit
     << " is " << sum(UpperLimit) << endl ;
```

Notice the way the call to `sum` is used in the stream of output. We could imagine that

```
sum(UpperLimit)
```

is simply a short-hand way of writing

```
1+2+3+4+5+...+UpperLimit
```

This is very convenient, as the code reads very intuitively. We want to print the sum of the numbers between `1` and `UpperLimit`, so we write an expression that *means* the sum of all the numbers between `1` and `UpperLimit`, and place this expression in an output statement. Compare this approach to the solution below, which we would produce using the version of `sum` given in Figure 9.2.

```
cout << "Type in a number" ;
cin >> UpperLimit ;
sum(UpperLimit,Global) ;
cout << "The sum from 1 to "
     << UpperLimit
     << " is "
     << Global
     << endl ;
```

This solution to the problem, although correct, is not as elegant (or efficient) as the version we were able to write using the version of `sum` given in Figure 9.2. The inelegance derives from two irritations with the way the reference parameter version of `sum` is written:

- it has to be called as a *statement*
- we require a *variable* to pick up the result of the function call

The fact that the function must be called as a statement means that we have no expression in the program which means the sum from one to `UpperLimit`, as we had with the other version of the function.

The fact that a variable is required to pick up the result of the function call makes our program less memory efficient, and increases the amount of irrelevant information which a programmer reading our program must consider in order to understand it.

The inelegance and inefficiency of Figure 9.2 is not peculiar to the problem we set out to solve. The problem involved printing out the result of the calculation embodied in the function, rather than storing the result in a variable. Surely if we wanted simply to call the function to store the result of the summation from `1` to, say `v`, then the version in Figure 9.1 will turn out to be less elegant than the version in Figure 9.2? In fact, the two versions are found to be equally efficient and readable. Suppose we want to store the result of the summation in a global variable called `global`. Here is the version we would write using the reference parameter version of `sum` given in Figure 9.2:

```
sum(v,global) ;
```

Now, we have called the function as a statement, and passed the limit, `v`, as a value parameter, indicating the upper limit of the summation, and we passed the variable name `global`, as the reference parameter, indicating that the result is to be stored in the variable `global`. The value-returning version of the function given in Figure 9.1 must be called in an expression, where an integer is required. We can write such an *expression* as the right-hand side of an assignment *statement* which stores the result of the call in the variable `global` like this:

```
global = sum(v) ;
```

In general it will always be true that a function which calculates a *single* result is better written as a genuine value-returning function, rather than as a function which 'returns' the result using a reference parameter. This raises the question as to when we should use reference parameters. The answer is simple: where *more* than one result is to be calculated by a function. In this situation, the use of a value-returning function becomes a matter of taste. That is, we could return one value as the result of the function and return the other values in reference parameters. We shall consider two problems, which indicate the issues to be considered when deciding whether to use a reference parameter or a value-returning function.

## The `find` problem

Consider the problem of finding the index number of a character in an array. Suppose that we want to return two results to the calling part of the program, one giving the value of the location of the character if it is found in the array, and the other, a *flag*[1], indicating whether or not the character is in the array.

---

[1]The word 'flag' is used in computing to indicate a boolean (that is, true or false) value which indicates (we say, 'flags') that some event has occurred. The concept derives from sport, where a flag may be raised to indicate an event in a game (such as the 'off-side rule' of soccer). In computing 'raising a flag' means setting the value of the flag to true.

We could write a function to find the character and return both the character and the flag in reference parameters. This version of the function, `find`, is given in Figure 9.3 below:

```
void find(char s[], char ch, int& location, int& found ) ;
//
// Pre-condition:
// s must contain a null character terminator.
//
// Post-condition:
// If ch occurs in the array s,
// then found is set to true,
// otherwise, found is set to false.
//
// If found is true,
// then location contains the index of the
// first occurrence of ch in s,
// otherwise the value of location is the
// index of the string termination character.
//

void find(char s[], char ch, int& location, int& found )

{
        location = 0 ;
        while (s[location] != '\0' &&
               s[location] != ch)
        {
              location++ ;
        }
        if (s[location] == ch)
              found = 1 ;   // True
        else
              found = 0 ;   // False
}
```

**Figure 9.3** The function `find` with two reference parameters

We could use this function in a fragment of code like this:

```
        cout << "Type in a string" ;
        cin >> AString ;
        find(AString,'X',index,WasItFound) ;
        if (WasItFound)
              cout << "This string contains a cross";
        else
              cout << "This string has no cross";
```

Notice that in this fragment of code we are not interested in the value of the variable index, but that we *have* to have this variable in order to make a valid call to the function find.

Now we could re-write the function find so that it returns one of the results it calculates in a reference parameter and one as the value returned by the function itself. A natural choice is to select the variable found as the value returned by the function, as we shall be able to write a statement like:

```
if (find(AString,ch,index))
        cout << "Found " << ch << " in "
             << AString ;
else
        cout << ch " is not in " << AString ;
```

Notice that in this version of find we only have *three* parameters, because the 'fourth parameter' is no longer needed (it is the value returned by the function). This version of the function find is given in Figure 9.4.

---

```
int find(char s[], char ch, int& location ) ;
//
// Pre-condition:
// s must contain a null character terminator.
// Post-condition:
// If ch occurs in the array s, then find returns true,
// otherwise, it returns false.
// If the result is true, then location will contain
// the index of the first occurrence of ch in s,
// otherwise the value of location is the
// index of the string termination character.
//

int find(char s[], char ch, int& location )

{
      location = 0 ;
      while ((s[location] != '\0') &&
            (s[location] != ch))
      {
            location++ ;
      }
      if (s[location] == ch)
            return 1 ;   // True
      else
            return 0 ;   // False
}
```

---

**Figure 9.4** A version of find with side-effects

## Side-effects

The example we have just seen in which the function `find` returns a value as its result and also returns another value via a reference parameter is an example of a function whose evaluation causes a *side-effect*. A side-effect is any change to the state of the computer that occurs when an expression is evaluated. Such a change might, for example, take the form of an assignment that occurs when the expression is evaluated or, perhaps, something is printed on the screen, changing the state of the output device.

Side-effects should be used with caution. The essential beauty of an expression is that it *mimics* the properties of *mathematics*. For example, we know that addition is commutative, that is, we can re-write the expression

$$x + y$$

as

$$y + x$$

It is often useful to be able to exploit these properties of arithmetic operators in the process of understanding or improving the way a program behaves. The more closely an expression involving arithmetic operators mimics the properties of the mathematical counterparts, the better, because we can then rest our analysis and understanding of our program upon thousands of years of mathematical knowledge.

Side-effects have the rather unfortunate consequence that they make the properties of the arithmetic operators *deviate* from their mathematical interpretation. Consider the two function definitions in Figure 9.5.

```
int f(int i) ;

int g(int i) ;

int f(int i)
{ v = 1 ;   return i+1 ; }

int g(int i)
{ return v*i; }
```

**Figure 9.5** Side-effects in functions

Notice that both these functions have a formal value parameter called `i`, but as we have discussed, these value parameters are entirely *independent* of each other, as the formal parameter name serves only as a way of naming the actual parameter supplied to the function when it is called.

More importantly, notice that the function `f` assigns the value `1` to the global variable `v`, and that the result returned by the function `g` *depends* upon the value of the global variable `v`. The function `f` has a side-effect, the assignment to `v`, whereas the function `g` does not, but its evaluation will be affected by the value of a variable, `v`, over which it has no control.

Now the expression

```
f(x) + g(x)
```

does not mean the same thing as

```
g(x) + f(x)
```

for some value `x`.

For example, suppose the value of `v` is `42`, before each expression is evaluated. In both cases, the evaluation of the expression will store a `1` in `v`, but in the first expression, the value of `v` used in the evaluation of the function call to `g` is `1`, whereas in the second expression the value of `v` used in the function call to `g` is `42`. Each expression will therefore evaluate to a *different* result, breaking the commutative law of mathematics.

Although side-effects may make a program harder to understand, many programmers use them, because they have two advantages over side-effect free programs:

- programs with side-effects are sometimes evaluated faster by the computer than equivalent side-effect-free versions
- programs with side-effects can often be written with fewer characters and occupy less space in the memory of the computer

These advantages have to be weighed against the disadvantages:

- side-effects destroy many of the mathematical properties of the expressions used in a program
- side-effects typically make programs harder to understand

The decision as to whether or not side-effects should be used is therefore a trade-off between efficiency and understandability of programs. This form of trade-off occurs frequently in programs, and the way one balances the trade-off depends critically upon the application for which the program is being developed. We call a function which contains no side-effects a pure function, because it is almost identical to a function in mathematics. Experience gathered from programming practice over the past three or four decades has indicated that side-effects in functions make programs harder to understand and maintain.

# Mental execution again

Consider the function `sum` defined in Figure 9.1. This function could be used in an expression such as:

```
sum(5) + 3
```

In order to mentally evaluate this expression we must execute the body of the function `sum` on our ' work sheet'. The execution of the body of the function is only required in order to calculate the value of the expression used in the `return` statement, so having executed the body of the function, we are *only* interested in the value returned, which we substitute for the entire call.

Remember that we have to add an initialiser for the value parameter `n`. This gives us the body of the function (plus initialiser) below:

```
{
        int n = 5 ;

        int fred,i;   // a loop variable

        fred = 0 ;
        for(i=1; i<=n; i++) fred = fred + i;

        return fred;
}
```

The loop will be executed five times producing the sequence of additions:

```
fred = fred + 1;
fred = fred + 2;
fred = fred + 3;
fred = fred + 4;
fred = fred + 5;
```

Now as the initial assignment to `fred` stores a `0`, we can see that the effect of these five assignments is:

```
fred = 0 + 1 + 2 + 3 + 4 + 5 ;
```

which we can now simplify to

```
fred = 15 ;
```

The expression returned by the function is the result of looking up the value of `fred` at the end of the execution of the body, thus the value returned is `15`. We can now replace the call to `sum` in the expression `sum(5) + 3` with the result, `15`, giving the expression `15 + 3`, which we can evaluate to `18`.

Notice that the meaning of the expression `sum(5)` *is* `15`, and the effect of writing the expression `sum(5)` is *equivalent* to the meaning of writing `15`. We have calculated the meaning of the entire expression by mimicking the behaviour of an *imaginary computer*. The principle of encapsulation allows us to think of `sum` as a 'built-in' feature of all programs which use it, and once we are sure we understand its meaning perfectly, we can dispense with the need to mentally execute it each time we see a call to it.

In this case we may assume that

```
sum(n)
```

for some expression *n*, is merely a short-hand way of writing

```
0+1+2+3+...+n
```

## Examples of value-returning functions

Remember that we decided that a good principle in deciding whether to use a reference parameter or whether to have a function return a result was that any function which calculates a single result should be written without any reference parameters. We may thus re-write the functions we defined in Chapter 8 which used a single reference parameter, so that they simply return the result required.

For example, the function `FindBiggest`, defined earlier using a reference parameter in Chapter 8, Figure 8.7, can be written as a 'pure' function. This pure version of `FindBiggest` is given in Figure 9.6 below:

```
int FindBiggest(int A[10]);
//
// Post condition:
// returns the value of the biggest element in A.
//

int FindBiggest(int A[10])
{
        int i;
        int result ;
        result = A[0];
        for(i=1; i<=9; i++)
              if (result < A[i]) result = A[i] ;
        return result ;
}
```

**Figure 9.6** Function to return the biggest element of an array

Notice that the swap function of Chapter 8 is *not* a suitable candidate for re-writing as a pure function, because it has two results (the new values of the two variables to be swapped). The function GetValidFloat does return a single result (in a reference parameter), however, and we can re-write it as a pure function. This version of GetValidFloat is given in Figure 9.7.

```
float GetValidFloat(float  bottom, float  top);
//
// Post-condition:
// Returns a float read in from the keyboard.
// The value returned is guaranteed to be no
// smaller than bottom, and no larger than top.
//

float GetValidFloat(float  bottom, float  top)
{
      int result;
      do
      {
            cout << "Type a number in the range ";
            cout << bottom << " to " << top;
            cout << " (inclusive)" ;
            cin >> result ;
      } while ((result < bottom) || (result > top)) ;
      return result ;
}
```

**Figure 9.7** Pure function to return a validated float from the keyboard

The 'pure' version of Locate is given in Figure 9.8.

## Valid return types

The function ReadArray, defined in Figure 8.12 of Chapter 8, is also a candidate for re-writing as a pure function, because it returns only a *single* value in a reference parameter (the value is the array read in from the keyboard). Unfortunately, we *cannot* re-write this function in a 'pure' style, because C++ does not allow arrays to be returned as the result type of a function. C++ restricts the type of value that can be returned from a function, quite considerably. The restriction makes it a lot easier to write compilers for C++ (though it arguably makes it harder to write programs), because a simple mechanism can be used to return the result of a function to the part of the program where the result is required. A compiler merely has to leave the result on the top of the stack at the end of the function's execution.

```
int Locate(char s[], char ch ) ;
//
// Pre-condition:
// s contains the character ch.
//
// Post-condition:
// The function returns the index of the first
// occurrence of ch in s.
//

int Locate(char s[], char ch )
{
      int i ; // A loop counter

      i = 0 ;
      while (s[i] != ch)
      {
            i++ ;
      }

      return i ;
}
```

**Figure 9.8** A pure function which returns the location of a character in an array

The types which can be returned from a function are

```
int
float
char
```

and

pointers

A function which calculates a value other than these must store the result in a reference parameter.

## Returning arrays from functions

The functions `Sort` and `CopyArray` of Chapter 8 like `ReadArray` from Figure 8.12 of Chapter 8 have a single array-valued result. Because the array's name is a pointer to the first element of the array, we might consider defining the return type to be a pointer to an integer. We could then return the array as the value of the function by returning the pointer to the first element of the array. This is possible, but we shall have to consider the crucial difference between a pointer to an array and the array that it points to.

Suppose we define ReadArray like this:

```
int* ReadArray() ;
//
// reads in elements into and array.
// The array is returned as the result of
// the function.
//
// This version of the function does not
// work properly.
//

int* ReadArray()
{
        int result[10] ;
        int i=0 ;

        do
        {
                cin >> result[i] ;
                i++ ;
        } while (i <= 9);

        return result;
}
```

This function will return a pointer to a part of memory which is no longer used. This is because local variables mean anything inside the body of a function. During the execution of the body of the function ReadArray, the value stored in result will be the address of the first element in the locally defined array. However, when the function terminates, the memory used for the local array will not be retained, so the pointer will point to 'rubbish'.

Remember that, in Chapter 5, we discussed how an array can be allocated dynamically at run time. Using this method of memory allocation we *can* return an array from a function. The body of the function will contain a pointer as a local variable, which we shall call p. The function uses the new instruction to allocate enough storage for the array at run time. The value of the pointer is returned at the end of the function. This version of the function looks like this:

```
int* ReadArray() ;
//
// reads in elements into and array.
// The array is returned as the result of
// the function.
//

int* ReadArray()
{
        int* result;
```

```
        int i=0 ;

        result = new int [10];

        do
        {
              cin >> result[i] ;
              i++ ;
        } while (i <= 9);

        return result;
}
```

The memory allocated by the new instruction is retained until the program explicitly relinquishes it using the `delete` command. This means that the value returned by this version of `ReadArray` will be a pointer to memory that still exists when the function terminates.

## Exercises

9.1 Why is `fred` a rather unhelpful name for a variable? What kind of variable names are most appropriate? Is `i` a good name for a local variable that controls the execution of a loop? Why is the name of a local variable unimportant as far as the 'client' is concerned?

9.2 What is the value returned by each of these function calls?

```
square(3)
square(0)
square(-4)
square(2+2)
square(2+square(2))
square(square(2))
```

9.3 Write down as many expressions involving calls to `square` which return the same values as the call[2] `square(10)`.

9.4 What is wrong with each of these program fragments involving a call to the function `square`?

[2]As there are infinitely many such expressions, you should not take 'as many as you can' literally, or you will not complete the exercise!

A)
```
int x[10] ;
x = square(10);
```

B)
```
int x;
x = square("10");
```

C)
```
int x ;
x = square(10,2);
```

D)
```
int x[10] ;
square(10) = x;
```

9.5 Adapt `sum`, so that it takes a number, `n`, as its parameter, and returns the factorial of `n`. (The factorial of a number, *n*, is obtained by multiplying all the numbers between 1 and *n*.)

9.6 Write a function which takes two numbers and returns the bigger of the two.

9.7 Use your answer to the last question to write a function which takes three numbers and returns the biggest of the three.

9.8 Write a function which takes a string and returns the number of characters in the string.

9.9 Write a function which takes a string, `s`, and a character, `c`, and returns the number of times that `c` occurs in `s`.

9.10 Using your answer to Exercise 9.9 write a function which takes a string and a character and returns the value true if the character occurs in the string and returns the value false otherwise.

# 10

# Classes and Objects

## Aims

The aim of this chapter is to explain, in more detail, the concept of a class, how it is used in object-oriented programming to create objects and how these objects can be used in programs.

After reading this chapter you should be able to:

- understand the concept of a class
- understand the relationship between classes, objects and class members
- understand the difference between attributes and operations
- create classes and objects in a C++ program
- understand the need for and be able to use constructors and destructors
- develop and use objects in a real program context
- create objects at run-time and access them via pointers to those objects

## Introduction

At last, we arrive at the heart of object-oriented programming: objects, themselves.

Using the word in the broadest sense, the whole world, including computers and programming, is made up of objects. As you read this book, you are surrounded by objects: a desk, perhaps, the chair that you are sitting on, pens and pencils, and the book itself. An object is simply a self-contained entity that has an existence independent of other entities, so trains, buildings, paper cups and software can all be regarded as objects. We naturally describe our environment in terms of entities such as these.

Another thing that we naturally do is classify objects: the Golden Gate belongs to the class of bridges; the Sydney Opera House belongs to the class of buildings; and Margaret Thatcher belongs to the class of ex-Prime Ministers of Britain. A class can be regarded as a blue print for an object. It describes the objects that belong to it in terms of their properties. For example, we can describe the class, Dog, as having the following properties:

- four legs
- carnivorous
- furry
- wags tail when happy
- chases sticks

This set of properties describes all dogs and, if it were a complete set of properties (a difficult thing to achieve for real-life objects), it would define what a dog is.

So a class can be thought of as an abstract description of an object, whereas an object is an actual entity that is a member of a class. For example, suppose your neighbour's dog is called Teddy. Teddy can be regarded as an object that is a member of the class Dog. He has all the properties of the class Dog but, in addition, he has an identity; he is Teddy, a real dog.

## Classes in computer programs

The ability to describe the class Dog, in a computer program, is of dubious benefit. However, to be able to describe the class Employee, in a personnel record system, or the class Sensor, in a building security system might well be useful. Using classes and objects, we can write our computer programs as models of the real-life problems.

As we have seen, in Chapter 4, classes allow the programmer to define new data entities that are combinations of other, simpler entities. These are relatively simple data structures whose properties are other data.

However, you may have noticed that in the class Dog above we have mentioned two types of property: things that describe what the object is, e.g. 'furry', and things that describe what the object does, e.g. 'chases sticks'.

Object-oriented languages allow us to define these two types of property in a class; in the object-oriented jargon they are called *attributes* and *operations* (or *methods*). Attributes are the data only, descriptions of an object, whereas operations are the behavioural descriptions of what an object can do (or what can be done to it).

The class Employee, mentioned above, would have both attributes and operations. Table 10.1 shows a set of potential properties for Employee.

**Table 10.1** Properties of the class Employee

| **Attributes** | **Operations** |
|---|---|
| Name | Hire |
| Employee number | Promote |
| Job title | Give pay rise |
| Salary | Fire |
| Length of employment | |

As you can see, the attributes are simply data and the operations are actions, or functions, that are appropriate to objects of the class.

Once a class has been defined, it can, potentially, be reused in other programs by simply including the class definition in the new program. However, it is not necessary for the programmer who uses a class to know how it works; they should simply need to know how to use it. Most, if not all, object-oriented languages, support this sort of use by allowing the implementation of an object to be hidden from the outside. Only functions and data that are specifically declared as being available to external programs are, in fact, available.

To give an analogy: a car engine can be designed for, and used in, a number of different models of car. But the designer of a car does not need to know how an engine works; indeed the design of an engine is a complex business and is best left to experts in the field. The car designer only needs to know how to use the engine, i.e. its size and shape, its power output, etc. A car engine is a reusable object that has a specification independent of the car in which it is used.

In object-oriented programming we can aim to do the same sort of thing: design useful classes of object that can be reused in other programs.

# Classes in C++

So classes are what makes C++ object-oriented; they are used to specify objects. An object's class is similar to a variable's type, it specifies the characteristics of an object in the same way that a type tells us what characteristics a variable has. Those characteristics are the attributes and operations that belong to the class and, in C++ classes, these are represented by data declarations and function definitions, respectively.

An object is a program entity that is a particular instance of a class. Once you have specified what an object is (what it looks like and what it is composed of) by defining a class, you can declare objects of that class in the same way you would declare a variable.

# Class members: attributes and operations

As we have said, a class is made up of data and functions. In C++ we call these components *members*: we have *data members* and *member functions*. Data members are the attributes of the class and member functions are the operations or methods of the class.

Members may be accessible to the program that uses an object of a particular class, i.e. they may be *public* or they may be only usable within an object, itself, i.e. they are *private*.

Here is what a class declaration looks like:

```
class Name {

public:
      // Public members go here

private:
      // Private members go here
};
```

It consists of the word `class` followed by the name of the class that we are declaring. The members of the class follow enclosed in braces and, like all declarations, it is terminated by a semicolon.

The member declarations are divided into `public` and `private` sections, each section being labelled by the word itself, followed by a colon. It is quite legal to have several `public` and `private` sections, as long as they are correctly labelled, but it is considered good practice to have only one of each.

The following declaration is of a class called `Time`.

```
class Time {
public:
      Time();
      void setTime(int, int, int);
      void print24hour();
      void print12hour();
private:
      int hour;
      int minute;
      int second;
};
```

`Time` is a class that stores a value that represents a time (e.g. 23:45); it has four member functions, all of which are accessible to the program, outside (i.e. public) and three data members that are private to objects of this class.

The data members are all integers; they are named `hour`, `minute` and `second`, and can be seen in the latter half of the declaration. These data members will store the time data.

The member functions are `Time`, `setTime`, `print24hour` and `print12hour`; we will ignore the first one, `Time`, for the moment.

The function `setTime` is a `void` function that takes three integers as parameters; these will represent the time in hours, minutes and seconds. `setTime`'s purpose is simply to copy these values to the appropriate data members. `print24hour` and `print12hour` are both `void` functions that take no parameters. Their purpose is to use `cout` to display the time in 24 and 12 hour formats, respectively.

Notice that in this class declaration, the member functions are not defined, they are declared only as function prototypes. We must, of course, define them *somewhere*, and when we do this, we must also identify that they are members of the class `Time`.

The complete definition of the class `Time` is given in Figure 10.1.

Notice the notation that we use to denote that a function is a member of a class: we precede the function name with the class name and two colons, e.g.

```
void Time::print12hour()
```

The `::` symbol is called the scope resolution operator. When we define a member function of a class we must use this operator, along with the class name, to identify which class the member function belongs to. This gives us the flexibility to have member functions from different classes with the same name.

```
#include <iostream.h>
class Time {
public:
      Time();
      void setTime(int, int, int);
      void print24hour();
      void print12hour();
private:
      int hour;   // 0 - 23
      int minute; // 0 - 59
      int second; // 0 - 59
};

// Constructor simply initialises to zero
Time::Time()
{
      hour = 0;
      minute = 0;
      second = 0;
}

// setTime sets a time using 24 hour notation
void Time::setTime(int h, int m, int s)
{
      if ((h < 24) && (h >= 0)) hour = h;
      if ((m < 60) && (m >= 0)) minute = m;
      if ((s < 60) && (s >= 0)) second = s;
}

// Print time in 24 format
void Time::print24hour()
{
      cout << hour << ":" << minute << ":" << second ;
}

// Print time in 12 format
void Time::print12hour()
{
      if (( hour == 0) || ( hour == 12 ))
            cout << 12 << ":" ;
      else
            cout << hour % 12 << ":";

      cout  << minute << ":" << second ;
      if (hour < 12)
            cout << " AM";
      else
            cout << " PM";
}
```

**Figure 10.1** The `class Time`

A class that represents a file system might, for example, have a member function called 'select' that would enable a set of files to be chosen before performing a certain operation on them (e.g. deleting them), whereas a class that represents a database might need a member function called 'select' that would choose a particular data item from the database. The definitions of these functions might look something like this:

```
void FileSystem::select()
{
        // Program code to implement the File System
        // member function goes here
}

void Database::select()
{
        // Program code to implement the Database
        // member function goes here
}
```

Thus we can see that there is no difficulty in deciding which class the two functions belong to.

We use classes by creating objects of the class and then calling their member functions:

```
void main()
{
        Time t;

        // Set the time to midday
        t.setTime(12,0,0);

        cout << "The time in 24 hour format is: ";
        t.print24hour();
        cout << endl;

        cout << "The time in 12 hour format is: ";
        t.print12hour();
        cout << endl;
}
```

In the program above we have created an object, `t`, of the class `Time`. This declaration is syntactically identical to those that we have been using for variables where the variable name is preceded by its type. Here, the name of the object that we are declaring is preceded by the class that the object belongs to.

We use the function `setTime` to give a value to an object. In order to specify which object we are referring to, we must precede the function name with the name of the object to which it belongs, i.e. `t.setTime(12,0,0)`. Next, we use the two other member functions `print24hour` and `print12hour` to print the value of `t` on the display.

# Constructors

But we have missed out something that is important: what is the function, `Time`, that has no return type?

This is called a *constructor*, and apart from having no return type, a constructor must also have the same name as the class to which it belongs. The job of a constructor is to provide initialisation for an object. When an object is declared, this constructor function is automatically called in order to perform whatever initialisation is necessary. In the case of the class `Time`, it simply initialises all the data members to zero (i.e. midnight).

Of course, any constant value could be chosen to initialise data members, but what if we need to initialise an object to a value chosen by the programmer? We can do this by declaring a constructor with parameters, e.g.

```
// Constructor with parameters
Time::Time(int h, int m, int s)
{
      hour = h;
      minute = m;
      second = s;
}
```

But to use this we must provide actual parameters when the object is declared, e.g.

```
Time t(12,0,0);    // t initialised to midday
```

By using this constructor we can initialise the object, `t`, to any value. But you should notice that this particular constructor will allow the time to be set to an invalid value (e.g. 25 o'clock) because no validation is performed on the actual parameter values. A more sensible approach would be something like this:

```
Time::Time(int h, int m, int s)
{
      if ((h < 24) && (m < 60) && (s < 60))
      {
            hour = h;
            minute = m;
            second = s;
      }
      else
      {
            hour = 0;
            minute = 0;
            second = 0;
      }

}
```

# Destructors

A destructor is, not surprisingly, the opposite of a constructor; it is called when the program ends or the object goes out of scope. For example, when an object is declared locally, within a function, and that function terminates, the local object goes out of scope and the object is destroyed.

Destructors are used to do any housekeeping work that is required before the object is destroyed. This is typically required when the object uses data that is dynamically created with `new`. The memory used for data created in this way should be released using `delete`, before the object that uses the data is destroyed.

Often, simple class definitions do not require the use of a destructor.

The destructor function is given the same name as the class but preceded by the tilde character (e.g. `~Time()`); it can return no value and so has no type and cannot have any parameters. It is usually good practice to place the destructor immediately after the constructor in a class declaration.

# Example: objects for a car hire company

The aim of this example is to give you a flavour of how objects can be useful in constructing real programs. Of course, we cannot give you a real application, that would take most of a book of this size, but the High Performance Car Hire Company example will show you how such an application might be constructed.

The program in Figure 10.2 consists almost entirely of the definition of the class `HireCar`. The aim of this class is to enable the programmer to create objects that encapsulate the attributes and the behaviour of the cars that are available for hire. The attributes of the class represent the data which we shall want to associate with each object. For a hire car, each object will represent a single car and will have six attributes:

| | |
|---|---|
| `carExists` | a status value that shows whether the object is in use |
| `make` | a character string that contains the make of the car |
| `model` | a character string that contains the model of the car |
| `hireStatus` | another status variable that shows whether the car is on hire or not |
| `hirer` | a character string containing the name of the person who has hired the car (if any) |
| `returnDate` | the date when the car is due to be returned by the hirer; it is represented as a character string |

In addition to the attributes, five operations (member functions) are provided:

| | |
|---|---|
| `newCar` | this sets the attributes of the object to describe a new car |
| `rentCar` | this records the customer name and return date and also sets the `hireStatus` attribute |
| `returnCar` | this is invoked when the car is returned from being hired; it simply sets the `hireStatus` attribute appropriately |
| `onHire` | this allows access to the `hireStatus` attribute |
| `printDetails` | this outputs to the screen all the current details of the car |

## Overloaded constructors

Apart from these operations, you will notice from the listing in Figure 10.2 that there are *two* constructors declared in the class: this repetition of a function definition is known as function *overloading*. As we will see later, this is something that can be applied to any function but it can be particularly useful for constructors.

Having two constructors allows us to create an object in two ways; one where no car details are associated with the object and only the `carExists` attribute is set to `false`, and another where the attributes that describe the car are initialised and the `carExists` attribute is set to `true`.

Of course, in order for the compiler to understand which of the two constructors should be invoked, there must be some way of distinguishing between them. In the predecessor to C++, the C language, the only way to distinguish one function from another was by their names, which had to be unique.

In C++ we have the concept of a function's *signature*, of which its name is only a part. The signature is made up of the name of the function, the number of parameters that the function takes and the types of those parameters. It is the function's signature that must be unique in C++.

Our two constructors have the same name but different sets of parameters. The first has no parameters at all, while the second has two parameters, each of which is a character array. This difference makes the signature of the two constructors different and so they may exist as separate functions. However, since they both have the same name as the class itself, they are both recognised as constructors.

The ways in which the two constructors are used is shown in the `main` function of Figure 10.2. The first two declarations of `HireCar` objects are given actual parameters for the make and model of the car. These will, of course, invoke the constructor which has matching formal parameters. The third declaration of a `HireCar` object has no actual parameters; this matches the constructor that has no formal parameters and so will invoke that version of the constructor.

```
//
// The high performance car hire company program
//

#include <iostream.h>

// Declare some useful constants
const int True = 1;
const int False = 0;
const int strnlen = 20;        // the maximum length of all
                               // strings in the program

// Function to copy one character string into another
// Pre-conditions:
//    source is a null terminated character string
//    destination is the same length or longer than source
// Post-condition:
//    destination will contain a copy of source
void scopy(char source[], char destination[]);

// The class HireCar and its member function definitions

class HireCar
{
private:

   int carExists;          // true = object is in use,
                           // false = object is not in use

   char make[strnlen];  // holds the manufacturer's name
   char model[strnlen]; // holds the model name

   int hireStatus;         // true = on hire,
                           // false = not on hire

   char hirer[strnlen]; // the last name of the hirer
   char returnDate[strnlen];
                           // a string representing the return
                           // date

public:

   // Constructors
   HireCar();
   HireCar(char make[], char model[]);

   // Assign the make and model for the car and set the
   // exists attribute to true
   void newCar(char make[], char model[]);

   // Get and set the hire attributes
```

```
   void rentCar();

   // Set the hireStatus to false
   void returnCar();

   // returns hireStatus
   int onHire();

   // Display all car details
   void printDetails();

} ;

// Member function definitions

HireCar::HireCar()
{
   carExists = False;
}

HireCar::HireCar(char newmake[], char newmodel[])
{
   // This constructor uses another member function
   newCar(newmake, newmodel);
}

void HireCar::newCar(char newmake[], char newmodel[])
{
   // Set the attributes of the car
   scopy(newmake, make);
   scopy(newmodel, model);
   carExists = True;
   hireStatus = False;
}

void HireCar::rentCar()
{
   // Do not use spaces or other white space in the strings
   cout << "Enter Customer's last name: ";
   cin >> hirer;
   cout << "Enter return date: ";
   cin >> returnDate;
   hireStatus = True;
}

void HireCar::returnCar()
{
   hireStatus = False;
}

int HireCar::onHire()
{
```

```
   return hireStatus;
}

void HireCar::printDetails()
{
   // Only print out the details if there are some!
   if (carExists)
   {
      cout << "Make  : " << make << endl
         << "Model : " << model << endl;

         if (hireStatus)
         {
            cout << "The on is on hire to : " << hirer <<
                 << endl << "and is due back on "
                 << returnDate << endl << endl;
         }
         else
         {
            cout << "This car is not on hire." << endl
                 << endl;
         }
   }
   else
   {
      // The object has not been initialised
      cout << "Object not in use" << endl << endl;
   }
}
// End of class HireCar

void scopy(char source[], char destination[])
{
   int i = 0;
   do
   {
       destination[i] = source[i];
   } while (source[i++] != '\0');
}

//
// The main program starts here
//
void main()
{

   // Declare some objects of class HireCar
   HireCar car1("Ford", "GT40");
   HireCar car2("AC", "Cobra");
   HireCar car3;          // this one is not initialised

   car1.rentCar();        // rent out car1
```

```
    // Print the details of each car
    car1.printDetails();
    car2.printDetails();
    car3.printDetails(); // this one has no details yet

    // Set new attributes for cars 3 and 2
    car3.newCar("Austin-Healey", "3000");
    car2.newCar("Jaguar", "E Type");

    // Print the details again - note the changes
    car1.printDetails();
    car2.printDetails();
    car3.printDetails();
}
```

**Figure 10.2** The car hire program, version 1

## Arrays of objects

The example in Figure 10.2 declares objects individually. However, in a real application of this type it is likely that a data structure would be used to hold the objects. For example, an array of `HireCar` objects would allow them to be used more flexibly. The `main` function in Figure 10.3 shows how an array of objects might be used in a program. (Note that this `main` function uses the class definition for `HireCar`, as before. You should imagine that it replaces the `main` function of Figure 10.2.)

```
void main()
{

    // Declare an array of objects of class HireCar

    const int FleetSize= 20;

    HireCar carFleet[FleetSize];
    int i;

    // Print the details of all the cars in the fleet
    for (i = 0; i < FleetSize; i++)
    {
        cout << "Car number " << i << endl;
        carFleet[i].printDetails();
    }
}
```

**Figure 10.3** Using an array of objects

The program in Figure 10.3 simply declares an array of 20 `HireCar` objects and then uses a loop to print the details for each of the objects. If you try this program you will see that the result of calling the `printDetails` member function is, for each object, to print `"Object not in use"`. This is because the `carExists` member of each object has been initialised to `False` and no car has been assigned to any of the objects as yet.

A car may be assigned to an object in one of two ways: either the member function `newCar` must be invoked for that object, or the appropriate constructor (the one with formal parameters) must be invoked when the object is created. In this program, `newCar` is not invoked at all but when the array of objects is declared a constructor is called for each one. As no parameters are given for the constructor it must be the parameterless constructor function that is invoked, hence the `carExists` member is initialised to `False`.

## Creating new objects as the program is running

Consider the operation of a real car hire company. It is likely that during the life of the company the fleet of cars for hire will grow (if the company is successful) or, perhaps, shrink. We could design our program such that an array is used to hold the car objects, as in Figure 10.3. This would mean that the array would have to contain enough objects to cater for the maximum number of cars that might be required. This is an inefficient approach because we will always be using the maximum amount of memory (for the whole array of objects) no matter how many are actually in use. While efficiency should not be our prime concern when writing programs[1], if we can easily make our programs more efficient, then we might just as well do it.

A more efficient approach is to create an array of pointers to `HireCar` objects, create new objects as we need them and arrange for one of the pointers in the array to refer to that new object. We create a new object at run time (i.e. while the program is running) using `new`, as we have seen in Chapter 5.

You will remember that `new` creates a new entity of the type specified and returns the address of that object; the function `addNewCar`, in Figure 10.4, does just this. It uses the variable `lastCarIndex` as the index to the next unused pointer in an array of pointers and then increments this variable so that it then refers to the next free pointer.

The program in Figure 10.4 again uses the class definition of `HireCar` that we developed earlier. The program implements a simple menu system that allows the user to perform a number of functions pertaining to a car hire company. Yet again this is a deliberately simple program (indeed some of the functions are left for you to define) so that we can more easily concentrate on the use of pointers.

---

[1]Correctness and maintainability (i.e. having the attribute of being easily changed or updated) should be our main concern when writing programs and these should not normally be compromised for the sake of efficiency.

```
const int FleetSize = 100;// Maximum number of cars
int lastCarIndex = 0;       // index to the last in the array
                            // also the number of cars

// Declare an array of pointers to HireCar objects
HireCar * fleet[FleetSize];

// Display a menu of options and return the
// users choice
char menu()
{
   char choice;

   cout << "Enter 'a', 'h', 'r', 'p', 'x'" << endl
        << "for Add, Hire, Return, Print or Exit"
        << endl;

   cin >> choice;
   return choice;
}

// Find the next free car in the array
// and invoke its hire member function
void hireACar()
{
   // add your own code here
}

// Mark a particular car as being returned
// from hire
void returnACar()
{
   // add your own code here
}

// Print the details of all of the cars in the array
// up until the last car
void carDetails()
{
   int i;

   for (i = 0; i < lastCarIndex; i++)
   {
      fleet[i]->printDetails();
   }
}

// Create a new car and add it to the array of cars
void addNewCar()
{
   char make[strnlen], model[strnlen];
```

```
   cout << "Enter make then model: ";
   cin >> make >> model;

    fleet[lastCarIndex] = new HireCar(make, model);
    lastCarIndex++;

}

void main()
{
   char menuChoice;

   // The main program is a loop that
   // invokes a menu of options

   do {
      menuChoice = menu();
      switch(menuChoice)
      {
         // Add a new car to the array
         case 'a': addNewCar();  break;
         // Hire a car
         case 'h': hireACar();   break;
         // Return the car from hire
         case 'r': returnACar();  break;
         // Print the details of the fleet
         case 'p': carDetails(); break;
      }
   } while(menuChoice != 'x');
}
```

**Figure 10.4** Creating objects using `new`

The function that illustrates the use of pointers with objects is `carDetails`. This consists of a loop that iterates through the array of `HireCar` object pointers, invoking the member function `printCarDetails` for each object that has been created. The line that invokes the member function is:

```
fleet[i]->printDetails();
```

As you can see, the syntax is a little different from what we are used to. Instead of using the dot notation (e.g. `fleet[i].printDetails()`), an arrow separates the object from the call to the member function. This is used because we are not using the actual object name to invoke the function but a pointer to an object: when using the object name we must use the dot notation to refer to the object's members, but when using a pointer to an object, the arrow notation must be used. This is quite easy to remember because the arrow symbol looks like a pointer. (The arrow symbol is made up of a minus sign, -, and a right pointing angle bracket, >. The two elements must *not* be separated by a space.)

## Exercises

10.1 Write member functions for `Time` that will return the three parts of the time as integers. The function prototypes should look like this:

```
int Time::gethour();

int Time::getmin();

int Time::getsec();
```

10.2 Write a member function that will add a time to the current value. The time to be added will be given as an object of the class `Time` and passed as a parameter to the member function. The function prototype for this should look like this:

```
void Time::add(Time);
```

You will need to use the functions from Exercise 10.1. The function definition will look like this:

```
void Time::add(Time t)
{
	//
	// The rest of the code goes here
	//
}
```

10.3 Write a simple program that will declare two objects of the class `Time`, set one to 11 o'clock in the evening and the other to 2 o'clock in the morning. Add them using your solution to Exercise 10.2 and check that the result is correct.

10.4 Write a destructor function for the class `Time` that simply outputs a message, then write a function that includes a local `Time` object, and a program that calls the function. Note what happens when you run the program.

10.5 Write the code for the missing functions in Figure 10.4.

# 11 Inheritance

## Aims

This chapter explores how we, as humans, group classes of objects into higher order classes and describes the nature of the hierarchies of classes so produced. It then goes on to show how these classes inherit properties from each other and how the concept of inheritance can be incorporated into object-oriented programming.

After reading this chapter you should be able to:

- explain the nature of inheritance
- understand the relationship between base classes and derived classes
- understand how inheritance can be incorporated into a `C++` program
- write a `C++` program that uses base and derived classes
- understand the concept of polymorphism
- use overloaded and virtual member functions

## Classification hierarchies

In Chapter 10 we suggested that the way that human beings understand and communicate about their environment is by grouping the objects that surround them into classes. But we also group similar classes into higher order classes and divide broad classes into more specialised ones. For example, the class of trees belongs to the higher order class of plants, but within the class of trees we also have the sub-classes of evergreens and deciduous trees.

So we end up with a hierarchy of classes that objects can belong to. A hierarchy based on the one that we have just described is shown in Figure 11.1.

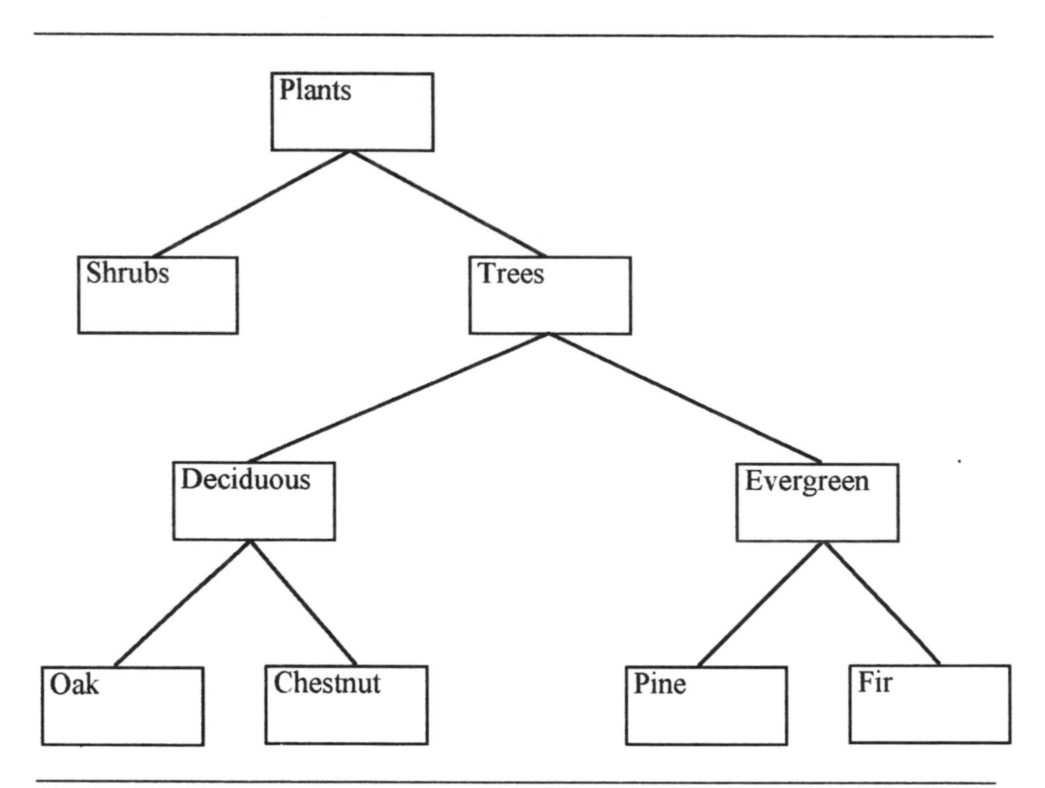


**Figure 11.1** A partial hierarchy of plants

## Inheriting properties

In a hierarchy of classes, the classes towards the top are known as *base classes* or *super-classes*, whereas those further down are the *derived classes* or *sub-classes*. Derived classes are specialisations of base classes, sharing the properties of the base classes but adding their own properties that distinguish them from the base class.

Imagine an object that is alive, has four legs, is covered in fur, and is a carnivore. We cannot be sure exactly what this object is, given the description that we have, but we could certainly classify it as an animal of some sort.

If we are told that a another property is that it may be kept as a pet, then we can further classify it as a domestic animal. And so it is fairly clear that we are talking about either a cat or a dog (there are sure to be many people that keep bears, wolverines, hyenas, kangaroos and many other weird and wonderful pets, but for the sake of simplicity we shall ignore such deviancy).

If the animal had the property of purring when content, then we would know that we were talking about a cat. If on the other hand it had the property of liking to chase sticks, then we could be fairly certain that it was a dog.

Here we have identified four different classes that form a hierarchy: furry animal, domestic pet, cat and dog. Each class *inherits* the properties of the class above it in the hierarchy (e.g. all of them have the property of being furry) but each of the lower level classes incorporates some properties of its own that distinguish it from the class above (i.e. *chases sticks* is not a property shared by objects further up the hierarchy). This 'pet hierarchy' is displayed pictorially in Figure 11.2.

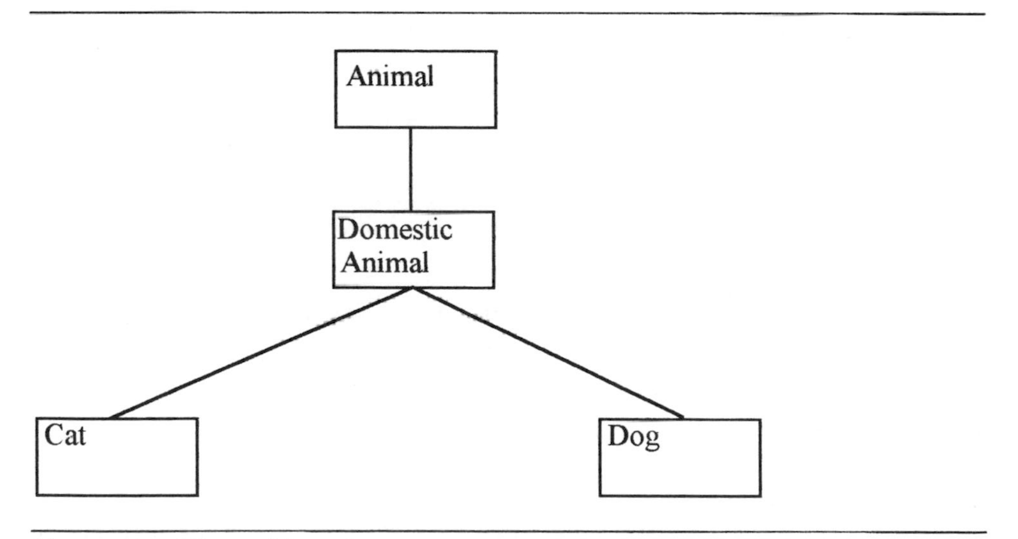


**Figure 11.2** The pet hierarchy

## Inheritance in C++

In C++, as in all other object-oriented languages, we are able to use classes that we have already declared as base classes and derive specialisations from them.

Let us assume that we need to write a program that will calculate the pay for the employees of a company. The employees may be of two types, salaried staff that get paid the same every month, and hourly paid staff that get paid for the hours that they have worked. Let us further assume that in all other respects these two types of employee are the same, unrealistic though this may be.

A convenient way to approach the program would be to define a class that incorporates all the attributes and behaviour of an employee, and use this as the base class for two specialised classes, one for each type of employee. The two derived classes would inherit all of the members of the base class and would only need to specify the differences between themselves and the base class (in this case the two different methods of payment).

Thus having defined the base class we reuse it in the definitions of the derived classes. This has two advantages. First it saves the effort of duplicating the program code, and, second, we can be sure that once the base class has been tested and works for one derived class, it will work for any subsequent classes. Furthermore, if at a later date, we need to create a class for another type of employee (e.g. piece workers), much of the work will have been done already.

The following declaration is for a class, `Employee`, that we shall use as a base class.

```
class Employee {

public:
   Employee(int number, float sal);
                        // Constructor - set the employee
                        // number and salary
   void pay();          // Calculate monthly pay
   void identify();// show employee number and type

protected:
   int empCode;         // code that describes the type
                        // of employee (e.g. salaried)
   int empNumber;       // Each employee has a unique
                        // employee number
   float salary;        // the annual salary
};
```

It is deliberately simple and consists of only a few members. The member functions consist of the constructor, which initialises the employee number, salary and employee type, and two other functions, `pay()`, which will calculate the pay for an employee and, `identify()`, which will simply print the employee details (employee number and code). These last two functions have been chosen because one will be common to both employee types, and so can be inherited from the base class, while the other will change depending on the employee type and so will have to be defined for each of the two derived classes.

The data members are in a *new* section of the declaration. We have already seen `public` and `private` sections where members are either available to the program outside of the class (those in the `public` section) or are only available to the functions within the class declaration (those in the `private` section). This new `protected` section allows the members to be kept private from the rest of the program (i.e. `private`) but allows the members of derived classes to access them.

Table 11.1 gives a summary of the meanings of these, so-called, *access specifiers*.

**Table 11.1** Access specifiers

| If a member is... | It may be used by... |
|---|---|
| `public` | any function inside or outside the class declaration |
| `protected` | any member function of the class or member functions of classes derived from it (but see types of inheritance, later) |
| `private` | only member functions of the class |

The next program fragment shows a class derived from the base class `Employee`.

```
class SalariedEmp:public Employee {
public:
   SalariedEmp(int number, float salary);
   void pay();
};
```

Here we have a class `SalariedEmp` that is derived from `Employee`. The name of the class is followed by a colon, the type of inheritance (`private`, `protected` or `public`) and the name of the base class.

The members that are specified are only those that differ from the base class (as we shall see later). Objects of derived classes will possess all the data and function members that are specified in the derived class declaration together with those that are inherited from the base class.

## Types of inheritance

When declaring a derived class, the base class may be specified as being `public`, `protected` or `private`. By using these specifiers, the data members and member functions of the base class which may be accessed in the derived class will be affected. Table 11.2 shows the effect of each of the three forms of inheritance. Anything other than `public` inheritance is rare and you will find only examples of `public` inheritance in this book.

**Table 11.2** Types of inheritance

| Access of base class member | Type of Inheritance<br>`public` inheritance | `protected` inheritance | `private` inheritance |
|---|---|---|---|
| **`public`** | `public` members in the base class will be `public` in the derived class | `public` members in the base class become `protected` in the derived class | `public` members in the base class become `private` in the derived class |
| **`protected`** | `protected` members in the base class become `protected` in the derived class | `protected` members in the base class will be `protected` in the derived class | `protected` members in the base class become `private` in the derived class |
| **`private`** | `private` members in the base class are always hidden from the derived class | `private` members in the base class are always hidden from the derived class | `private` members in the base class are always hidden from the derived class |

## The `Employee` class

The complete definitions of the example base class, `Employee`, and the derived classes, `SalariedEmp` and `HourlyEmp`, are shown in Figure 11.3.

```
#include <iostream.h>
const int Unknown = 0;
const int Salaried = 1;
const int Hourly = 2;

class Employee{

public:
   Employee(int number, float sal);
   void pay();
   void identify();

protected:
   int empCode;
   int empNumber;
```

```
   float salary;
};

Employee::Employee(int number, float sal)
{
      empNumber = number;
      salary = sal;
      empCode = Unknown;
}

void Employee::pay()
{
   cout << "Annual salary " << salary << endl;
}

void Employee::identify()
{
   cout << "Employee: " << empNumber << endl
      << "Type: " << empCode << endl;
}
```

**Figure 11.3(a)** The Employee base class

```
class SalariedEmp:public Employee {
public:
   SalariedEmp(int number, float salary);
   void pay();
};

SalariedEmp::SalariedEmp(int number, float salary):
Employee(number, salary)
{
   empCode = Salaried;
}

void SalariedEmp::pay()
{
   cout << "Annual salary " << salary << endl
      << "This month " << salary/12 << endl;
}

class HourlyEmp:public Employee {
public:
   HourlyEmp(int number, float salary);
   void pay();
};

HourlyEmp::HourlyEmp(int number, float salary):
Employee(number,salary)
{
```

```
   empCode = Hourly;
}

void HourlyEmp::pay()
{
   int hours;
   cout << "Annual salary " << salary << endl;
   cout << "Enter hours worked: ";
   cin >> hours;
   cout << "This month " << hours * salary/2080 << endl;
}
```

**Figure 11.3(b)** The derived classes `SalariedEmp` and `HourlyEmp`

```
void main()
{
   int i;

   // Declare a couple of employees
   SalariedEmp sEmp(123, 50000);
   HourlyEmp hEmp(456, 30000);

   // Now see how the object's behaviour changes
   // depending on which class it is

   cout << endl
        << "Monthly pay" << endl
        << "-----------" << endl
        << endl;

   sEmp.identify();
   sEmp.pay();

   cout << endl;

   hEmp.identify();
   hEmp.pay();
}
```

**Figure 11.3(c)** A program to use the previously defined classes

Figure 11.3(a) shows the complete definition of the base class `Employee`, while Figure 11.3(b) shows the definitions of the derived classes `SalariedEmp` and `HourlyEmp`.

There are a couple of things to note in this second part of the program. First, you should notice that the member function `pay()` is redefined for each derived class.

This is because the functionality of this member is different for each class. Second, the constructors are different for each derived class, as they assign different values to the data member empCode. However, we also wish to invoke the constructor from the base class and provide it with some parameter values.

In fact we *must* call the base class constructor in some way, because there will be additional data members for it to initialise. This is done using the syntax shown below:

```
HourlyEmp::HourlyEmp(int number, float salary):
Employee(number,salary)
{
    empCode = Hourly;
}
```

The constructor Employee (with parameter values from the parameter of HourlyEmp) is invoked by placing it in a *member initialisation list*, following a colon after the derived class constructor's name.

If there had been a base class constructor that required no parameters, then the compiler would ensure that it would be called automatically, before the derived class constructor. However, even if no parameters are required, it does no harm to invoke the base class constructor explicitly, as we have done here.

Figure 11.3(c) is a program that uses the derived classes by creating an object of each class, and then invoking their member functions. If you run the program, you will see that when identify() is called, the member function from the base class Employee is invoked (there is no other, of course) but when the function pay() is called, it is the one from the appropriate derived class that is invoked.

From this example, we can see how the member functions of a base class can be overridden by member functions of the same name but which are also defined in a derived class. This mechanism allows us to define true specialisations of a base class.

## Arrays of mixed object types

We saw in Chapter 10 how we could use an array of pointers to access objects that we created at run time. Using this technique, we can perform the same operation on each of a set of objects no matter how many objects are contained in the array. It would be very convenient, for example, to be able to put our SalariedEmp and HourlyEmp objects in a *single* array and call the member functions to calculate pay, etc. in a loop. The problem is that since each member of the array must be of the *same* type we cannot place a mixture of the different employee types in one array. However, we can achieve a similar effect by declaring an array of pointers to the *base* class whilst assigning objects of a *derived* class to it. In this way, we treat objects of the derived classes as if they were objects of the base class.

Usually, of course, we cannot assign an object's address to a pointer of another type but here we are able to do this because the object is a specialisation of the base class, i.e. a derived class. We can always use a pointer to a base class to refer to an object of another class that is derived from that base class.

The program in Figure 11.4 uses the same class definitions as Figure 11.3. This time, however, it declares pointers to the base class and assigns them to objects of both `SalariedEmp` and `HourlyEmp`. The function of the program is the same as Figure 11.3. It prints out the identity of the employee and then the month's salary.

---

```
void main()
{
   const int NumOfEmployees = 2;
   int i;

   // An array of pointers to Employee objects
   Employee* e[NumOfEmployees];

   // Assign a couple of employees
   e[0] = new SalariedEmp(123, 50000);
   e[1] = new HourlyEmp(456, 30000);

   // Now see if the behaviour changes depending
   // on which class it is
   cout << endl
        << "Monthly pay" << endl
        << "-----------" << endl
        << endl;

   for(i = 0; i < NumOfEmployees; i++)
   {
      e[i]->identify();
      e[i]->pay();

      cout << endl;
   }
}
```

---

**Figure 11.4** Using base class pointers to refer to derived class objects

Unfortunately, the program does not behave in exactly the way that we want it to. While the correct data is placed in the object's data members, the member functions which are invoked are those from the *base* class, `Employee`, not the *derived* classes of `SalariedEmp` and `HourlyEmp`. This should not be a surprise. The array is one of pointers to the class `Employee` and not to its derived classes. Thus when a member function is accessed via one of the pointers, it is that of the base class that is invoked.

What we would *like* is for the program to be clever enough to know which of the derived classes is being referred to by the base class pointer, and invoke the correct member functions for this class. We can solve the problem of invoking the correct derived class member function when using base class pointers by using *virtual functions*. Virtual functions are a form of *polymorphism* and we will discuss the meaning of this term first.

## Polymorphism

The word 'polymorphism' means having many shapes and it refers to the ability to use the same name to perform different functions in different classes. Virtual functions are one form of polymorphism but we have already seen a simpler type of polymorphism in overloaded functions. We shall discuss these two concepts in the following sections.

### Virtual functions

Virtual functions provide a mechanism that allows us to ensure that the member function from the relevant derived class is invoked, whether we are calling it directly, or whether we are referring to the object via a base class pointer. So, for example, in Figure 11.4, were the member function `pay()`, in the base class, to be made into a virtual function, the correct derived class member function would be invoked by the main program.

Figure 11.5 shows a similar program to that in Figure 11.3 but using virtual functions. The main difference is that the declaration of each member function, `pay()`, is preceded by the word `virtual`.

---

```
#include <iostream.h>

const int Unknown = 0;
const int Salaried = 1;
const int Hourly = 2;

class Employee{
public:
   Employee(int number, float sal);
   virtual void pay();
   void identify();
protected:
   int empCode;
   int empNumber;
   float salary;
};
```

```
Employee::Employee(int number, float sal)
{
      empNumber = number;
      salary = sal;
      empCode = Unknown;
}

void Employee::pay()
{
   cout << "Annual salary " << salary << endl;
}

void Employee::identify()
{
   cout << "Employee: " << empNumber << endl
      << "Type: " << empCode << endl;
}
```

**Figure 11.5(a)** The `Employee` base class

Figure 11.5(a) is the definition of the `Employee` class again but with the member function `pay()` declared as `virtual`. Figure 11.5(b) defines the derived classes. In each of these the function `pay()` is declared as `virtual` too.

```
class SalariedEmp:public Employee {

public:
   SalariedEmp(int number, float salary);
   virtual void pay();
};

SalariedEmp::SalariedEmp(int number, float salary):
Employee(number, salary)
{
   empCode = Salaried;
}

void SalariedEmp::pay()
{
   cout << "Annual salary " << salary << endl
      << "This month " << salary/12 << endl;
}

class HourlyEmp:public Employee {
public:
   HourlyEmp(int number, float salary);
   virtual void pay();
};
```

```
HourlyEmp::HourlyEmp(int number, float salary):
Employee(number,salary)
{
   empCode = Hourly;
}

void HourlyEmp::pay()
{
   int hours;

   cout << "Annual salary " << salary << endl;
   cout << "Enter hours worked: ";
   cin >> hours;
   cout << "This month " << hours * salary/2080 << endl;
}
```

**Figure 11.5(b)** Derived `SalariedEmp` and `HourlyEmp` using virtual functions

```
void main()
{
   const int NumOfEmployees = 3;
   int i;

   // Declare an array of pointers to the
   // base class, Employee

   Employee *e[NumOfEmployees];

   // Assign new objects of both the base class
   // and the derived classes to the array
   e[0] = new SalariedEmp(123, 50000);
   e[1] = new HourlyEmp(456, 30000);
   e[2] = new SalariedEmp(789, 10000);

   // Now see how the behaviour changes depending
   // on which class it is
   cout << endl
        << "Monthly pay" << endl << "-----------" << endl
        << endl;

   for(i = 0; i < NumOfEmployees; i++)
   {
      e[i]->identify();         // called from base class
      e[i]->pay();              // called from derived class
      cout << endl;
   }
}
```

**Figure 11.5(c)** A program to test the new class definitions

The program in Figure 11.5(c) does exactly what we want it to. Even though we are using base class pointers to refer to derived class objects, the correct member functions are invoked for the objects that are being used. So in this example, the code in the loop in the `main` function will first refer to an object of the class `SalariedEmp`, then to an object of `HourlyEmp`, and finally to an object of `SalariedEmp`, again. Furthermore, the correct member function, `pay()`, will be invoked from the appropriate derived class in each case.

## How virtual functions work — static and dynamic binding

The explanation for the difference in behaviour between virtual and non-virtual member functions lies in how the compiler refers to them. When non-virtual functions for an object are used in a program, the actual function to be invoked (i.e. the one for the appropriate base or derived class) is fixed at the time that the program is compiled, and the code produced by the compiler contains a specific reference to the function. This is called *static binding*, i.e. the program code for a function is directly bound to the name that invokes it, by the compiler.

However, when *virtual* member functions are used, the compiler produces code that will invoke the correct function for the object that is being referred to while the programming is running. If a base class pointer is being used to refer to a number of different derived class objects during the course of a program, then, when a member function is called the correct function for the appropriate derived class is invoked. This may not be known at the time that the program is compiled and so the binding of the correct member function to its name is performed as the program is running and is, therefore, known as *dynamic binding*.

It is the declaration of the base class member function `pay()` as `virtual` that produces this functionality. However, you will have noticed that `pay()` is declared as virtual in the derived classes, too. This is done so that these classes can, themselves, be used as base classes that further specialist classes can be derived from. By declaring `pay()` as `virtual` in `SalariedEmp` and `HourlyEmp` we can ensure that the virtual function mechanism will work throughout the hierarchy of classes.

## Function overloading

Another form of polymorphism is achieved via function overloading. In Chapter 10, we saw that one class can have a number of constructors that perform different types of initialisation. As long as each function signature is unique, the correct function will always be invoked. In this chapter, we have seen that non-virtual member functions defined in a derived class will override those in the base class so the member function `pay()`, in our previous examples, invokes a different response depending on whether it is invoked for a base class object, or a derived class object.

In each of these cases we are overloading the functions. This simply means that the same function name can refer to more than one function definition. When we call an overloaded function the compiler therefore has to decide which of the function definitions applies. Function overloading is a feature of C++ that can be used in many situations, whether the functions be members of classes or not.

We have been used to function overloading from the very first chapters of the book — we were simply not aware of it. For example, if we write expression x+y at two points in our program, the types of x and y may be int on the first occasion and float on the second. For each type the compiler will call a *different* function to perform the addition, but the programmer need not be concerned with this when writing either of the expressions, both of which will use the same syntax — x+y.

The use of function overloading can help make a program more readable and intuitive to write by using the same name for a number of functions that perform similar operations but on different types of data. For example, when using arrays, initialising each element at the time they are declared is both tedious and error prone. One might prefer to use a function to initialise them instead. The following code fragment is a function that will initialise an integer array or a given length, such that all its elements are set to zero.

```
void initialise(int a[], int len)
{
    int i;

    for (i = 0; i < len; i++)
        a[i] = 0;
}
```

This might be considered a useful function, particularly if several integer arrays are declared in a program. Indeed, it might well be a function that we would want to include in a number of programs. But why stop at integer arrays? Character arrays are often initialised to a string but for those that are not, it would make sense to ensure that they are initialised to the null string (i.e. the first character being the null character) and if one is using an array of real numbers (i.e. float) it would also make sense to provide a similar function to initialise those as well. Figure 11.6 contains a set of overloaded functions that perform the initialisation of each of these types of array.

The functions in Figure 11.6 all have the same name but different signatures as they each have different numbers and/or types of parameters: the version for integers has one integer array and one integer as parameters, that for real numbers has one float array and one integer, while the final function has a single character array.

The compiler can therefore distinguish between the functions because they have different signatures but, as far as the programmer is concerned, only one name has to be remembered. Furthermore, any program that uses the functions will be more understandable than if three different function names had been used.

```
void initialise(int a[], int len)
{
    int i;

    for (i = 0; i < len; i++)
        a[i] = 0;
}

void initialise(float a[], int len)
{
    int i;

    for (i = 0; i < len; i++)
        a[i] = 0;
}

void initialise(char a[])
{
    a[0] = '\0';
}
```

**Figure 11.6** Overloaded array initialisation functions

## Exercises

11.1 Consider the class `Vehicle` and develop a class hierarchy that has `Vehicle` as a base class. Draw the hierarchy in the same form as Figure 11.1.

11.2 Describe a set of attributes for each of the classes that you have defined in Exercise 11.1. Are there any classes that have the same attributes as a class above or below in the hierarchy?

11.3 Declare a base class `Thermometer` that holds a temperature in degrees Kelvin. Provide methods that will allow a new temperature to be entered and another that will return the temperature in degrees Kelvin.

11.4 Declare two classes derived from the `Thermometer` class in Exercise 11.3 called `Celsius` and `Fahrenheit`. Each should use the same method for entering a new temperature as the base class but the function that returns the temperature should provide a Fahrenheit or Celsius value.

11.5 Write a program that uses the classes defined in Exercises 11.3 and 11.4 and uses an array of base class pointers to access the objects.

11.6 A library program uses a class that contains the details of an item in the library. Develop a set of class declarations that will represent the different types of item that can be found in a library (e.g. book, audio cassette, video, journal), their attributes (e.g. author, publisher) and their operations (e.g. create a new item, lend an item, return an item). You should first declare a base class that contains all of the common members for a library item.

11.7 Declare a class to represent a reference book. This should be derived from a class that represents a book from Exercise 11.6. The main difference between a normal book and a reference book is that the latter cannot be loaned, so you must override the member functions that are concerned with lending and returning the book.

11.8 Find as many syntax errors as you can in the following fragment of C++:

```
class SalariedEmp:public Employee {
public:
   SalariedEmp(int number; float salary);
   virtual void pay();
}

SalariedEmp:SalariedEmp(int number, float salary):
Employee(number, salary)
{
   empCode = Salaried;
}

void SalariedEmp::pay();
{
   cout << "Annual salary " << salary << endl
      << "This month " << salary/12 << endl;
}

class HourlyEmp:public Employee {
public:
   HourlyEmp(int number, float salary);
   void pay(); virtual
};
HourlyEmp::HourlyEmp(int number, float salary):
Employee(number,salary)
{
   empCode = Hourly;
}
```

```
void HourlyEmp:pay()
{
   int hours;

   cout << "Annual salary " << salary << endl;
   cout << "Enter hours worked: ";
   cout >> hours;
   cout << "This month " << hours * salary/2080 <<
endl";
}
```

# 12

# Files

## Aims

In this chapter the concept of a file is introduced and we explore how files may be used in C++ programs.

After reading this chapter you should be able to:

- understand the nature of a file
- write C++ programs that read from, write to and append to files.
- write programs that detect when the end of the file has been reached
- write programs using the functions `getline` and `get` to retrieve data from files

# An introduction to files

So far, the only data that we have come across has been stored in a program's variables and therefore exists only while the program is running. This has worked well enough for our example programs but in many real-world programs data must be stored independently of the program that creates, or uses them.

For example, a retailer who uses a stock control program does not want to lose the inventory data if the computer is switched off, or if the program is terminated in order to run another program. Also, a program that calculates monthly salaries may need to use the same data as a personnel record system. Rather than duplicate the data (and also, therefore, any changes that need to be made to that data), it makes sense to keep the data independent of, but accessible to, both programs.

A permanent record of data is achieved by storing it in files that reside on some form of (usually) magnetic medium, such as an internal hard disk or external diskette. The files are stored similarly to the way audio cassette tapes have music or speech stored on them, so once they have been created, files continue to exist whether or not the program that created them is running or, indeed, whether the computer is functioning or not.

# Using files in C++

The creation and maintenance of files on a computer is the responsibility of the computer's operating system. This will contain the facilities for creation, deletion, reading and writing. In order to distinguish one file from another they are given names when they are created. The exact form of that name depends on the particular operating system, but they are often in the form of *name.ext*, where *name* is a description of what the file contains and *ext* denotes the type of file. Table 12.1 contains a few examples of file names and what they might contain.

To use a file in a C++ program we first create an object to represent that file and then give the name of the file to that object. The file object contains member functions that communicate with the operating system and will allow us to read data from files and write data to them.

Of course, in order to create an object of the required type, we first need to define an appropriate class with the correct members. Luckily, every C++ compiler comes with a set of classes that define the objects that we need to use. These pre-defined classes take care of the necessary interaction with the operating system.

The definitions of file manipulation classes are in a file themselves, called `fstream.h`, which we have to include in any program that uses files.

In order to use the file classes in our programs we write something that should look very familiar:

```
#include <fstream.h>
```

Including this line in our programs allows us to declare the objects that we need to manipulate files.

**Table 12.1** Examples of file names

| File name | Contents of the file |
|---|---|
| chap12.doc | a word processor file that contains Chapter 12 of a book |
| payroll.cpp | the source code of a C++ payroll program |
| payroll.exe | the executable payroll program |
| empl.dat | a data file that contains details of employees |
| readme.txt | a text file containing instructions about how to install a program |

Before we use a file we must *open* it. This simply means giving the file object the name of the file which associates the object (a logical entity) with the file (a physical entity). When we open a file we also decide in which *mode* we will use it. The two basic modes are *read* and *write*, meaning that we can open a file in order to read data from it or open one to write data to it.

If we open a file for reading, then clearly it must exist. However, if we open a file for writing then it may or may not exist. Also, when writing to a file, we may wish to add new data to the end of an existing file or we may wish to create a new file. There are, therefore, two modes of writing: starting from scratch with a new file and 'appending' to the end of an existing file. Table 12.2 summarises the modes for file access.

**Table 12.2** Basic file modes

| Mode | Description |
|---|---|
| `in` | open an existing file to read data from |
| `out` | create and open a new file to write data to (if the file already exists then it will be deleted) |
| `app` | open an existing file to append data to (if the file does not already exist, then the effect is the same as write) |

## Reading from and writing to files

The program in Figure 12.1 should look very familiar. If it does not, take a quick look at the very first program in this book. That program printed out the result of adding 2 and 2 on the screen, here the only difference is that the output goes to a file.

```
// A program to write 2 + 2 to a file
#include <fstream.h>
void main()
{
      fstream outFile;

      outFile.open("test.txt", ios::out);
      outFile << 2 + 2;
}
```

**Figure 12.1** Writing an integer to a file

If you run the program in Figure 12.1 you will end up with a new file called `test.txt` that will contain the character '4' (you can look at it with a text editor to make sure). There are three differences between this program and the first one in the book, which writes 4 to the screen: the first is that the `#include` line now refers to `fstream.h` instead of `iostream.h`; the second is that there is the declaration of an object of the class `fstream`; and third the member function `open` is called with the name of the file to be created and the access mode.

However, there is a major similarity in that the statement that does the writing to the file is identical in form to the statement that writes to the screen. Instead of `cout`, however, we have the name of the file object, `outFile`.

The reason for the similarity is that keyboard and screen are treated as special types of file which are automatically opened in the appropriate mode and the names `cin` and `cout` refer to the objects that represent these special 'files'. So you will not be surprised by the program, in Figure 12.2, which reads the file that we created with the program from Figure 12.1.

```
// A program to read an integer from a file
#include <fstream.h>
void main()
{
      int number;

      fstream inFile;
      inFile.open("test.txt", ios::in);
      inFile >> number;
      cout << "The number read from 'test.txt' is "
           << number;
}
```

**Figure 12.2** Reading an integer from a file

Here we create an object of the class `fstream` called `inFile`, open a file `test.txt` (the one we created with our first program) and read an integer from it. The value of the integer is then displayed using `cout`. Notice that the way we read from the file is the same as when using `cin`, except that the name of the file object is used instead of the 'special file' `cin`.

You should notice that we do not have the line:

```
#include <iostream.h>
```

in our program, even though we have used `cout`. This is because `fstream.h` already includes `iostream.h`, so when using `fstream.h` we automatically get everything that is in `iostream.h` and do not have to `#include` it specifically.

To summarise, we open a file for writing by declaring an object of the class, `fstream`, and then open it using the member function `open` giving the file name as the first parameter and the special term `ios::out` as the second parameter, to specify write mode. We open a file for reading by declaring an object of the class `fstream`, and then open it using the member function `open` again, giving the file name as the first parameter but this time with the special term `ios::in` as the parameter that specifies the mode. We can then use the file object names to read and write data in the same way as when using `cin` and `cout`.

We can also write to, and read from, the same file in a single program. But we cannot have one file open for both reading and writing at the same time. The program, in Figure 12.3, illustrates the technique.

```
// A program to write 4 + 4 to a file
// and then read it again.
#include <fstream.h>
void main()
{
	int num;
	fstream dataFile;

	dataFile.open("test.txt", ios::out);
	dataFile << 4 + 4;
	dataFile.close();
	dataFile.open("test.txt", ios::in);
	dataFile >> num;
	dataFile.close();

	cout << "The number read from 'test.txt' is " << num;
}
```

**Figure 12.3** Writing to, and reading from, the same file

This is a combination of the first two programs. First we open the file `test.txt` for writing and put some data into it, then we open it for reading and extract the data from it. However, before we can open the file in a new mode, we must close it first. This is done by invoking the member function `close`. You can see that this is done after writing data to the file and before opening it for reading. (Also, for neatness, the file is closed after reading from it. This is not strictly necessary in this program, as all files are automatically closed when a program terminates.)

## Appending data to a file

Appending data to a file is done in the same way as writing to a file, except that the mode parameter used is `ios::app`. The program in Figure 12.4 illustrates how data can be appended to an existing file.

```
// Create a new file and put some data into it
// then open it for appending and add more data
// display the result
#include <fstream.h>

void main()
{
        int i, number;
        fstream dataFile;

        // First create the file and write 3 integers
        dataFile.open("test.txt", ios::out);
        dataFile << 1 << endl << 2 << endl << 3 << endl;
        dataFile.close();

        // Now open it again and write 3 more integers
        dataFile.open("test.txt", ios::app);
        dataFile << 10 << endl << 20 << endl << 30 << endl;
        dataFile.close();

        // Now read the 6 integers and display them
        dataFile.open("test.txt", ios::in);
        for (i = 0; i < 6; i++)
        {
                dataFile >> number;
                cout << "Number " << i << " is " << number
                     << endl;
        }
}
```

**Figure 12.4** Appending data to a file

Notice that when writing integers to the file, each one is followed by `endl`. This is the equivalent of hitting the return key after entering a number from the keyboard and provides a separator between the integers in the file. If this were not done then the data stored in the file would look as if it were one long number and reading from the file would give us only one, rather strange, value.

We need not necessarily use `endl`, any 'white space' character would have done, such as a tab or a space, e.g.

```
dataFile << 1 << " " << 2 << " ";
```

## Detecting the end of the file

It is often the case that we do not know how much data there is in a file before we start to read from it. If we try to read more data from the file than it contains then we will not get sensible values. Therefore, there is a mechanism for *detecting* that we have reached the end of the file so that we can stop reading data at the appropriate time.

The member function, `eof`, will return true if we have read all of the data from the file; if there is more data to be read it will return false. The next program (Figure 12.5) uses the file, `test.txt`, created previously (by the program in Figure 12.4) but does not 'know' the number of integers it will be required to read. It uses a `while` loop to read the data and stops only when the end of file is reached.

```
// Read integers until the end of file is reached
#include <fstream.h>
void main()
{
	int i=1, number;
	fstream dataFile;

	dataFile.open("test.txt", ios::in);
	// While NOT end of file...
	while(!dataFile.eof())
	{
		dataFile >> number;
		cout << "Number " << i << " is " << number
			<< endl;
		i++;
	}
}
```

**Figure 12.5** Detecting the end of file

## The member function `getline`

So far we have read only *integers* from a file and we have seen that in order to distinguish between one and the next integer, they must be separated by white space — spaces, tabs or new line characters. The same is true of character strings; the program in Figure 12.6 illustrates a potential problem with this approach.

```
//
// Create a new file and put character strings
// into it. Then read the file and display the result
//
#include <fstream.h>
void main()
{
	int i = 1;
	char str[80];
	fstream dataFile;

	// First create the file and write strings to it
	dataFile.open("test.txt", ios::out);
	dataFile << "Hello how are you?" << endl
	         << "I hope you are well";
	dataFile.close();

	// Now read the string and display it
	dataFile.open("test.txt", ios::in);
	while(!dataFile.eof())
	{
		dataFile >> str;
		cout  << "Character string " << i
		      << " is " << str << endl;
		i++;
	}
}
```

**Figure 12.6** Reading and writing strings

If you run the program, you will see that what is written to the file is not exactly the same as what is read in again. This is because the original strings that were written to the file contained spaces. These are treated as separators by the >> operator, and so several strings are read from the file instead of the original two.

Clearly, in order to make sense of the data that we read from a file we must have some idea of the *format* in which it was written. But if that format was plain text, it may not be convenient to read it back as single words with all of the formatting (i.e. spaces, new lines and tabs) removed.

The member function getline allows us to preserve the formatting of character strings by reading in character strings one line at a time. Figure 12.7 is similar to the previous program in Figure 12.6, but using getline in place of >>.

```
// Create a new file and put character strings
// into it. Then read the file with getline and
// display the result
#include <fstream.h>
void main()
{
	int i = 1;
	char str[80];
	fstream dataFile;

	// First create the file and write strings to it
	dataFile.open("test.txt", ios::out);
	dataFile << "Hello how are you?" << endl
	         << "I hope you are well";
	dataFile.close();

	// Now read the string and display it
	dataFile.open("test.txt", ios::in);
	while(!dataFile.eof())
	{
		dataFile.getline(str, 80, '\n');
		cout  << "Character string " << i
		      << " is " << str << endl;
		i++;
	}
}
```

**Figure 12.7** Reading strings with getline

If you run this program you will see that the strings that are displayed are exactly the same as those which were written to the file, complete with spaces. The general form of the getline function is:

```
stream.getline(string, size, delimiter)
```

where:

| | |
|---|---|
| stream | is the input stream from which the data is to be read, |
| string | is the character array that the line will be read into, |
| size | is an integer that limits number of characters that will be read, and |
| delimiter | is a character that will be used as the character to read up to. |

So the line:

```
dataFile.getline(str, 80, '\n');
```

from Figure 12.7, reads a line of characters from `dataFile` into the character array `str`, until it reaches a new line (`'\n'`) character or until the number of characters read is 79 (i.e. 80 minus 1), or until it reaches the end of a file. The purpose of the size parameter (80) is to ensure that we do not read more characters from the file than we have space for in the array. It is for this reason that the size parameter is usually set at the same as the size of the array.

The function `getline` always terminates the string that is read with the null character (the usual string terminator) and this is why `size - 1` is the maximum number of characters that will be read. If `getline` reaches the delimiting character, this is replaced by the null character (i.e. the delimiter will *not* appear in the character array).

Since `'\n'` will usually be the character at which we will wish to stop reading, the third parameter defaults to this value. So we could have used the form:

```
dataFile.getline(str, 80);
```

if we had wished.

## Using `getline` with `cin`

Because `getline` is a member function of the `stream` class, we can also use it with `cin`. In fact, if we wish to input a complete line of information from the keyboard, then this is often the most convenient way of achieving it (see Figure 12.8).

## The member function `get`

Another member function that can be used to read files (or with the stream `cin`) is `get()`. This function returns the next character from the file, or the special character, `EOF`, if the end of the file has been reached.

The program in Figure 12.9 asks the user to enter data in a variety of forms and stores this data in a file. The file is then read as characters and displayed. If you run this program you should see that the data have been stored as characters, exactly as if they had been typed from the keyboard (although you may find that the `float` has been rounded).

```
//
// Using getline with cin
//
#include <fstream.h>

void main()
{
	const int SIZE = 80;
	int i = 1;
	char str[SIZE];
	fstream dataFile;

	cout << "Please enter your full name: ";
	cin.getline(str, SIZE);

	dataFile.open("test.txt", ios::out);
	dataFile << str;
	dataFile.close();


	dataFile.open("test.txt", ios::in);
	while(!dataFile.eof())
	{
		dataFile >> str;
		cout  << "Name " << i
		      << " is :" << str << endl;
		i++;
	}
}
```

**Figure 12.8** Using `getline` with `cin`

## Exceptions and errors

An exception is something that occurs that is out of ordinary. We have seen one sort of exception already, that is, encountering the end of a file. When this happens we have to stop normal processing and do something different.

Reaching the end of a file is not an error; all files must end somewhere. But there are occasions when we shall reach the end of a file before we had expected to and this 'exception' should be catered for.

For example, it may be that file names on your computer must be no longer than eight characters, but this restriction will not stop you using a longer name in your C++ program (the compiler does not know about the restrictions that your operating system imposes). Also, you may try to open a file for reading that does not exist.

```
//
// Using get() to see how data is stored in a file
//
#include <fstream.h>

void main()
{
   fstream f;
   int i;
   float m;
   char s[20];
   char c;

   f.open("test.txt", ios::out);

   cout << "Enter an integer: ";
   cin >> i;

   // write it to the file
   f << i << endl;

   cout << "Enter a number with a decimal part: ";
   cin >> m;

   // write it to the file
   f << m << endl;

   cout << "Enter a string: ";
   cin >> s;

   // write it to the file
   f << s << endl;

   f.close();

   // Now read the entire file as characters
   // and display them

   f.open("test.txt", ios::in);

   do
   {
      c = f.get();
      cout << c;
   } while ( c != EOF);

}
```

**Figure 12.9** Using the member function `get()`

There is a mechanism that will allow the programmer to find whether a particular file operation has been successful. Consider the following fragment of code:

```
fileName.open(f, mode);

if (!fileName)
      cout << "Could not open file";
else
      cout << "File opened OK";
```

After an attempt has been made to open a file, we can test whether it was successful or not by using the `fstream` object's name as a logical value. If it is true then the operation was successful, if it is false then the operation failed for some reason.

Normally, we must test for the successful opening of files. If we do not and an error occurs, then the subsequent read or write operations will not behave as we would expect them to.

## A telephone book program

The final program is a simple case study using files. It incorporates many of the techniques described thus far in the book. It is a telephone book system that stores names and numbers as strings in a file. The program allows the user to open a file for reading or writing, and then to add names to the file, or display the entries in it.

Figure 12.10 contains the telephone book program. It is in four parts. Figure 12.10(a) shows the class declarations for `Entry` and `TelBook`. `Entry`, a simple data structure consisting of two strings, will be used to hold a telephone book entry (i.e. `name` and `number`). `TelBook` is the telephone book itself and handles all of the file opening, reading and writing.

Figure 12.10(b) consists of the member function definitions for the class `TelBook`.

Figure 12.10(c) is the main program that consists of a menu-style user interface and provides the appropriate actions for the user to choose from.

Figure 12.10(d) consists of the functions used in the main part of the program, which implements the telephone book.

Figure 12.10(a) shows the declarations in the program. Two classes are required, and the first is a simple class that has no member functions. This class is called `Entry` and it consists of two character strings, one of which will contain a name and the other a telephone number. Each object of this class will represent a single entry in the telephone book.

```
//
// Telephone Book and Entry classes
//
#include <fstream.h>

const int TRUE = 1;
const int FALSE = 0;
const int fieldLength = 20;

class Entry{
public:
   char name[fieldLength];
   char number[fieldLength];
};

class TelBook{

public:
   ~TelBook();

   int open(char * filename, char openMode);
   void close();
   int nextEntry(Entry &e);
   int addEntry(Entry &e);

private:
   char mode;
   fstream fileName;
   int fileOpen;
};
```

**Figure 12.10(a)** The telephone book program

The second class is called `TelBook` and represents the telephone book itself. This provides four member functions that allow the programmer to control access to the telephone book file. The function `open` will open an existing file or create a new one, while the function `close` simply closes the telephone book file. The two other functions `nextEntry` and `addEntry` allow the programmer to get the next entry in the file or add a new one, respectively.

The implementation of the member functions can be seen in Figure 12.10(b). These are quite straightforward and need little explanation. However, note that the `addEntry` and `nextEntry` functions both check to see whether the file is open in the correct mode before attempting to perform their respective operations; if this were not done the operations could fail. Also worthy of note is the way that the function `nextEntry` copies the next telephone book entry read from the file into a reference parameter of type `Entry` provided by the calling function (in this case `main`).

```
//
// Member functions for TelBook
//

TelBook::~TelBook()
{
   close();
}

int TelBook::open(char * f, char openMode)
{
   if (fileOpen) close();

   if (openMode == 'w') mode = ios::app;
   else mode = ios::in;
   fileName.open(f, mode);

   if (!fileName) fileOpen = FALSE;
   else fileOpen = TRUE;
   return fileOpen;
}

void TelBook::close()
{
   fileName.close();
}

int TelBook::nextEntry(Entry &e)
{
   if(fileOpen && mode == ios::in && !fileName.eof())
   {
      fileName.getline(e.name, fieldLength);
      fileName.getline(e.number, fieldLength);
   }
   return !fileName.eof();
}

int TelBook::addEntry(Entry &e)
{
   if (mode == ios::app && fileOpen)
   {
      fileName << e.name << endl
               << e.number << endl;
      return TRUE;
   }
   return FALSE;
}
```

**Figure 12.10(b)** The telephone book program

```
//
// Main program starts here
//

void open(TelBook &t, char mode);
void addentry(TelBook &t);
void showbook(TelBook &t);

void main()
{
   TelBook tbook;
   Entry e;
   char choice;
   int finish = FALSE;

   while (!finish)
   {
      cout  << endl
            << "R - open a book for reading" << endl
            << "W - open a book for writing" << endl
            << "A - add an new entry to book" << endl
            << "D - display book" << endl
            << "C - close book" << endl
            << "Q - quit" << endl << endl
            << "Enter your choice (capital letter): ";

      cin >> choice;

      switch (choice)
      {
       case 'R':
          open(tbook, 'r'); break;
       case 'W':
          open(tbook, 'w'); break;
       case 'C':
          tbook.close(); break;
       case 'A':
          addentry(tbook); break;
       case 'D':
          showbook(tbook); break;
       case 'Q':
          finish = TRUE; break;
       default:
          cout << "Invalid entry. Try again" << endl;
      }
   }
}
```

**Figure 12.10(c)** The telephone book program

Figure 12.10(c) of the program is the `main` function. Note that this function is preceded by prototypes for the functions that it uses; these are defined later in Figure 12.10(d). The `main` function implements a menu that allows the user to open a file in the correct mode (i.e. for reading or writing), add a new entry to the file, or display the entire contents of the file. Options for closing the file and quitting the application are also provided. For most user selections a function is called which will, in turn, call the appropriate member functions from the telephone book object. However, the close option of the member function is invoked directly and the quit option simply sets a flag that will terminate the loop.

```
//
// Functions used by main()
//
void open(TelBook &t, char mode)
{
   char name[20];
   cout << "Enter the name of the book to open:";
   cin >> name;

   if(!t.open(name, mode))
      cout << "Could not open file" << endl;
}

void addentry(TelBook &t)
{
   Entry e;

   cout << "Enter name:  ";
   cin >> e.name;
   cout << "Enter phone number:  ";
   cin >> e.number;

   if(!t.addEntry(e))
      cout << "Could not add entry" << endl;
}

void showbook(TelBook &t)
{
   Entry e;

   while (t.nextEntry(e))
   {
      cout  << "Name   :  " << e.name << endl
            << "Number:  " << e.number << endl;
   }
}
```

**Figure 12.10(d)** The telephone book program

The final part of the program in Figure 12.10(d) contains the three functions invoked by the main function; these perform the operations corresponding to the user options.

## Exercises

12.1 Write a program that will accept and then store a set of integers in a file that represent exam marks. The program should have two main functions, one to allow the addition of data to the file and the other to read all the data from the file and display it on the screen.

12.2 Write a program that will accept text typed from the keyboard and then store it in a file. Use the `getline` function to read each string and then write it to the file followed by a new line (i.e. `endl`). The program should stop when the user enters an empty string (i.e. presses the return key twice). You can check that your program works by inspecting the file that you have created with a text editor such as the one you use to write your programs.

12.3 Modify the answer to Exercise 12.1 to record the names of the students in another file. The order of the names in the student file should correspond to the order of the integers in the marks file. Change the function that displays the results so that it reads both files and displays something like this:

```
Arthur Average     50
Betty Brainbox     99
Clive Clever       75
Dan Dire           10
```

You should use `getline` to read the strings from the file.

12.4 Use the function `get`, in a program, to read a file of text (i.e. character strings) and count the number of vowels the file contains.

12.5 Define a class that represents the rainfall for a month. It should contain data members for the month name and the rainfall in inches. The class should also contain a function that writes the data to a file and one that reads data from a file. In each case the file object should be passed to the member function. Write a program that uses an array of 12 objects of the class to represent the rainfall for a year. The program should allow the input and storage of data for 12 months and/or the reading and display of the same data from a file.

# Appendix A
## Recursion

### Aims

The aim of this appendix is to explain how recursive functions can be used to achieve repetition.

After studying this appendix you should be able to:

- mentally execute recursive functions
- write and understand programs which contain recursive functions
- convert a `while` loop into a call to a recursive function

# Introduction

A recursive function is one in which the body of the function contains a call to the function itself. At first this may seem a strange thing to do, and the reader might suspect that a recursive function would naturally go on calling itself *forever*, and would therefore be of little value.

It is true that a recursive function *may* go on calling itself forever, if care is not taken. Figure A.1 below contains an example of a recursive function which does just that.

```
int sum(int n) ;
//
// A recursive function that never terminates
//

int sum(int n)
{
	return n + sum(n-1) ;
}
```

**Figure A.1** A recursive function which fails to terminate

The program is supposed to calculate the sum of all numbers between zero and `n`. We can use the substitution method to evaluate a call. We shall try the call to this recursive version of `sum`, with the actual parameter `4`, that is, we shall attempt to evaluate the call:

```
sum(4)
```

Replacing this call by the expression used in the `return` statement we obtain:

```
4 + sum(3)
```

This substitution still contains an occurrence of a call to the function `sum`, so we may apply the substitution process once again, substituting the actual parameter `3` for the formal parameter `n`, in the call `sum(3)`. Replacing the call `sum(3)` with the result of this substitution, we obtain:

```
4 + 3 + sum(2)
```

Once again we have a call to `sum`, which we can unfold, using substitution, to obtain:

```
4 + 3 + 2 + sum(1)
```

The process goes on:

```
4 + 3 + 2 + 1 + sum(0)
```

*and on*:

```
4 + 3 + 2 + 1 + 0 + sum(-1)
```

*and on*:

```
4 + 3 + 2 + 1 + 0 + -1 + sum(-2)
```

Now, although this was a bad way to write a function, we can see a pattern emerging, which is very close to the result we are seeking in writing the function `sum`. If only the function would stop calling itself after it has reached the last number to be added into the summation then we would have the correct answer to the calculation.

Notice that whatever number we start off with in the initial call to the function `sum`, the function starts at that number and proceeds to count down from it adding each number in turn to a result which is accumulating the summation. As we said earlier, addition is commutative, so it is of no importance that the numbers are added together starting off with the largest. We will obtain the same answer as we would get by starting with the smallest number and counting up to the largest.

Now the smallest number in the summation is always 0, and no matter where the summation begins the 'count down', the number zero will, eventually, be reached.

This is the point at which we want the function to stop calling itself.

We can re-write the function `sum`, still recursively, but so that it does terminate, by making the function only call itself when it is passed an actual parameter which is *not* zero. When the actual parameter zero is passed to the function it will not call itself, but will return `0` (which is the correct answer for the sum from zero to zero is zero). The correct way to write a recursive version of `sum` is given in Figure A.2 below:

---

```
int sum(int n) ;
//
// Pre-condition:
// n >= 0
//
// Post-condition:
// The function returns the sum 0+1+...+n
//

int sum(int n)
{
```

```
        if (n==0)
                return 0;
        else
                return n + sum(n-1) ;
}
```

**Figure A.2** A correct recursive summation function

Now we can, again, try the call:

```
sum(4)
```

using the substitution method.

The first steps produce the same expanding expression that we encountered with the non-terminating version of `sum` defined in Figure A.1.

The first call is evaluated by substituting `4` for `n` in the body of `sum`. As the expression `4==0` used in the `if` statement is false, we obtain the result returned by the `else` part of the `if` statement, giving us:

```
4 + sum(3)
```

Once again, when we substitute the actual parameter `3` for the formal parameter `n` in the call `sum(3)`, we execute the `else` statement, which gives us the expression:

```
4 + 3 + sum(2)
```

Further unfolding the function call `sum(2)` we obtain:

```
4 + 3 + 2 + sum(1)
```

This still contains a call to `sum`, which unfolds to give us:

```
4 + 3 + 2 + 1 + sum(0)
```

Now, when we substitute the actual parameter `0` for the formal parameter `n`, we do *not* execute the `else` part of the `if` statement, but instead return the result `0` giving:

```
4 + 3 + 2 + 1 + 0
```

This expression does *not* contain a call to `sum`. We can evaluate it completely to get:

```
10
```

which is the correct answer to the summation from `0` to `4`.

## The two important ingredients for successful recursion

We have seen that it is possible to write a recursive function which terminates and which performs a useful calculation. There are two important ingredients which make this possible, and *all* recursive functions will have to contain these two ingredients if they are to terminate.

### Base case

The base case of a recursive function is the value of the parameter(s) for which the function does not perform a recursive call. Without a base case the function will always perform a recursive call and will thus not terminate. The base case is usually a value of the parameter(s) for which the solution to the problem is trivial.

In the recursive function `sum`, the base case is the number zero, for which the result of the `sum` is, indeed, trivial.

There may be more than one base case in a recursive function, but there *must* be *at least* one.

### Recursive case

In addition to a base case, a recursive function will have one (or more) recursive case(s), which is the value(s) of the input parameter for which the function calls itself to form a part of the answer. The recursive call must pass a parameter to the function which represents some form of progress towards the value of one of the base cases. For example, in the recursive case for the function `sum`, the recursive call passes `n-1` as the actual parameter to the recursive call. This represents progress, because the value passed on is one step closer to arriving at the base case, zero.

Suppose we did *not* pass on a smaller value in the recursive call to the function. If we do not, then once again, we would find that our function will not terminate. For example, suppose we define the function `sum` so that the recursive call is correct, but makes no progress towards the base case. We might write something like this:

```
int sum(int n)
{
        if (n==0)
                return 0;
        else
                return sum(n) ;
}
```

The function will only terminate if we pass it the value of the base case as the actual parameter.

If we call the function with another actual parameter, for example `4`, then the recursive call will make no progress towards the base case. To see this happen, consider the call:

```
sum(4)
```

In order to evaluate this call, we must mentally execute the `else` part of the `if` statement in the body of `sum`, giving

```
sum(4)
```

Now we are evaluating the *same* expression that we started with, and will continue to evaluate the same expression for ever.

Let us consider another problem, which can be written recursively to see how the base case stops the process of recursive calls and how the recursive case makes progress towards the goal of arriving at the base case. The problem is to write a function which calculates the number of characters in a string. The solution is given in Figure A.3 below:

---

```
int Length(char AString[]) ;
//
// Pre-condition:
// The array AString must contain a
// '\0' character terminator.
//
// Post-condition:
// The function returns the number of
// characters in the string
// (not including the terminator).
//

int Auxiliary(char s[], int count) ;
//
// An auxiliary function used by Length
// Pre-condition:
// The array s must contain a '\0' character at
// an index whose value is greater than or
// equal to count.
// count must be greater than or equal to zero.
//
// post-condition:
// The function returns the count + the number
// of characters between the index count and
// the '\0' character in s.
//

int Length(AString)
{
```

```
        return Auxiliary(AString, 0) ;
}

int Auxiliary(char s[], int count)
{
        if (s[count] == '\0')
                return count ;
        else
                return Auxiliary(s, count+1) ;
}
```

**Figure A.3** An accumulating parameter function

Notice that the function `Length` does not perform the task of finding the length of the array *itself*, but passes this problem on to an auxiliary function (called `Auxiliary`). The function `Auxiliary` has an extra parameter, in which it 'accumulates' the result in the (value) parameter, called `count`. A function such as this, which accumulates its result in a parameter, is called an 'accumulating parameter function'.

The base case for the function `Auxiliary` is when the character at the position `count` in the array `s` *is* the termination character, in which case the value of the accumulating parameter is returned.

The recursive case for `Auxiliary` is when the character at the position `count` in the array `s` is not the termination character, in which case the recursive call to `Auxiliary` passes the same array (this clearly must *not* change), and a new value for `count`. Notice that the new value passed as an actual parameter for the formal parameter `count` makes *progress* towards the base case, because it is increased, thus the next call to `Auxiliary` will consider an element one place further on in the array `s`. The pre-condition guarantees that the base case will eventually be reached, because it assures us that we shall eventually reach the termination character.

We have chosen this point to introduce you to recursion because it is important to be familiar with the principle of functions in general, and to be fluent in the terms and uses of functions to be in the best position to understand the concept of recursion. However, we should stress that recursion is not an idea that is *exclusively* associated with functions which return a value. *Any* function can be written in a recursive style (indeed in some languages, the *only* way of achieving repetition is via recursion). We shall now consider a recursive function which does *not* return a value at all, but which prints out a shape on the screen.

Suppose we want to write a (recursive) function called `Triangle` to draw a right angled triangle of height `n` characters where `n` is the parameter to the function `Triangle`.

The picture will look like this (if called with the actual parameter `4`):

```
****
***
**
*
```

We can use the function `line` which we introduced in Chapter 7, Figure 7.2, to draw a single line of asterisk characters. This allows us to define the function `Triangle` in terms of the function `line`. The solution is given in Figure A.4 below:

---

```
void Triangle(int n);
//
// Draws a right angled triangle
//
// Pre-condition:
// n>=0.
//
// Post-condition:
// A right-angled triangle of n characters
// high is drawn on the screen.
//

void Triangle(int n)
{
      if (n!=0)
      {
            Line(n,'*') ;
            cout << endl;
            Triangle(n-1) ;
      }
}
```

---

**Figure A.4** Recursive function to draw a triangle

The base case of the function `Triangle` is when `n` is zero, in which case there is *nothing* to draw[1]. The recursive case is where `n` is not zero, in which case we draw a line of `n` asterisk characters, produce a carriage return and then call the function `Triangle` with `n-1` to complete the triangle. Notice that the recursive call does make progress towards the base case[2], as we know it must in order for the recursion to terminate.

---

[1]Notice that if we were to call the function with the actual parameter zero, then we would get a triangle of zero height — i.e. nothing.

[2]It is also interesting to compare this function with the recursive function `sum(n)`, which adds the numbers between 0 and `n`. The base case and recursive case for the two functions are identical, which comes as no surprise since the number produced by `sum(n)` is the $n^{th}$ *triangle* number. The connection between the two functions is that the call `Triangle(n)` will draw `sum(n)` asterisks on the screen.

## A way of understanding (and verifying) recursive functions

Beginners sometimes find recursion hard to understand, because of the way in which a function appears to depend upon itself. In order to escape this brain-bending self-referentiality we can bear a simple rule in mind which prevents us having to consider the unfolding of the recursion in order to understand the meaning of the function[3].

We have already seen that a recursive function must contain one (or more) base case(s) and one (or more) recursive case(s). All that we have to do in order to see that our recursive function is correct is to consider each case in turn and verify that it is correct. For the base case(s) we must check that the function behaves correctly if the parameter passed is (one of) the base case(s). For the recursive call, we may legitimately assume that the recursive call produces the correct answer, and simply attempt to see that the expression in which the recursive call is contained is correct.

For example, consider the summation function `sum`. The base case is zero, in which case the function returns zero, and the summation of all the numbers between zero and zero is *indeed* zero, so the base case is correct. The recursive case is `n + sum(n-1)`. Now we shall (legitimately) assume that `sum(n-1)` produces the correct answer, that is, we shall assume that

`sum(n-1)` *is* `0 + 1 + 2 + ... + (n-1)`

We want to see that this recursive call is contained in an expression which will evaluate to the correct answer for `sum(n)`. Well, it does, because

```
n + sum(n-1)
```

will be

```
n + (0 + 1 + 2 + ... + (n-1))
```

because we are assuming that the recursive call `sum(n-1)` returns the correct result, i.e. `(0 + 1 + 2 + ... + (n-1))`.

Now we know that the order in which we perform the addition of several numbers makes no difference, so we could write that expression like this:

```
0 + 1 + 2 + ... + (n-1) + n
```

without affecting the result. But we know that `0 + 1 + 2 + ... + (n-1) + n` is the correct value of `sum(n)`, which is what we wanted.

---

[3]This rule is justified by the mathematical principle of induction, but we shall not pursue this justification here.

## Pros and cons of recursion

The advantages of recursion derive from the way in which, as we have shown, we can verify that a recursive function behaves correctly in a relatively straightforward manner. It is a matter of taste as to whether or not one considers a recursive form of a function definition to be easier to understand than a version written with loops.

The disadvantage of recursion is that it is typically less efficient in both memory and speed, as the recursive calls of a function involve an overhead in passing the actual parameters for the formal parameters. As the number of times a recursive function will be called may not be known when the program is written it will also not be known when the program is written exactly how much storage is required.

## The connection between recursion and looping

There is a strong connection between a function with a `while` loop and one which is written recursively. In fact we can always re-write a `while` loop as a recursive function according to a rule.

Consider the while loop template below, in which `<statement>` stands for any C++ statement, including the possibility that `<statement>` is a sequence of statements in curly brackets, and `<expression>` is the boolean expression controlling the termination of the `while` loop.

```
while (<expression>)
      <statement>
```

This `while` loop can be replaced by a call to the recursive function `f`, where `f` is defined to be:

```
void f()
{
      if (<expression>)
      {
            <statement> ;
            f();
      }
}
```

Now we know, from Chapter 3, that `for` loops and `do ... while ...` loops can be rewritten as `while` loops. Since we now also know that a `while` loop can be rewritten as a call to a recursive function, we know that we could, if we chose to, always and only use recursion to achieve repetition.

# Exercises

A.1 Write a recursive version of the factorial function and call it `fac`.

A.2 Use the unfolding technique to mentally evaluate the following expression:

```
10 * fac(4)
```

A.3 Here is a function to locate the first occurrence of the character `ch` in the array `A`, whose index is greater than or equal to `i`:

```
int locate(char ch, int i, char A[]) ;
//
// pre-condition: there is an occurrence of the
// character ch at or after the index i
// within the array A.
// post-condition: locate returns an integer l.
// l is the index of the first occurrence of the
// character ch after the index i in the array A.
//

int locate(char ch, int i, char A[])
{
      if (A[i] == ch)
            return i
      else
            return locate(ch,i+1,A) ;
}
```

Re-write the recursive function `locate` using a loop.

A.4 What does this function do?

```
void Rev() ;

void Rev()
{
      int i;
      cin >> i ;
      if (i!=-1)
      {  Rev() ;
         cout << i ; }
}
```

A.5 Can you rewrite a call to the function in Exercise A.4 as a loop construct?

A.6 Write a recursive function which takes a string and a character and returns the index of the first occurrence of the character in the string. For this, you will need to use an auxiliary function which contains an extra accumulating parameter which contains an index to the 'current' element of the string under consideration.

# Appendix B
# Template Classes

## Aims

This appendix explains the concept of container classes and shows how generic container classes may be constructed using the `C++` template mechanism.

After reading this appendix you should be able to:

- understand the nature of a container class
- construct and use a template class to build a container class

## Introduction

Template classes are a special type of class definition that allow the creation of generic classes. A generic class is one that can be used to store different types of data. Instead of having to define different classes that handle integers, characters or user defined objects, a single class template can be defined that will define the functionality required of the class, irrespective of the type of data that its objects contain. Objects can thus be created for any data type that the client might require.

A typical use of template classes is in the creation of *container classes*, so we shall discuss these first.

## Container classes

A container class is one which is used to instantiate objects that will act as containers for other data. We have already come across one sort of container, the array. A container class can perform a similar function to an array and can be made as flexible as the programmer requires.

Typically, a container will be something like a list, a queue or a stack. It will contain a private data structure that holds the required values and a set of *access functions* which are member functions that allow the stored data to be manipulated.

Figure B.1(a)–(c) is the definition of a class `IntegerQueue`. This is a container that maintains an ordered queue of integers. When an object is created the constructor may be given a parameter that specifies the size of the queue. If the parameter is not given, the size of the queue will be ten.

The constructor obtains an integer array for the queue dynamically, using `new`, and assigns the address of this to the pointer `queuePtr`. Having done this the pointer may be used as a reference to the array.

Because the array holding the data is created when the object is instantiated, it is good practice to free the memory used when the object is destroyed. This is the function of the destructor: it disposes of the array created by the constructor, using `delete` to achieve this.

There are five access functions in `IntegerQueue`. The first two, `length()` and `used()`, simply return the total length of the queue and the number of used elements (these can be used to determine whether the queue is full). The other three are used to put data into the queue, remove it from the queue, and to look at a particular element in the queue (note that items added go at the end of the queue and items removed are taken from the front).

```
#include <iostream.h>

class IntegerQueue{
public:
      IntegerQueue(int s = 10);      // constructor
      ~IntegerQueue();               // destructor

      int length();                  // return size of queue
      int used();                    // return number of
                                     // used elements
      int getItem(int index, int &item);
                                     // get the value of
                                     // item at position
                                     // index in queue

      int add(int item);             // add item to end
                                     // of queue
      int remove(int &item);         // remove first
                                     // item from queue

private:
      int size;
      int FirstFree;
      int *queuePtr;                 // pointer to first
                                     // element of queue
};
```

**Figure B.1(a)** The class declaration for `IntegerQueue`

```
IntegerQueue::IntegerQueue(int s)
{
      size = s;
      FirstFree = 0;                 // empty queue
      queuePtr = new int[size];      // create queue of
                                     // required size
}

IntegerQueue::~IntegerQueue()
{
      delete [] queuePtr;
}

int IntegerQueue::length()
{
      return size;
}
```

```
int IntegerQueue::used()
{
	return FirstFree;
}

int IntegerQueue::getItem(int index, int &item)
{
	if (index >= 0 && index < FirstFree)
	{
		item = queuePtr[index];
		return 1;
	}
	return 0;    // no such item
}

int IntegerQueue::add(int item)
{
	if (FirstFree < size - 1)
	{
		queuePtr[FirstFree] = item;
		FirstFree++;
		return 1;
	}
	else return 0;
}

int IntegerQueue::remove(int &item)
{
	if (FirstFree == 0) return 0;

	item = queuePtr[0];
	for (int i=0; i < FirstFree; i++)
		queuePtr[i] = queuePtr[i+1];
	FirstFree--;
	return 1;
}
```

**Figure B.1(b)** The member function definitions

```
void main()
{
	int i;
	int queueItem;

	IntegerQueue integerQueue(5);

	cout << "Add numbers to the queue,"
	     << "the last one should fail"
```

```
            << endl << endl;

    for(i = 0; i < 5; i++)
    {
        cout << "Enter an integer: ";
        cin >> queueItem;
        cout  << "Adding "
              << queueItem << " to the queue"
              << ", the result is: "
              << integerQueue.add(queueItem)
              << endl;
    }

    cout << endl
         << "Print out the queue: ";

    for(i = 0; i < integerQueue.used(); i++)
    {
        integerQueue.getItem(i,queueItem);
        cout << queueItem << " ";
    }
    cout << endl << endl;

    cout << "Remove an item" << endl;

    integerQueue.remove(queueItem);
    cout << "Removed: "
         << queueItem
         << endl << endl;

    cout << "Show the changed queue: ";
    for(i = 0; i < integerQueue.used(); i++)
    {
        integerQueue.getItem(i,queueItem);
        cout << queueItem << " ";
    }
}
```

**Figure B.1(c)** A program to use the class `IntegerQueue`

## Class templates

Container classes can be very useful constructs and may be needed in a number of different programs. We could build a library of such useful classes for use in future programs but it might quickly become extremely large. The queue that we have defined can only store integer values. It would seem rather silly to have to write almost identical queue classes for queues which contain other types of data.

To solve this problem, we need a generic queue class that does not specify the *type* of data that it stores. This is what a template class will provide.

Figure B.2(a)–(c) shows another version of the queue class in the form of a template. You should notice that the class declaration and each of the member function definitions are now preceded by `template<class T>`, and many of the occurrences of the word `int` have disappeared, to be replaced by `T`. The name `T` represents the type of data that the queue is going to hold and this can be any normal C++ type such as `int`, `float` or `char`, or it can be any user defined class, such as `Time`.

To create an object of the class `Queue`, we must tell the compiler the type of data that the template is to be instantiated for. This is done by placing the required type in chevrons after the class name in the declaration, i.e.

```
Queue<float> floatQueue(5);
```

This declaration can be seen in the test program for the template class in Figure B.2(c): it will create an object called `floatQueue` which can contain up to five values of type `float`.

```
#include <iostream.h>
template<class T>
class Queue{
public:
      Queue(int size = 10);     // constructor
      ~Queue();                 // destructor

      int length();       // get queue size
      int used();         // get number of used elements
      int getItem(int index, T &item);
      // get the value of item at position index in queue

      int add(T item);                     // add item to end
                                           // of queue
      int remove(T &item);                 // remove first item
                                           // from the queue

private:
      int size;
      int FirstFree;
      T *queuePtr;                         // pointer to first
                                           // item in queue
};
```

**Figure B.2(a)** The `Queue` template class

```
template<class T>
Queue<T>::List(int s)
{
      size = s;
      FirstFree = 0;                  // empty queue
      queuePtr = new T[size];         // create queue of
                                      // required size
}

template<class T>
Queue<T>::~Queue()
{
      delete [] queuePtr;
}

template<class T>
int Queue<T>::length()
{
      return size;
}

template<class T>
int Queue<T>::used()
{
      return FirstFree;
}

template<class T>
int Queue<T>::getItem(int index, T &item)
{
      if (index >= 0 && index < FirstFree)
      {
            item = queuePtr[index];
            return 1;
      }
      else return 0;    // no such item
}

template<class T>
int Queue<T>::add(T item)
{
      if (FirstFree < size - 1)
      {
            queuePtr[FirstFree] = item;
            FirstFree++
            return 1;
      }
      return 0;
}
```

```
template<class T>
int Queue<T>::remove(T &item)
{
      if (FirstFree == 0) return 0;

      item = queuePtr[0];
      for (int i=0; i < FirstFree; i++)
            queuePtr[i] = queuePtr[i+1];
      FirstFree--;
      return 1;
}
```

**Figure B.2(b) The member functions for the template class**

```
void main()
{
      int i;
      float queueItem;

      Queue<float> floatQueue(5);

      cout << "Add numbers to the queue,"
           << "the last one should fail"
           << endl << endl;

      for(i = 0; i < 5; i++)
      {
            cout << "Enter a float: ";
            cin >> queueItem;
            cout  << "Adding "
                  << queueItem << " to the queue"
                  << ", the result is: "
                  << floatQueue.add(queueItem)
                  << endl;
      }

      cout << endl
           << "Print out the queue: ";

      for(i = 0; i < floatQueue.used(); i++)
      {
            floatQueue.getItem(i,queueItem);
            cout << queueItem << " ";
      }
      cout << endl << endl;

      cout << "Remove an item" << endl;
```

```
        floatQueue.remove(queueItem);
        cout << "Removed: "
             << queueItem
             << endl << endl;

        cout << "Show the changed queue: ";

        for(i = 0; i < floatQueue.used(); i++)
        {
              floatQueue.getItem(i,queueItem);
              cout << queueItem << " ";
        }
}
```

**Figure B.2(c)** A program to use the template class

# Exercises

B.1 Write the declaration for a `char` queue that can contain up to 100 characters.

B.2 What is the difference between the queue that you created in answer to Exercise B.1 and a string of 100 characters?

B.3 What would be the effect of not having a destructor function in the `Queue` class?

B.4 Write a member function for the `Queue` class called `isIn` which takes a single parameter and returns true or false depending on whether the value of the parameter is in the queue.

B.5 Write a template class for a container class called stack. The operation of a stack is like that of a stack of plates in a self-service restaurant. Values are stored in the order in which they are entered but when they are removed they are produced in the opposite order, i.e. the last item to be placed on the stack will be the first to be removed and the first item placed on the stack will be the last one removed.

The class should contain four member functions:

| | |
|---|---|
| `int push(T item)` | this places an item on the stack and returns true if successful and false if the stack is full |
| `int pop(T &item)` | this removes the top item from the stack and returns true if successful and false if the stack was empty |
| `int full()` | this returns true if the stack is full and false otherwise |
| `void clear()` | this empties the stack |

# Index